P9-DIH-764

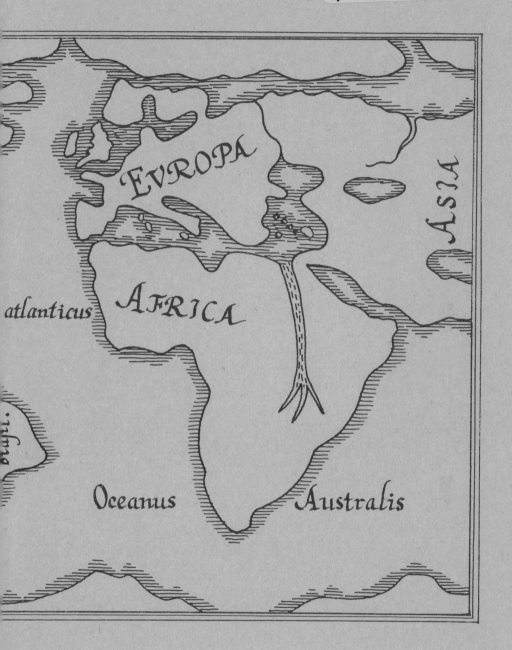

Samford University Library

Gift of
MRS. ELIZABETH M. HACKER

AMERICAN
GENESIS

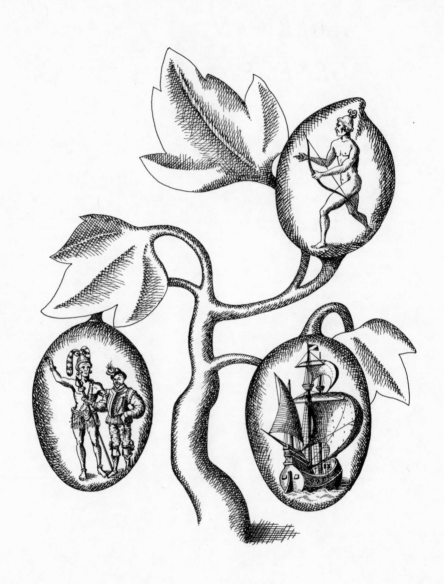

AMERICAN GENESIS

Pre-colonial Writing in the North

By EVELYN PAGE, *1902 –*

Released from
Samford University Library

Gambit   Boston   1973

Samford University Library

FIRST PRINTING

Copyright © 1973 by Evelyn Page
All rights reserved including the right to
reproduce this book or parts thereof in
any form
International Standard Book Number: 0–87645–072–9
Library of Congress Catalog Card Number: 72–94004
Printed in the United States of America

Annex
970.01

E
101
.P33

In honor of
Cornelia Meigs
who, in interest and encouragement,
presided over the genesis of this book

76—04541

Foreword

The study of the origins of American literature has ignored the earliest writing of America, giving it over to history. Professor Randolph G. Adams' "Reports and Chronicles," in *The Literary History of the United States*, begins to repair the neglect and to suggest further examination of "our first literature." Other distinguished critics echo his interest in the early American work not only of writers in the English language, but also in Spanish, Italian, Portuguese, and French. Professor Robert E. Spiller points to a whole new development of American criticism when he calls the Columbus "Epistola" of 1493 "the beginning of the written record" of America, setting its form and pattern.

American Genesis presents a survey of this "written record" in the sixteenth century, whatever the European background, national or international. Like its subject, its purpose is discovery—to investigate and to trace an evolution, where such exists. In the outcome, the development turns out almost never to be the patterning of one piece of writing upon another. The fundamental pattern, that of the voyage, persists. It evolves, not by example and the elaboration of earlier handling, but in the evolution and elaboration of event. As the experience changes, usually becoming more complex, so the writer changes his sequences and techniques and interpretations, in order to do justice to his complexities.

Such a process of evolution precludes the appearance of "sources," in the usual critical definition. The historians did indeed use earlier work, but for compilation, not for re-representation. The sixteenth-century writer, by the evidence, offered no model to his contemporaries or his successors. Moreover, the whole body of sixteenth-century writing has offered few, if any, sources to later American centuries. Indeed, the influence is far more profound and pervasive. Once again, it is the impact of a whole, continuous, recorded, and imaged experience, in its chapters of genesis. Smith, Lescarbot, and Champlain, who bring these chapters to a culmination rather than a conclusion, have traveled far from Columbus, in a changed direction, but Columbus still provides the course to their understanding. So, to propose a still wider range, he also does to that of John Dos Passos and Ernest Hemingway.

A general discussion of a subject so broad, in its origins so diverse, is necessarily tentative. It is hoped that authorities in the literatures and languages of Spain, Italy, Portugal, France, and England will begin or continue studies in the European antecedents and complements of American writing. Gilbert Chinard, for the French, offers an example which few have followed. Whole areas wait for close attention. The carrying over into America of stories of the Orient and of western Europe; the contemporary scrutiny of nature—plants, animals, landscapes, men; the relationships between Latin American writing and that of the North; sixteenth-century Utopian concepts and their American counterparts—these topics and their like call for examination.

Meanwhile, risks of error and misjudgment must be accepted. Authorities in the fields encroached upon here will find corrections to make and disagreements to offer. A survey such as this is premature, but justifies itself by providing a sequence and a summary, both capable of betterment.

To those who in the future may help to correct and clarify my statements, I offer my thanks; to those who have already so contributed, I wish to extend my appreciation and make my acknowledgments, always accepting my own responsibility for the outcome. Dean Alice Johnson of Connecticut College, Mrs. Millicent Beausoleil of the Putnam Public Library, and Miss Dorothy Blair, former reader at Smith College, have generously spent time and attention in reading and criticizing my manuscript. Professor Glen L. Kolb has reviewed my translations from Spanish, and offered suggestions to enlarge my limited knowledge of Latin-American epics and Spanish prosody. Señor Don Ernesto de la Torre Villar, Director of the Biblioteca Nacional de México, with equal scholarly courtesy has solved my perplexities in regard to Urdaneta, that "friar of Mexico" who neither sailed the Strait of Anian nor claimed to have done so, though others made the claim for him. Miss Helen K. Aitner, Reference and Documents Librarian at the Palmer Library of Connecticut College, has been my unfailing help, her range of information being exceeded only by her liberality in increasing mine.

Among institutions, I am deeply indebted to the Inter-library Loan Center of the Connecticut State Library, the Putnam Public Library, the Palmer Library of Connecticut College, the Beinike and Sterling Libraries of Yale University, the Library of the New-York Historical Society, the New York Public Library, the Watkinson Library

at Trinity College, the Pierpont Morgan Library and the
John Carter Brown Library of Brown University. To the
skillful and patient staffs of all of these, I extend my
gratitude.

Certain practices which I have followed in the text call
for explanation. For the reader's comfort, the typography
and spelling in quotations in English follow modern
standards. Quotations in other languages are given according to the original, and translated or paraphrased into
modern English. The original spellings and styles are
adhered to in all titles, for bibliographical convenience.
I have kept to sixteenth-century usage in proper names, or,
lacking reasonable consistency there, follow the *National
Union Catalogue* of the Library of Congress.

Ordinarily restricted to primary sources, a brief bibliography for each chapter appears at the end of the text.
Whenever possible it gives the first printing of each item
and further references to reasonably accessible reprints in
the language of origin and in English. I also list expertly
edited, definitive texts, for close annotation and extended
bibliography. The principal bibliographical purpose is to
assist those who wish to study this literature in either its
European derivations and relationships, or in an American
context. In the citation of modern reprints, authority and
availability have been the main considerations.

Repeated reference must be made to the great voyage
collections. These sometimes offer the first publication of
the particular narrative, and sometimes remain the printing
most easily reached. In order to avoid a tedious repetition
of long titles, these collections are referred to by short title
in the chapter bibliographies. Workably full titles will be
found in a listing at the end of this volume.

The scholar will judge these bibliographical efforts to be
primitive, but he does not need guidance to the work of
Evans and Sabin, nor does he require reminders about

standard reference works. For extended bibliography in both primary and secondary texts, he is referred to the biographies, histories, and editions of such scholars as David Beers Quinn, Howard Mumford Jones, Samuel Eliot Morison, John Bartlet Brebner, George P. Hammond, Agapito Rey, W. L. Grant, H. P. Biggar, James Phinney Baxter, Herbert E. Bolton, and the editors of the Hakluyt Society publications. The chapter bibliographies provide specific references to appropriate books of theirs. The *Bibliography* of the *Literary History of the United States* (volume III) provides a necessarily selective listing of titles, in first publication and edited reprint.

Contents

He who would see the New World
The Golden Pole, the second,
Other seas, other lands,
Achievements great, and wars,
And such things attempted
As alarm and give pleasure,
Strike terror and lend delight;—
Read of the author this pleasing story,
Where nothing fabulous is told,
All worthy of being esteemed,
Read, considered, used.

> —Epigram to the *Relaçam verdadiera* of
> the Gentleman of Elvas, to which is
> added the note: "Golden Pole is used
> because the region is rich."

1 / *The Golden Pole*

In the study of American culture, too much is known about too little, and too little is known about too much. For a demonstration, take a quick glance at the *Bibliography Supplement* to the *Bibliography* of the *Literary History of the United States*. Covering the publications in the field between 1948 and 1962, the *Supplement* offers two pages of critical reference, or somewhat too much of a good thing, under the name of William Faulkner. For the whole of the sixteenth century, a close reader, scanning such general categories as "The Colonial Period to 1760: General Studies," will find an occasional, possible reference. Checking the book or essay referred to, he will most likely find that it has nothing to do with anything written before 1600. By implication, the discoverers and occupiers of the northern continent above Mexico between 1493 and 1599 were men of silence, or— where they can be shown to have voiced their experiences— unworthy of intellectual consideration. Neither is true. With all admiration for Faulkner, he himself could not have written as he did if earlier writers had not exercised for him his aboriginal materials and his voyage forms. The sensitive, well-read critic who links Faulkner's "The Bear" to Homer has ignored the closer background of American Indian animism.

American Genesis, in the attempt to bring before an American reader the literature of his first hundred and twenty-five years from Columbus to John Smith, has a moral as well as a critical purpose. The argument takes, for departure, the position that without a knowledge of the beginnings, understanding of later outcomes is distorted and limited. The modern critic, unless he is a specialist in the seventeenth and eighteenth centuries, will have been dragged through John Smith, William Bradford, Cotton Mather, and Jonathan Edwards as an undergraduate, and has probably come out of the misbegotten assignment with the firm plan never again to read, study, or take into account anything composed before 1790 at earliest. *Genesis* agrees with him that his experience has likely been void of interest or enlightenment, but suggests that a start in the 1490s will serve him better, and that with such a start Smith, Bradford, Mather, and Edwards will gain significance and excitement. For the general, should-be audience of American literature, it suggests a duty as well as a pleasure. Here our physical, social, intellectual, and cultural marches are first compassed about. To obey the commandment of Alexander Pope and the Delphic oracle surely requires their resurveying. If Sad Sack, blurred by his daily battles, rejects the duty and finds no pleasure in self-knowledge, surely he can respond to the action of other men's battles—conquests, defeats, starvations, survivals, sudden wealths, and sudden impoverishments, along with visions of golden men and cities, high offices under grateful kings, principalities over subject peoples, the establishment of true faiths, and the gaining of glory. Such are the subjects his earliest literature offers him.

If the accepted chronology is arbitrary, geography too has set up a fence against the study of our particular landscape or landscapes of man. Apparently nothing ever writ-

ten by one who sailed the St. Lawrence River can be called
"American," that term having become the adjective for the
noun United States. Nor can anything west of the Mississippi (until 1803), or south of the Rio Grande, or in Florida
until long after the colonial period. The St. Lawrence, by
the evidence, is particularly restrictive. Champlain may be
in Maine, or New York, or Massachusetts, but his writing is
irretrievably Canadian, and Canadian writing is not
"American." And so for many of the Jesuit "Relations."
The Spanish narratives of the Southwest have gained regional acceptance, but not national. They belong to the literatures of California and New Mexico, but not to "America." The absurdities multiply as the criticism of literature is
closed in by boundaries which did not exist for hundreds of
years, and when they do finally exist establish loci for customs houses, not for libraries.

One part of the geographical discrimination comes out of
language. The Atlantic seaboard contributes without question to American literature because its language is English.
This is not true, of course. The shared, and largely dominant language of the seaboard is English. But in any corner
of the northern Atlantic area, French, Italian, Portuguese,
Finnish, Polish, or what have you, may now be spoken, and
may have been spoken since the 1500s. French, Italian, and
Portuguese were certainly written, along with the to-be-
come-prevalent English tongue. "America" and the stu-
dents of "American" culture are going to have to work up
their languages, or make do with translations, because
theirs is a polyglot inheritance.

Polyglot in society and politics, in religion, in cultural acceptances and rejections, in speech and writing—with such
a syndrome, a nation in the making inevitably creates a
polyglot literature. *Genesis* not only records this imperative,
but celebrates it, insisting that the multilingual texts hitherto assigned to history alone belong to imaginative writing

as well, in whatever language they may have been composed or printed. In the assemblage, English takes an honorable, but not a ruling, place, and John Smith the Englishman wisely borrows and develops the ideas of the Frenchman, Marc Lescarbot.

What is the outcome of such a study, in brief? In the broad range of culture, the text itself is an epitome, and must stand as such. In the narrower area of literature, certain abbreviations are possible. For structure and form, the voyage governs the sixteenth century. Most readily identified there, it continues for three later centuries to provide the distinctive American pattern, even after the domestic and the logical designs have become its rivals. The sixteenth century's approach to presentation is journalistic, in all of the meanings of the adjective. (Dos Passos might have got his techniques from the sixteenth century, but it is very unlikely that he did—he no doubt adopted them, as his forebears did, because they were inherent in his subjects.) One specifically American genre manifests itself—the short story. Certain kinds of action appear or foreshadow themselves, such as the martyrdom, the Indian captivity, the Indian battle, and the search for the mine. Others—the sea passage, piracy, and the slave ship, for instance—are touched upon, but have to wait for development. Along with dramatic confrontations, the literature makes manifest American archetypes in their many behaviors, concepts and percepts present or in the making, the shaping and misshaping of traditions, the alchemical revelation of truth through falsehood, of good success through failure and defeat. All these join together to show the processes by which life and writing define a new civilization. The large general process is the negation of static being, and the affirmation of becoming.

The great spectacle is the one before which, in its earliest years, Peter Martyr rejoiced. "Every day the harvest in-

creases, and overtops that of the last. The exploits of Saturn
and Hercules and other heroes, glorified by antiquity, are
reduced to nothing." With the same pen, he reported the
extermination of the Lucayan natives, death and disease
among the Spaniards under Bartholomew Columbus—his
three hundred men sick and starving, with everything lacking, "even the necessities of life"—and the even worse stress
of the seven hundred colonists at Veragua, of whom only
some forty survived. By no stretch can Peter Martyr be
called an American writer. America contributes the experience. He reads it, and reflects the American paradox,
which other writers, more truly native, could express less
well, perhaps, but had themselves undergone. *Genesis* makes
their work its subject, a "pleasing story," as the sponsor of
the Gentleman of Elvas says,

> "All worthy of being esteemed,
> Read, considered, used."

2 / *Eastward in Eden*

This study of the pre-colonial writing of northern America finds its texts in history, examining them as works of art which unfold in dramatic action and imagery and idea and interpretation. Its central statement is simple enough to be made at once. The sixteenth-century documents of Western exploration, by definition a record of voyages by sea and land, make the first development of a new literature indigenous to the general area which is now the United States and inseparable from the historic experience undergone there. In that "pleasing story," the arts of information and those of imaginative involvement take part. Both treat of discovery in its literal meaning, and share the disclosure. The most florid piece of poetic embellishment has its historic attribute, while the official report can generate emotion and show forth comedy or tragedy.

The time under consideration, something more than a hundred years, stretches from 1493 to the early 1600s. It makes a single epoch, most conveniently named the "sixteenth century." The terminology is loose, as is that of the appropriate geography. Since political boundaries had no existence, the boundaries of the American north are taken to be cultural. Northern Mexico (Upper California, New Mexico, and the other Hispanic territories), the central and eastern stretches of the present United States, and the contiguous lands and seas of Canada offer something of a unity which a Spaniard might well call Florida, an Englishman Virginia, and a Frenchman the "Pays des Basques" or Nouvelle France. Once again, pleasingly enough, within the unity lies diversity.

Indeed, the beginning of both literature and history occurs outside the continent, to the east and south, when Columbus makes his landfall in the Caribbean, duly recorded in his journal. His justly famous letter of 1493, endorsed to Luis de Santangel, announces what he thought he had done. It is as well an outcry of jubilation. He is in Asia. By sailing west, he has reached the East and found there Paradise, a garden of fruit and gold.

Such glorious claims show only part of his entitlement to be considered the originator of a new body of writing. Beyond them, the form which circumstances forced upon him, the report which he had to provide, and his manner of presenting it make the letter not only a beginning but a prototype, a design which like the maps of the time has digressions and lacks, but nevertheless indicates a course for other men to follow and enlarge upon. Not, it should be said at once, through any so-called influence of the Santangel letter upon them, but because their trials and purposes were those which Columbus had undergone. Baldly put, they too had voyages and discoveries to report to princes and potentates remote from them.

The Columbus letter announces an achievement so magnificent, an event so astounding, that the writer had no need to stimulate excitement. If Columbus was aware that the letter was already highly developed as a European literary genre, he made no use of the knowledge. He writes informally, with a certain calculation to be sure, but not of a literary sort. Instead he keeps to his purpose, to communicate information which he himself was prevented from delivering. His voyage nearly over, he gives first its great result—"in thirty-three days I passed over to the Indies . . ." The words ring with a triumph untempered by art or artifice.

He follows the statement with a hurried account of his voyage which drastically abbreviates the calendar sequence of the journal he had kept, and thereafter quickens into a lyrical description of the newly discovered island landscapes and their inhabitants. Of La Spagnola (Haiti), he writes, "The lands thereof are high, and in it are very many ranges of hills, and most lofty mountains . . . all most beautiful in a thousand shapes, and all accessible, and full of trees of a thousand kinds, so lofty that they seem to reach the sky . . . And some of them were in flower, some in fruit . . . And the nightingale was singing, and other birds of a thousand sorts, in the month of November, there where I was going." Intoxicated with the paradise of his finding, he is little less so with its people, naked, timid, ignorant, and easily cheated though they be. Still he finds in them "subtle wit" and "wondrous lovingness" and an inclination for "love and service" towards the beings whose arrival they proclaim with loud cries of "Come! come to see the people from Heaven!"

In the last part of the letter, Columbus scatters his attention. He has looked for the monsters he was prepared to see, but has found none. However, he is told that one island which he has not yet visited is inhabited by ferocious cannibals and another, entirely by women. The people of a third (where there is incalculable gold) "have no hair." These legacies from Mandeville or Pliny or other tellers of tales, mixed as they are with actualities, show a process which manifests itself again and again in American writing. Columbus and his sailors expected the marvelous; the natives, always obliging and quite familiar with monstrosities of their own creation, were quick to satisfy the expectation. Columbus, beyond the range of his vision, perceives the extraordinary—anthropophagi, the depilate, Amazons— while he sees before his own eyes a people "very comely."

He returns finally to a celebration of his victory "over things which seem impossible," and to promises of future glory and wealth. He will give "their Highnesses" gold and valuable goods, and slaves from among the idolators "as many as they shall order."

Ending in haste, he thanks God who has given the "victory," and rejoices for Christendom and the Holy Trinity in the conversion to be accomplished "of so many peoples to our holy faith." His piety is beyond question, and yet he leaves one dilemma unmet and probably unrecognized. If these people as idolaters can legitimately be enslaved, will they as Christians gain the right to freedom?

He gives still another sign of the tragedy which would almost at once corrupt his idyl. His sailors had found that they could swindle the natives by trading trash for gold. Columbus forbade it and required fair dealing, but did not realize—could not, within his culture—that when he promised his royal patrons this empire with all its wealth, he doomed himself as well to a guilt of huge robbery. Again without understanding, he pointed to the future in speaking of the Spaniards he left to garrison a fort there. They are safe from attack by the unarmed, timorous savages, he says; yet, if by chance they are attacked, they are—however few —"sufficient to destroy all that land." In the event, Columbus was mistaken. On his second voyage, he found the fort destroyed and the garrison killed; later garrisons destroyed not the land but its peoples.

Such observations as those of Columbus, the dramatic development of which is a part of history, present or suggest the first subjects and statements of the literature of explora-

tion. The establishment of empire and the prospect of
wealth, a romantic utopianism and a vision of innocence,
the right to the conquest of bodies for labor, the winning of
souls to a true faith, the Christian entitlement to "pure"
land (land, that is, not held by other Christians, whose territories must by ironic extension have been termed "im-
pure"), and the prefiguring of the potentially dangerous
and monstrous unknown—these and other matters, explicit
or inherent, appear at once as topics or assumptions, though
not as images or interpretations such as other writers—some
of them contemporaries—were to offer. Later, when Columbus speaks of the Golden Chersonese and the Garden of
Eden, he is not metaphoric but literal. He believed Cuba to
be the former, and used topographical proof of the location
of the latter in Venezuela. "The Indies" meant Asia to him,
and gold a precious metal; neither carried any sort of sym-
bolism. For his monsters, he made no discrimination between the cannibals who did exist among the natives, and
the Amazons and bald men who did not. Within his defini-
tions he remains a strict realist.

The question of style is more complex, and further com-
plicated by translation. Speaker of a dialect Italian, with
little or no formal education, he had as a grown man
learned Latin, Portuguese, and a faulty Castilian Spanish,
in which he wrote all his letters. The first, inaccurate printing of the "Epistola" used his Spanish, to be followed immediately by a Latin translation and in the course of time by
translations into other European tongues. Out of the differences between the texts come many questions of correct-
ness.

That he was describing a situation for which no European vocabulary provided, made for inevitable distortion.
Occasionally he avoided it by using Indian terms; sometimes he committed himself, or his translators committed
him, to deceptive European phrasing. He gives the Indian

"canoa" for the dugout, but puts "heaven"—with all its Christian and European connotations—into a native context. "Town" appears in the letter, although Columbus more often uses "village" or "hamlet" for the native settlement. "King" substitutes for "cacique." Quite unconsciously used, his terms put a gloss of familiarity upon an experience never undergone before, and thereby interpret rather than signify.

Columbus himself was little likely to make such distinctions. He was a gifted writer, but not—even in the generous humanistic sense—a trained writer. He was rather luckily an amateur who took his structure from his subject, making with his pen as well as with his ships a venture in discovery. He is colloquial rather than formal, freely expressing emotion and enthusiasm; fluent and highly personal, sometimes to disorder and confusion. Nothing in his presentation supports his claim to have used the *Commentaries* of Julius Caesar as a model. The journal, with its day by day sequence, yields to the letter and its rearrangements. Beyond these Columbus did not go, but let such men as his own son, Ferdinand, Peter Martyr, and Bartolomé de Las Casas take his writings into more complex designs.

Just as the full dramatic implications of his explorations were hidden from him, so too he records rather than develops the drama of his career. No one composition of his portrays his rise to pre-eminence, his overthrow, and his downfall. Yet, in another letter, he recognizes his tragic reversal in his abandonment by his royal sponsors, and reaches literary consciousness and high eloquence. "I am indeed in as ruined a condition as I have related; hitherto I have wept over others;—may Heaven now have mercy upon me, and may the earth weep for me."

During the century after Columbus's death, American writing divides itself into two literatures, the one of the area of Mexico, the Caribbean, and Central and South America, Spanish-Portuguese in origin and elaboration; the other, cruder and still more varied, created by the Spanish, French, English, and Italians who traveled the North Atlantic and the Pacific coasts and explored far inland, across the Rio Grande and the Gulf of Mexico. Only the second of these is ancestral to the culture and the course of colonial literature in northern America, though the Spanish of the south and southwest provide a fortunate overlapping of the two. In its beginning, the discrimination is geographical, but without restriction to modern boundaries. At a time when Spanish "Florida" reached as far towards the Arctic as the ventures and imaginations of Spaniards could take it, while "Virginia" ran as far toward pole and tropic as English claims and ambitions dared to go, map lines were fictions. The written story accrues to the community shaped by it.

. In northern writing, the immediate successors of Columbus were the coastal explorers, keepers of sea journals. Like him of European birth and language, they were like him also in being little trained in rhetorical formalities. As writers they shared a single purpose—the communication of "true" discovery.

For the earliest northern voyages, from the mid-1490s to 1524, no narratives survive. The Italian Cabots, sailing under the English flag, and the Portuguese pilots, sailing sometimes for England and sometimes for Portugal, left nothing of literary significance, nor did the Spanish explorers of the area, nor the fishermen who frequented the northern latitudes. Practical individuals and professional seamen had no wish to divulge the secrets of their trade; nations in rivalry with each other were likely to withhold newly gained knowledge, hoarding it in archives which may still hide some of the prime classics of exploration.

In a later period some of these were reasonably soon

made public by compilers such as the Italian Ramusio, printer in 1556 of the first of the known "relations" of such a voyage—that of his fellow-countryman Giovanni da Verrazzano (1480?–1527?), who sailed for France to the "north parts" to establish a French claim to that country. Whatever the scholarly questions about his account, in its several versions, Richard Hakluyt included the Verrazzano narrative in his *Divers Voyages* of 1582.

The Verrazzano "Relation," dated July 8, 1524, is a straightforward report made to Francis I at the end of a voyage along the North Atlantic seaboard, probably from the Carolinas to Newfoundland. Verrazzano develops his subject as his voyage has developed, necessarily chronologically. He makes two kinds of interpolation, the one to describe the Indians, the other the "new land," which, he inaccurately boasts, was "never before seen of any man, either ancient or modern." Unlike Columbus he knew that he was not in Asia, although one version of his text comes close to stating that he is; like Columbus, but with less reason, he is sure that the sweet-smelling forests cannot be "altogether void of drugs or spicerie and other richesse of gold." Again, his landscape has the beauties of a paradise. Its people are "nimble" and "sharp witted"; indeed, they have the qualities of the Chinese "of the uttermost parts of China." He does not say by what evidence he makes this identification, but expresses himself as though he could count upon the king's understanding.

He varies his account with scenes and anecdotes as he progresses northward. One such describes a young sailor rescued from drowning by the natives, who cries out piteously in fear of them. Believing that he is to be roasted over the fire they build to warm him, he finds himself instead comforted and restored, whole and undevoured, to his shipmates. Another episode gives a charming sketch of the "sport" by which an Indian "king" and his "gentlemen" entertain the sailors, while "the queen and her maids" watch at a distance.

Fact and fancy are congenial enough in his text, probably because Verrazzano saw no conflict between them. The Asian geographical confusion (or perhaps intentional misguidance) is curiously clarified in the so-called "cosmographical appendix" of one of the Verrazzano manuscripts. As fantasy, his Asia joins such terms as "king," "queen," "gentlemen," and "maids" to invest a rather close, literal description with an air of illusion. His vocabulary and his preconceptions take him into unrealities, when he plainly meant to deal with the actual. He is clear of all deception, however, in reporting that towards the end of his passage off the coast of Maine, he found hostile savages, who had probably been preyed upon often enough by kidnapping fishermen. Verrazzano marks the hostility, but offers no reason for it—his own sailors had already, without any particular animus, tried to catch two Indian women, and succeeded in making off with the child of one of them. He is so little concerned that he does not say what became of the boy.

Verrazzano's successor in French exploration, Jacques Cartier (1494–c. 1553), likewise contributes to the sea narrative. For each of his three proven voyages to the area of the St. Lawrence in Canada, there remains an account of which he may or may not have been the author. The relations are commonly ascribed to him, however, and are assumed to be his by such near-contemporaries as Ramusio and Hakluyt. The third among them, of the voyage of 1541–1542, is fragmentary and in a literary sense negligible. The "First Voyage" or "Discours" or "Relation Originale" for 1534, and the "Second Voyage" or *Brief Récit* for 1535–1536, on the other hand, offer valuable evidence of development. Whether Cartier wrote them or not, their phrasing indicates that they are by the same writer, who in the first instance kept close to the pattern of the sea journal, with its sequence of dates and its movement forward according to the movement of time and the voyage. The second relation, though the order is still broadly chronological, adopts a different and more ambitious arrangement, in an attempt to build to a dramatic climax the fear of an attack by the Indians of the St. Lawrence. Historic truth defeated the effort— Cartier escaped the feared uprising by sailing for home— and so the carefully built and heightened threat comes to nothing.

The "First Voyage," of which a French manuscript version was not known or printed until 1867, was first published in Italian (1556) by Ramusio. The text is that of a professional pilot who, except for certain significant interpolations, concentrates upon his course. For his patron, the King of France, or for other pilots its interest is high. For the modern reader, inexpert in the detailed geography of the Gulf of St. Lawrence and in navigation, the result is confusion to the point of incoherence, and a sense of hidden purpose. The political purpose was indeed concealed. Verrazzano having disappointed him, Francis I was again looking for a route by land or water to Asia, or—perhaps more accurately—a way to penetrate this outthrust, eastern projection of Asia and reach the wealth of Cathay, and had chosen Cartier to search for it. After three months, Cartier had to return to France, the exploration incomplete, its success not despaired of but not achieved.

What Cartier did find was a huge land and seascape, in the north a barren country which he calls "the land God gave to Cain" but to the south richly fertile. There he describes meadows bright with flowers and berries, forests magnificent with trees "wonderfully fair and of excellent odor," and islands as covered with birds "as a field of grass." The beaches show "many great beasts, like great oxen, which have two teeth in their chops, like teeth of the elephant, that go in the sea." White bears and black rival the walruses as wonders. The seas and ponds swarm with fish, and the woods offer fruits and nuts.

Cain's land, then, and a garden. Significantly, he looks at the people he meets with the same doubleness. They are now wholly genial innocents, singing and dancing in joy; now wild, thievish, and ungovernable. Such contradictions were to appear and reappear in the writings of three centuries.

In shape, the "First Voyage" is a simple continuity, with little indication of planned structure. Hints of possible elaboration exist, however, in the graceful paragraphs descriptive of the landscape and its inhabitants. Pointing towards their extended counterparts of the "Second Voyage," these show pictorial freshness and stylistic purity.

"The said savages passed over with one of their boats and fetched us some pieces of seals all cooked, which they put upon pieces of wood and then withdrew, making us a sign that they gave them to us. . . . And they were in number, of men, women, and children as well, more than three hundred, of which part of their women, who did not pass over, danced and sung, standing in the sea up to their knees. The other women, who had passed to the other side where we were, came freely to us and stroked our arms with their hands, and then raised their joined hands to the sky, making many signs of joy. . . ."

The far more ambitious *Brief Récit* or "Second Voyage" of 1535–1536, first published in 1545, sets a definitely literary and philosophic tone in the dedicatory address "To the most Christian King." Its author (Cartier is especially doubted here) makes a metaphor of the westering course of the sun and the westering course of "our most holy faith . . . the Church Catholic." A man of piety, he offers Francis "sure hope" in evangelism; a man of the world, he promises the king an equal assurance of increase in "your seigno-

ries" and in fame. A man of learning, he challenges the
philosophers who without direct evidence declare this "arctic" zone uninhabitable. Against them he quotes Aristotle—
"Experientia est rerum magistra"—and "simple sailors"
who "have known the contrary . . . by true experience."

Upon the truth of experience his story both stands and
falls. Offering at first much the same sort of pilot's journal
as the "First Voyage," he stays throughout with act and observation, but increasingly elaborates upon them, writing
with ease and flexibility within planned divisions. His Indians begin to have at least a composite personality, while two
of them, Donacona of Stadacone (Quebec) and Taignoagny
the deceiver, are characters in outline. The scenes of greeting in the Indian towns are dramatized, as is an innocent
trick in which the usually honest Donacona joins. To keep
hold on the French and their valuable trinkets, and to prevent them from dealing with western Indians further up the
St. Lawrence, the savages produce a veritable play with
three horned "devils" sent by the Indian deity to warn the
French that upriver they will die in ice and snow. "And
suddenly came the said boat wherein were the three men
appearing to be three devils, having great horns on their
heads, and he in the midst made a marvelous speech in
coming, and they passed along our ships with their said
boat, without in any wise turning their looks toward us, and
went on striking and running on shore with their said boat,
and, all at once, the said lord Donacona and his people
seized the said boat and the said three men, the which were
let fall to the bottom of it like dead men, and they carried
the whole together into the woods, which were distant from
the said ships a stone's throw; and not a single person remained before our said ships, but all withdrew themselves."

Taignoagny and Dom Agaya, the two Indians whom
Cartier on the first voyage had snatched off to France, interpret the little piece of theatre for the Frenchmen. The two

march out of the woods "having their hands joined, and
their hats under their elbows, causing great admiration.
And the said Taignoagny began to speak and cry out three
times, 'Jesus! Jesus! Jesus!' raising his eyes toward heaven.
Then Dom Agaya began to say, 'Jesus Maria! Jacques Cartier,' looking toward heaven like the other. The captain,
seeing their gestures and ceremonies, began to ask what was
the matter, and what it was new that had happened, who
responded that there were piteous news, saying, 'Nenny est
il bon.' "

The warning, "No ways is this good," followed by the explanation that the Indian god sent his message by these en-
voys, did not hold back the adventurers from the golden
possibilities of Cathay, whatever the danger of death. They
laughed at the warning and went on their way towards "Cibola," that dream and drama of European making which
was to destroy many lives. Soon disenchanted of the visionary Seven Cities, they found consolation—proffered by the
always obliging and equally wonder-loving Indians—in a
new dream kingdom, the "Kingdom of the Saguenay." Up
the Ottawa River, a month's journey to the north, or up the
Saguenay River and by the west, they would come to a
country whose people dressed like them "in cloth," who possessed many virtues, many towns, and much copper and
gold; a country watered like Eden—"the whole . . . an
island, the which is encompassed and surrounded by the
said river and streams; and . . . beyond the said Saguenay
the said stream flows, entering into two or three great lakes
of water very wide; then . . . one finds a fresh-water sea of
which there is no mention of having seen the end, as they
have heard by those of the Saguenay; for they have told us
that they have not been there."

Even in a translation, the sorcery of the tale comes
through. Something of truth and something of mirage, part

hearsay and part wish, under many names—Saguenay, Cibola, the Seven Cities, the grand Copal, Lago de Oro, the
Island of the Amazons, California, Anian, Cosa—the
golden, unreachable country becomes part of the American
prospect, never to be dispelled, as fresh and firm to Mark
Twain's Colonel Sellers as to Jacques Cartier and his crew.

Perhaps actuality had less effect, although the narrator
celebrates the grandeur and beauty and abundance of the
land which he had himself seen, with its mountains and
plains, its rivers and lakes, its vines and trees, grains and
fruits, its birds and beasts and fishes. Adding only one touch
of fantasy—"a beast which has but two feet . . . the form
and size of a palm and more"—he offers his lists: stags,
bears, foxes, wolves, hares, martens; cranes, swans, bustards,
wild geese, ducks, wild pigeons, nightingales; whales, sea
hogs, seahorses, salmon, mackerel, mullet. At the end of
each series, he has to add "and other beasts," "and other
wild things," "and other birds," "and other fish," marveling
at their numbers and sizes and kinds, both known and new.

Summer passed. With winter, Cartier beached his ships
and built a fort. There he was to undergo the other aspect of
the wilderness, its deadliness. Though the narrator makes
little of the threat of hunger, he cannot put aside the horror
of the cold. Listening to stories of a country, a month's traveling away, "where there is never ice or snow," and where
"oranges, almonds, nuts, plums" grow in abundance, he
suffers and tries to survive the frozen earth and water, exist-
ing five months "locked up in ice, the which was more than
two fathoms in thickness, and over the land there was the
height of four feet of snow and more, so that it was higher
than the sides of our ships . . . insomuch that our drink-
ables were all frozen within the casks. And throughout our
said ships, as well as above, the ice upon the sides was four
inches in thickness, and all the said river was frozen . . . at

which time there deceased among us even to the number of twenty-five persons of the chiefest and best companions that we had. . . ."

Such is human physical endurance that these mourned companions died not of cold but of scurvy, from which one hundred of Cartier's one hundred and ten sickened; and all were threatened with death as they watched over those who succumbed. Here is Florio's sixteenth-century rendering:

"That day Philip Rougemont, born in Amboise, died, being twenty-two years old, and because the sickness was to us unknown, our Captain caused him to be ripped to see if by any means possible we might know what it was, and so seek means to save and preserve the rest of the company: he was found to have his heart white, but rotten, and more than a quart of red water about it: his liver was indifferent fair, but his lungs black and mortified, his blood was altogether shrunk about the heart, so that when he was opened great quantity of rotten blood issued out from about his heart: his milt toward the back was somewhat perished, rough as it had been rubbed against a stone. Moreover, because one of his thighs was very black without, it was opened, but within it was whole and sound: that done, as well as we could he was buried."

If the luxuriant scene, praised for its summer kindness, in winter turned murderous, so too might the savages change. Friendly, humorous, gay, generous, and simple, they could hide and nurse anger, and plan revenge. They could teach a cure for scurvy and plot a massacre, deceiving without scruple. The French, now paternally kind, now mercilessly self-interested, outdid them in trickery and outrage, kidnapping their chief men once more and sailing off for France beyond the range of retribution.

The Cartier author largely tells his story as a journalist. He is likely to offer juxtapositions rather than significant comparisons. In certain discrete passages, he shows his sense of comedy or his awareness of tragedy. He is not yet able to sustain the achievement which is within his possibilities.

He takes his place then not as the creator of a body of writing which establishes his individual claims, but as one of many men who, in an almost genealogical linkage, join to bring about a long slow growth both of culture and of literature.

3 / *Passage, O Soul to India!*

Variously placed in the various editions of the Cartier narratives, but always part not of the narrative but of a list of Indian terms, there appears a curious, unexplained entry—"Ceux de Canadas disent qu'il faut une lune à naviger depuis Hochelaga, jusques à une terre ou se prend la canelle et la girofle." . . . you must sail beyond Montreal for a month to reach a land of cinnamon and cloves. Vocabulary entry or no, to the sixteenth-century knowledgeable the statement was a dramatic culmination. So placed, it might give evidence of a writer's ineptitude in arranging his materials. It remained, nevertheless, testimony to Cartier's near achievement of the spice islands of the South Sea with their precious crops. To his own mind, he was only a month away, and yet, as it had eluded Columbus and Verrazzano, the Cabots, and many another, the plunder of the East, however close at hand, lay beyond the grasping.

It would be difficult to establish exactly when—if such a moment occurred—the American coast ceased to be outer Asia, and became a reef forbidding a direct course there. The references of contemporary texts waver, to obscure rather than clarify such identifications. Certainly Cartier by

the end of his voyage of 1535–1536 had convinced himself
that he must penetrate the known shore to find his Oriental
destination. Within a few years after Cartier had ended his
search, new explorers were to try to pierce the barrier—to
their judgment narrow—which lay between the Atlantic
and Pacific oceans, fending them off from India and Cathay.

Persuaded by the statements of ancient and contemporary authorities and by the reports of seamen, hopeful ven-
turers declared that the northern parts of America consisted
entirely of islands. Somewhere, through this archipelago or
to the north of it, a strait led to Asia. In 1566, Sir Humphrey Gilbert brought the evidences together in a com-
plexly reasoned essay which formulated the case for "a passage to the Northwest to Cathaia, and the East Indies." For
Gilbert the terms of the American voyage of discovery had
definitely changed. It no longer explored Oriental coasts,
but looked for a west-leading waterway to reach them. With
the shift, the sea journals take up a new subject and move
toward new designs. The conflict is that of men against the
hostile elements, with God the ruler of the outcome between
his two creations.

For many reasons, economic, political, and scientific, the
seekers for the passage took their way northward in the Atlantic. One school of opinion correctly held that the route
across the pole itself was the shortest, and (less correctly)
that the polar regions above the known ice fields rejoiced in
a mild climate. Attempts to reach that temperate zone invariably failed, so that the later voyagers tried to skirt or
force the ice, in the continuing search below the pole for the
"Strait of Anian," a waterway created by the single word
"Ania" in Marco Polo's *Travels.*

The same complex of reasons led English navigators,
rather than Spanish, Portuguese, or French, to take over the

search in the last half of the sixteenth century. Under the stimulus of Gilbert's "Discourse," and roused by a noble ambition, following charts which showed actual and legendary lands and seas with equal authority, they added to those of earlier voyagers their stories of fiery mountains, towers and islands of ice, mines of gold, and fearful skies and oceans.

What they did—such of them at least who tried to penetrate the arctic—is hardly conceivable to the more accurately informed mind. Only the limits of their knowledge can explain their extravagant courage and the endurances they demanded of themselves and their crews. Ignorance fortified them, then, along with an aspiration voiced by their predecessor, Sebastian Cabot, and reported to Hakluyt: ". . . all men with great admiration affirmed it to be a thing more divine than human, to sail by the West into the East where spices grow, by a way that was never known before, by this fame and report there increased in my heart a great flame of desire to attempt some noble thing."

The "great flame of desire" burned high in Martin Frobisher (1535?–1594) who in three successive voyages, all chronicled, tried to force his way "through so many and so great mountains of fleeting ice, with so great storms of cold" to the "temperate" zone he expected. Frobisher's harsh experiences destroyed the theoretical argument; yet, resolved to accomplish "the only thing of the world that was left yet undone, whereby a notable mind might be made famous and fortunate," he yielded only to physical impossibility, the close prospect of starvation, and—after his third failure to find ores of true gold or the passage he looked for—the refusal of the profit-minded to back him.

Of the narratives of the Frobisher voyages, George Best's, which covers all three and is prefaced by a learned cosmographical essay, is the most ambitious and the most extended. But Best's *A true discourse of the late voyages . . . of Mar-*

tin Frobisher, General . . . (1578) varies from the already
conventional form only in the introduction, and the three-
fold repetition of pattern. It is a grouping and a replication,
rather than—in literary aspects—a change or enrichment.

As drama and as writing, Thomas Ellis's *A true report of
the third and last voyage . . . atchieved by . . . Martine Frobisher
. . .* (1578) far surpasses anything of Best's. Simply, but still
in magnificent Elizabethan English, Ellis makes the struggle of men against a horrendous nature emotionally appalling. His is the confrontation, in an immensity of danger, between human effort, fortitude, and pride, with wholly destructive and irrational elemental forces. God alone, so
reads Ellis's thesis, governs the outcome between his two depraved creations. In the mercy of God alone, lies the redemption of men's frailty.

Much of Ellis's power comes from the singleness and seriousness of his text. His action is of the greatest significance,
heightened in his presentation by precision and economy of
wording, and the tensions of his conflict. He speaks not so
much for himself, or for Frobisher, as for the simple men of
the nearly doomed company.

His first climax builds upon these three: action, actors,
and statement. "The storm still increased and the ice en-
closed us, so that we were fain to take down top and top
masts: for the ice had so environed us, that we could see neither land nor sea, as far as we could ken: so that we were
fain to cut our cables to hang overboard for fenders, somewhat to ease the ship's sides from the great and dreary
strokes of the ice: some with capstan bars, some fending off
with oars, some with planks of two inches thick, which were
broken immediately with the force of the ice, some going
out upon the ice to bear it off with their shoulders from the
ships. But the rigorousness of the tempest was such, and the
force of the ice so great, that not only they burst and spoiled
the foresaid provision, but likewise so rased the sides of the

ships, that it was pitiful to behold, and caused the hearts of many to faint.

"Thus we continued all that dismal and lamentable night plunged in this perplexity, looking for instant death: but our God (who never leaveth them destitute which faithfully call upon him, although he often punisheth for amendment's sake) in the morning caused the winds to cease, and the fog which all that night lay on the face of the water to clear: so that we might perceive about a mile from us, a certain place clear from any ice, to the which with an easy breath of wind which our God sent us, we bent ourselves. And furthermore, he provided better for us than we deserved or hoped for: for when we were in the foresaid clear place, he sent us a fresh gale at West or at West Southwest, which set us clear without all the ice. And further he added more: for he sent us so pleasant a day as the like we had not of a long time before, as after punishment consolation."

So he continues in the alternation of despair and release with which the voyage itself provided him, until the final succor of the arrival in England.

If it be argued that the mere unfolding of his experience, which he himself thoroughly trusted for effect, makes his merit without selection or skill, then the comparison with the other Frobisher voyage narratives can be made to prove Ellis's quality. He was, after all, the one of these writers—none of them without their eloquences—who understood the dramatic values in the shifting chances of life and death, and the one who came closest to presenting the ironic contradiction which is to recur in American writing, between a hostile and nearly or quite overpowering nature created by the just God for the testing of his sinful peoples, and the merciful heaven which defends men from it.

For the late 1580s, the Northwest Passage cycle continues in the voyages of John Davis—brisk, direct, factual sea journals. Composed by various writers, without embellishment, they have their energies and effects, but make no variations upon already established statements and patterns. The abstract reads, we sailed, did and saw this and this, suffered and were saved or lost, made such and such encounters with the savages, hungered, thirsted, and were stormworn, but some among us came home. Yet in fresh scenes and stronger emphases upon such topics as Indian sorcery and Christian condemnation of it, the Davis authors give evidences that they too meant to go beyond the report, and tried to vary what had become a formula.

To this pattern, Ellis had supplied a controlling thesis. The later Edward Hayes, chronicler for Sir Humphrey Gilbert's voyage of 1583, breaks the design in his beginning by lack of control. His opening passages are confused and inept, in the attempt to provide facts. Gilbert, defeated in one attempt to sail to Asia, had launched another expedition of crossed aims. He proposed to found a colony on land granted him by Elizabeth; he wanted to find gold; and he meant ultimately to discover the Asian water road, the existence of which he had demonstrated in his highly academic and curious essay, the "Discourse" of 1566, which he printed ten years later.

Hayes, Gilbert's historian, in the early pages of his "Report" (1589), is still more divided than his subject. Nevertheless, he is a man of literary awareness, who finally achieves the expression of a classic as well as cosmic morality. From his early disjointment, he moves into a narrative of high action combined with ethical statement, and eventually into the presentation of a "character," in the literary form of the Elizabethan period. Thereby, he makes Gilbert the tragic hero spoiled by fault.

Before he arrives at his culmination, Hayes has to present the warnings of overthrow. Meticulous in detail, he reports the evening of Wednesday, the 28th of August, "fair and pleasant, yet not without token of storm to ensue." Gilbert himself by chance has boarded the frigate, the smallest of his fleet of three. On board the *Delight*, which was the "admiral" or commanding ship of the small fleet, the ship's company, "like the swan that singeth before her death, continued in sounding of trumpets, with drums, and fifes; also winding the cornets, hautboys," to be "in the end of their jollity, left with the battell and ringing of doleful knells." A school of porpoises "did portend storm." The crew of the frigate make "frivolous reports . . . of strange voices, the same night, which scared some from the helm."

The subsequent shipwreck of the *Delight* and the loss of nearly a hundred men, among whom died Stephen Parmenius of Buda, one of the few scholars who dared undertake the American voyage, ruined Gilbert's hopes of wealth, empire, and fame. Two of those who saved themselves from the wreck died of hunger and hardship. From the awful story, Hayes takes his argument. "Thus whom God delivered from drowning, he appointed to be famished, who doth give limits to man's times, and ordaineth the manner and circumstance of dying: whom again he will preserve, neither sea nor famine can confound."

The simpler seamen of the other vessels, hungry, naked, and fearful, understanding the hopelessness of their venture, wanted to go home, and Gilbert yielded to them. At the very instant of turning back, they saw—so Hayes writes—an apparition on the face of the water, "a very lion to our seeming . . . turning his head to and fro, yawning and gaping wide, with ugly demonstration of long teeth, and glaring eyes, and to bid us a farewell . . . he sent forth a horrible voice, roaring and bellowing. . . ." Refusing to name its spiritual shape, Hayes is reticent, but declares that Gilbert "took it for Bonum Omen, rejoicing that he was to war against such an enemy, if it were the devil."

Thereafter, "with God's ordinance upon him," for what

mysterious end Hayes does not yet try to say, Gilbert in au-
dacity and unreason prepares the circumstances of his own
death. In a rage of despair, he beats the serving boy who has
left his sample of "gold" on board the lost *Delight,* and
boasts inordinately of good success to come in a later attempt. The appearance of "a little fire by night" upon the
main yard Hayes calls "usual in storms," but the sailors
take it as "an evil sign." Finally, in "rashness" rather than
resolution, Gilbert trusts himself again to the frail, small
frigate instead of the larger surviving ship.

Gilbert's famous speech, "We are as near to heaven by
sea as by land," made before the frigate was "devoured and
swallowed up of the sea," takes on by his act a double significance. It attests, as Hayes himself does, to Gilbert's piety
and courage, but also marks him as one who is guilty of excess and presumption, in identifying the divine purpose
with his own. In the summary estimation, Hayes finds him,
"as it were impatient to abide in expectation better opportunity and means, which God might raise" so that he
"thrust himself" into a venture "for which he was not fit,
presuming the cause pretended on God's behalf, would
carry him to the desired end." The last emphasis lies, however, upon his correction, and the restoration of the divine
order. "Then as he was refined, and made nearer drawing
unto the image of God: so it pleased the divine will to re-
sume him unto himself, whither both his, and every other
high and noble mind, have always aspired."

Hayes has taken out of the inevitable American experience the equally inevitable voyage form. Having permitted himself a series of structural faults for information's
sake, he arrives at an imaginative heightening of fact by the
expression of moral and theological belief and by recourse
to a contemporary literary genre. His voyage is no longer a
simple sea journal, but a minor cosmology within which
"success" must be discovered by heroic and fallible man-

kind. His achievement in writing lies in the building of these interpretations, and in their enaction.

Henry Hudson (?–1611) is the last of the English voyagers to contribute, in the tradition of the sixteenth century, to the sea narrative as literature and literary form. Of his four voyages, he made the first two for the English Muscovy Company. They were attempts to reach the Orient by the North Pole, or more accurately by a northeast passage. The accounts which survive, written for the most part by Hudson himself, record course and compass readings, make note of fish to be found, and birds and animals, and provide such other facts as Hudson thought useful and interesting. The third voyage, of 1609, undertaken by Hudson for the Dutch East India Company, survives in a report of much the same order, written this time by Hudson's mate, Robert Juet. Again Hudson had undertaken to find a northeast passage, but once again confronting an impossibility, changed his course to the northwest, to find a passage where Gilbert and Davis and Frobisher and the other earlier explorers had failed to find it.

Juet's journal of the voyage along the American coast is chiefly known for its description of the river, later to be named for Hudson. As writing, it is undistinguished. Beyond the presentation of a few genial episodes, and a brutal conflict between the Indians and the sailors, it offers no novelty in development or subject. Its importance lies in history. The ending of the voyage, in which England reclaimed her navigator, ultimately has literary significance. Under English auspices once again, Hudson embarked in 1610 on his fourth and last voyage, on which his mutinous crew cast him adrift to die. For this voyage, there survives a significant piece of writing, whose author, sent on the disastrous journey by one of Hudson's patrons, carries further the pattern which Ellis and Hayes had enriched. By some latent talent, this Abacuk Pricket, less literate than Hayes but with as deep a moral concern, in order to disclose the even more terrible event of the casting away of Henry Hudson by his mutinous crew, guides his narrative to the planned effects of fiction, without betraying his facts.

His subject is not far from Hayes's, since on his fourth voyage Hudson pushed his search for the passage beyond the limits of God's will and of human capacity to suffer, and thereby drew upon himself a fearful punishment. Yet Pricket does not say so. He does not aim to teach, but to convince. In the admitted guilt of an unpardonable mutiny and murder at sea, he tries to gain pardon for the mutineers who survived, among them (unwillingly, he says) himself. Since no excuse of hunger or suffering or abiding terror could suffice to win release for the self-convicted men, his recourse is to a nearly legal pleading.

He writes after the return to England in Hudson's ship *Discovery* of the misery-ridden remnants of the crew, those whom he names as their leaders and instigators having died by violence on the way home. Here he is perhaps suspect as historian, and upon this "fact" his legal argument rests. Once he gains acceptance for their deaths, under the judgment of God, he can insist that God's will has shown itself, and that the lesser guilts have been absolved. "There are many devices in the heart of man, but the counsel of the Lord shall stand."

Pricket begins his "Larger Discourse" with the embarcation of the ship *Discovery*. Hudson, on his last voyage to find a passage to the East, in 1610, took a course by the Orkneys to Iceland, Greenland, and at last to the mainland at Hudson's Strait and Bay. For this part of the journey, Iceland's Mount Hecla gave the omen—it "cast out much fire, a sign of foul weather to come." Three whales threatened the vessel but did it no damage. West of Greenland the *Discovery* ran into ice, "the first great island or mountain of ice, whereof after we saw store."

Thereafter, indeed, the ice endangered them at every shift of course, and Pricket mentions it constantly, as though the word itself would force a recognition of human vulnerability and fear. Early, the crew saw one of the great islands of ice "overturn." He calls the spectacle "a good warning to us, not to come nigh them nor within their reach." A day later, a storm blew the ice down upon them, so that they had to use the biggest field for a harbor. "Some of our men this day fell sick, I will not say it was for fear, although I saw small sign of other grief."

As the voyage continues, and his story moves with it, Pricket speaks of the growing discontent of the crew, and Hudson's refusal to consider their sustenance. He would not let them rest a day or two on a pleasant shore where there was food to be had; he would have the anchor up in a storm, so that some were hurt; he would not listen when he was warned of rocks, but kept his course till the ship struck, to be got off "by the mercy of God"; he dealt uncharitably with John Williams, the gunner, who died in the month of November (Pricket does not say how), out of whose death came the "unhappy deed," as Pricket names it, cryptically adding "which brought a scandal upon all that are returned home, and upon the action itself, the multitude (like the dog) running after the stone, but not at the caster. . . ."

Promising "not to wrong the living nor slander the dead," he begins to trace the origins of the mutiny. Hudson had already displaced his mate, Robert Juet, in favor of one Robert Billet. This makes one thread of motive, as Pricket supplies it. Another came from the selling of the dead gunner's "gray cloth gown." Hudson would not let any of the crew have it, but allotted it to a certain Henry Greene, a retainer of his own who had already taken a share in every petty dispute that wracked the crew. Then, becoming displeased with Greene, Hudson gave it instead to Billet, and when

Greene protested "did so rail at Greene, with so many words of disgrace" that Greene—wrought upon by the devil—resolved to do Hudson "what mischief he could . . . and to thrust him and many other honest men out of the ship in the end."

Cold, hunger, and pain further the plot. Hudson, although he had supplies for only six months, determined to winter over on the shore of his bay, where the men managed to shelter themselves and were able to kill enough birds and catch enough fish to survive. They were even more fortunate to find a tree whose buds cured their scurvy. Still, their food ran short. Hudson had offended the only savage who came near them by making too shrewd a bargain; after that, the other natives kept away and would not deal with him.

Of the attempts to divide the remnants of bread and cheese, some of the food having been hidden and hoarded by the men, and perhaps by Hudson himself, Pricket writes confusedly and evasively. He is little clearer about the events of the night during which the mutineers hardened their intention to cast away Hudson and the sick and lame men of the crew, setting them adrift in the ship's boat. He is definite enough in his recognition of guilt. "It was dark, and they in a readiness to put this deed of darkness in execution. I . . . prayed them not to go hand in hand with it in the dark, but to stay till the morning. Now, every man (I hope) would go to his rest, but wickedness sleepeth not. . . ."

In the slow unfolding of detail, Henry Greene becomes the lawless executioner who is himself eventually executed, as are the other violent men who followed him. Of the castaways, the hero is not Hudson but the ship's carpenter who of his free will chooses to join Hudson and the other victims and disappears with them, while the mutineers make the ship "fly as from an enemy."

In the concluding pages of the narrative, Pricket completes his argument. Those whom he has shown deserving of the penalties of justice are killed. The rest, who had been led astray in their ignorance, become so weak from hunger that they cannot—or from despair will not—work the ship. Impotent though they are, winds and currents bring them to Ireland and survival. Pricket does not insist on the point of divine help, but lets the end of his story drift off in the arithmetic of bargaining for their travel to England. Nor does he word his underlying question—who can find it in his mind or heart further to condemn or punish such miserable victims as these, since God has let them live?

As with all the narratives of discovery, Pricket's considerable achievement as a writer depends upon the sense of actuality which he creates. He goes further than his fellow journalists, however, in presenting not only setting, act, and actor, but also tones of voice, essential among them his own. Early in the voyage, in volcanic Iceland, the Englishmen find hot springs to bathe in, and name the place Lousie Bay. Robert Juet, "when he was drunk," declared that Hudson "had brought in Greene to crack his credit that should displease him." Hudson "did so rail on Greene . . . telling him that all his friends would not trust him with twenty shillings, and therefore why should he."

As Pricket continues, he touches each accent. On the final night of the conspiracy, "Henry Greene came again and demanded . . . what I said. Wilson answered: He is in his old song, still patient. Then I spake to Henry Greene to stay three days . . . to forbear but two days, nay, twelve hours; there is no way then (say they) but out of hand." The hero-carpenter, taking his valiant chance with Hudson, makes his good-by to Pricket—"but (saith he) if we must part (which we will not willingly do, for they would follow the ship) he prayed me, if we came to the Capes before them, that I would leave some token that we had been there, near to the place where the fowls bred, and he would do the like for us: and so (with tears) we parted."

In the whole course of the sixteenth century, then, there is no planned aesthetic development of the sea journal. Development occurs, but not in order to meet the theories or manipulations of the arts. Pricket is not deliberate in writing fiction—he is presenting such a plea as might sway a court, and makes his effects in order to win an acquittal. He does notably manage his materials to this purpose, and thus far consciously arrives at the techniques of presentation. In so doing he becomes, unawares, an initiator of that specifically American literary invention, the short story.

Of all the early writers of the voyage, Hayes is best instructed in the literary devices of his era, but comes so late to his "character" that his is a sequence of methods rather than a synthesis. His attempt to hold together his fragmented beginning by his theme of religious determinism is only partly successful until he arrives at his culmination. Ellis is closer in fidelity to the voyage pattern, and by that virtue limits himself. Perhaps somewhat impertinently, an argument might be made that Hayes's scattering, Ellis's restriction, and his and Pricket's drift-off endings, along with the simple continuities of earlier writers, are native to the new world, and that much later American writing of one school and another shows an indifference to decoration and a carelessness of formal design, in part neglect, in part rejection. What was at first casually left undone towards the well-made and highly finished narrative becomes in the twentieth century a result of the strictest calculation.

In any case, the full use of the American sea voyage as literature was going to have to wait upon the development of the novel and the extended essay in the nineteenth century

when Melville, Poe, Thoreau, Dana, Mark Twain and
many others were to turn to it, in diverse interpretations.
Their linkage to the sixteenth century is not necessarily one
of source, though that too may be, but lies rather in a kinship in the American experience, which men from Europe
were the first to undergo.

4 / *Westward the Star of Empire*

While, along the Atlantic, the early author-explorers limited themselves to sea and river coasts, to the south and west the frontiers of New Spain provided different landscapes, different hazards and successes, and certain shifts of literary experiment. The Spanish who were established in the Caribbean and in Mexico early became restless there, and continually extended or tried to extend their fabulous wealth in metals and principalities, probing the shores of the Mexican gulf and those of California, and pushing north into the mid-continental deserts, traveling in the last instance almost entirely by land.

In 1527, by sea still, with a formidable convoy of ships soon diminished by storm, Pánfilo Narváez led an expedition to the west of Florida, one of whose officers became its chronicler. The treasurer, Alvar Núñez Cabeza de Vaca (c. 1490–1559?), is said to have written his *Relación* in 1537. It was first printed in 1542. Vaca relates a disaster brought about by Narváez's decision to put ashore three hundred of his men to explore and conquer the country and find a place suitable for settlement. Both landing party and ships

were to follow the coastline, finally meeting at a harbor believed to be not far off.

Vaca stood out against the order, and gave his reasons.
The Spaniards were wholly ignorant. Because they lacked
an interpreter, no one could communicate with the Indians.
Even the pilots did not know where they were, lacking anyone from whom the lay of the land could be learned—"we
were about entering a country of which we had no account,
and had no knowledge of its character, of what there was in
it, or by what people inhabited, neither did we know in
what part of it we were; and besides all this we had not food
to sustain us in wandering we knew not whither. . . ."

He is putting the dramatic as well as the factual terms of
the narrative, whose actors are the increasingly hostile Indians, and the violent, greedy, increasingly desperate Spanish.
Seduced by a story of a rich city, they began to explore their
illusions. They found a "town" of fifteen houses surrounded
by cornfields. Apalachen, the largest "city" of the region,
was little more. They raided it, and found themselves under
an attack which became "continual war," the hidden savages "wounding our people at the places where they went to
drink. . . ." Always under ambush, they struggled back
towards the sea and another illusory city, having against
them not only the frightened hostility of the Indians whom
they had robbed and victimized, but the tangled, sterile wilderness and disease and accident. On the coast again, they
built makeshift boats, in which they managed to reach
Texas and shipwreck. Under their many faults and afflictions, they shrank in number. The arrogant, brutal, incredi-
bly enduring company of conquerors diminished from the
three hundred who landed, to eighty survivors of invasion,
to fifteen spared by the sea, and at last to the four who were
to straggle back to Mexico.

These four, a Negro and three Spaniards, served their Indian captors for nine years, now as the lowest of slaves, now

as traders, now as healers, now as deities. The story of their
vagrant journey westward from the Texas coast nearly to
the Pacific, passed from Indian tribe to tribe, takes its quality from the honesty and restraint which Cabeza de Vaca
practices and from the experience itself. In a simple presentation of cursive sequence, he offers little comment upon the
happenings he records. Only here and there does he deliberately portray the destruction as well as the destructiveness
of the men of war, more powerful than their savage adversaries but inevitably brought down by wounds, accidents,
sickness, and starvation, winning every fight only to lose
every chance to survive. In an early battle, ". . . we came
to a lake difficult of crossing, the water reaching to the paps,
and in it were numerous logs. On reaching the middle of it
we were attacked by many Indians from behind trees, who
thus covered themselves that we might not get sight of them,
and others were on the fallen timbers. They drove their arrows with such effect that they wounded many men and
horses, and before we got through the lake they took our
guide. They now followed, endeavoring to contest the passage but our coming out afforded no relief, nor gave us any
better position; for when we wished to fight them they re-
tired immediately into the lake, whence they continued to
wound our men and beasts. The Governor, seeing this, commanded the cavalry to dismount and charge the Indians on
foot. Accordingly, the comptroller, alighting with the rest,
attacked them, when they all turned and ran into the lake
at hand, and thus the passage was gained."

Without any great emphasis upon the expense of such
victories, and with little condemnation of his leader's unwis-
dom or of the immorality of such invasions, he gives the cost
in men during helpless retreats and profitless advances.
Only by contrast, in recording an instance of Indian charity
to the survivors of shipwreck, does he—whether deliberately
or by chance—present a thesis.

"The Indians, at sight of what had befallen us, and our state of suffering and melancholy destitution, sat down among us, and from the sorrow and pity they felt, they all began to lament so earnestly that they might have been heard at a distance and continued so doing more than half an hour. It was strange to see these men, wild and untaught, howling like brutes over our misfortunes. It caused in me as in others, an increase of feeling and a livelier sense of our calamity.

"The cries having ceased, I talked with the Christians, and said that if it appeared well to them, I would beg these Indians to take us to their houses. Some, who had been in New Spain, replied that we ought not to think of it; for if they should do so, they would sacrifice us to their idols. But seeing no better course, and that any other led to a nearer and more certain death, I disregarded what was said, and besought the Indians to take us to their dwellings. They signified that it would give them delight, and that we should tarry a little, that they might do what we asked. Presently thirty men loaded themselves with wood and started for their houses, which were far off, and we remained with the others until near night, when, holding us up, they carried us with all haste. Because of the extreme coldness of the weather, lest anyone should die or fail by the way, they caused four or five very large fires to be placed at intervals, and at each they warmed us, and when they saw that we had regained some heat and strength they took us to the next so swiftly that they hardly let us touch our feet to the ground."

So rescued, the Spaniards had learned nothing. The clue to their obtuseness lies, ironically enough, in the word "Christian." The Europeans could not regard the heathen wholly as men. To Vaca even, himself a man of more than usual sensitivity and flexibility of response, the Indians howl "like brutes," and their sympathy brings the Spaniards not to a recognition of that sympathy but "to a livelier sense of our calamity."

In later gratitude, however, after years of living among the Indians, never fully understanding either their minds or their actions but protected by their reverence, Vaca did try to protect them in return. When he at last reached the Spanish settlements in Mexico with his three companions, under Indian escort, he held off his countrymen who "wished to make slaves of the Indians we brought." By Christian trickery, he was made to fail. Nor could he prevent the Spaniards from enslaving the local Indians, whom he had persuaded to return to their villages. He had to end his commentary in a bitter spirit, reproaching his own kind.

It is hard to think that Vaca is not presenting his own as well as the Indians' response when he gives their reasons for refusing to believe that the four Europeans they knew and revered belonged among the cruel Christian settlers.

"The Indians . . . conversing among themselves said . . . that we had come whence the sun rises, and they whence it goes down; we healed the sick, they killed the sound; that we had come naked and barefooted, while they had arrived in clothing and on horses with lances; that we were not covetous of anything, but all that was given to us we directly turned to give, remaining with nothing; that the others had the only purpose to rob whomsoever they found, bestowing nothing on anyone."

Vaca's narrative takes strength too from his sense of melancholy. "These things happened or were done; we can only weep." So he seems to say on every page, though he does not use the words. Nor does he achieve the depth or height of tragedy, held short perhaps by his own unawareness and lacks of skill, perhaps by the ideas inherent in his own culture. He may also have been restrained by expe-

dience, since a story stressing the sacrifice of some hundreds
of men, showing a Spanish failure brought on by Spanish ferocity, could hardly please a Spanish reader.

He sustains his integrity as a writer, nevertheless, in pa-
thos, in honest confrontation, and in the refusal to decorate
or touch up a narrative whose terrors and teachings are implicit, its realisms those of a man who would not have
claimed an aesthetic principle but did not swerve from the
real.

The same virtues pervade the *Relaçam verdadiera dos trabal-
hos* . . . (1557), or "true relation of the vicissitudes . . ." of
Hernando de Soto, by the Portuguese Gentleman of Elvas.
His epigram, already printed in full at the beginning of
American Genesis, invites the reader (who is hereby reminded)
to a "pleasing story

> Where nothing fabulous is told . . ."

This brief poem names the new world "the Golden Pole,"
and a note explains, "we inhabit the Northern Arctic Pole,
and that people [the Americans] inhabit the Southern Antarctic Pole. Golden Pole is used because the region is rich."

Whatever the geographical perplexity, the lines make
manifest De Soto's first aim. Settlement and any kind of rational exploration come second to the hunt for treasure. Although he had a license to colonize, he led his more than
seven hundred men on a marauding expedition which
lasted from 1539 to 1543, striking as far north as the Carolinas and Tennessee, then west to the Mississippi (which he
regarded not with admiration but distaste as so much more
water in his way), then on to Arkansas and Texas. De Soto
himself died and was buried in the river he disliked, leaving
fewer than half of his followers to struggle back to Mexico.

The Gentleman of Elvas was one of these, but for some
fourteen years either did not write down his adventures, or

waited to publish them. He is believed to have written entirely from memory, not from a diary or notes. If so, his rec-
ollection is remarkable in detail, though its impact dulls in
the repetition of event. The Spaniards make an approach to
an Indian settlement, where they levy food, slaves, and
whatever the soldiery consider of value. The Indians capitu-
late or resist. Plundering, or a senseless massacre of the natives—at the mildest judgment, wasteful—ends the typical
action. At the next town it repeats itself, as the Spaniards
force their way across the wilderness. Their progress was so
destructive that they were never able to return by the way
they came, the country they had once crossed having been
too thoroughly devastated.

To the loss of emotional response, the Gentleman ordinarily suspends comment, but in one instance he cannot
hold back. De Soto, in fear of the Indians by whom he was
surrounded, ordered an attack upon a neighboring town,
"treating the inhabitants there severely," so that "neither
town would dare to attack him. . . ."

His men carried out their duties to an extreme. "Some
persons were so cruel and butcher-like that they killed all
before them, young and old, not one having resisted little or
much; while those who felt it their duty to be wherever
there might be resistance, and were esteemed brave, broke
through the crowds of Indians, bearing down many with
their stirrups and the breasts of their horses, giving some a
thrust and letting them go, but encountering a child or a
woman would take and deliver it over to the footmen." In a
rare outburst, the Gentleman of Elvas condemns his kind.
"To the ferocious and bloodthirsty," he adds, "God permitted that their sin should rise up against them in the presence of all—when there was occasion for fighting showing
extreme cowardice, and in the end paying for it with their
lives."

Two other brief contemporary accounts, those of Biedma

and Ranjel, confirm the pattern of the voyage by land for
the De Soto expedition, but otherwise do not contribute to
the literary progress of such narratives. The final outcome,
Garcilaso de la Vega's *La Florida del Ynca*, most definitely
does so contribute, but was not to be begun for some twenty-
five years, or published for sixty. Moreover, it belongs to a
category other than that of the relations of direct observers.
These, with the hopes and visions of gold and empire, move
west, Vaca's tale of tried endurance having been sufficient
to revive an old legend, and with it the lusts for gold and
glory.

The progress westward of the utopian "seven islands of
Antilia" illustrates one of the incalculable phenomena of
the human mind. The fantasy, which may have some vague
historical or geographical source, has been traced to the
Moorish conquest of Spain, whereafter, according to the
tradition, seven bishops led their Christian congregations to
refuge across the western sea. Antilia—one island with
seven cities, or five islands, or seven, or nine—appears and
reappears on maps and in chronicles, always joined to gold;
the very sands of the beaches must be rich in gold. The
"seven cities," however, tend in story to detach themselves
from islands, and migrate to the mainland, at first along the
Atlantic seaboard from Newfoundland southward along
New England to Florida, while "Antilia" itself removes to
South America, and Cibola becomes its counterpart to the
north of Mexico.

Whatever the kinship between the golden city of the
southern continent—Antilia, Manoa, or El Dorado—and
the seven golden cities of the northern—Cibola and later
Quivira—they share one attribute in that they are always
beyond known country, but not impossibly far away. So
many days journey, so many leagues east, west, south, or
north, lie the gardens, treasuries, and palaces where the

fruits and flowers are gold, and the statues and furnitures, and the prows of boats, and the cups and plates of royal banqueting. To help in the placing of the American southwest, the Indians there told a story of seven caves. The mere number was convincing, taken along with the fact of Mexican and Peruvian gold.

Other motives added themselves to the appetite for wealth. The religious longed to convert the pagan Indians, and for themselves sought martyrdom. The secular wanted principalities in land and governorships and the fame of new discovery. They knew that in the effort many men would die, but put off that inevitability on other men. For those who managed to live, the promises were huge.

Earlier attempts having failed, the first successful emissary from New Spain to the fabulous New Mexican cities was a Franciscan monk, Fray Marcos of Nice (?–1558), who undertook the journey in 1539. With him went the Moorish Negro Estévan, erstwhile companion of Cabeza de Vaca. Victim of Indian anger, he was not so fortunate as Fray Marcos, who managed to survive the expedition and wrote an account of it which has the qualities of the fairy tale, ranging from the underlying horrors of death and the desert to the delicacies and charms of flowering gardens and the pastures of the unicorn.

"I followed my journey," he says, "as the holy Ghost did lead me. . . ." The friendly Indians along the way gave him "great entertainment, and provision of victuals, with roses, flowers, and other such things, and bowers which they made for me of chalk and boughs platted together. . . ." They told him about islands off the coast where there were a great many pearls. With unusual skepticism, Fray Marcos comments "howbeit I saw none of them." They were as entertaining about the "many great towns" inland, rich in gold and emeralds.

The "deserts" of Fray Marcos' outward progress were rel-

atively harmless; not so the inhabitants of the great city, Cibola, to which the monk had sent ahead the Negro slave.
That wanderer had perhaps become overconfident or perhaps overbearing or lustful. The suggestions differ. In any
case, the "magistrate" of Cibola killed him and drove off his
Indian escorts, a few of whom, bloody with wounds, escaped
to give the friar the terrifying news. Fray Marcos in spite of
them went on far enough to see the city from across its fruitful plain. Under an illusion of sight or wishes, or Indian fancies told to him (or indeed deluded by all three), he saw
what seemed "a fair city," its stone houses "builded in
order," of many stories, its people "somewhat white,"
clothed in cotton and leather and possessed of "emeralds
and other jewels." They prefer turquoises above all others,
he continues, and then—abandoning all realism of the
pueblo—he adds, "They use vessels of gold and silver, for
they have no other metal, whereof there is greater use and
more abundance than in Peru. . . ."

In his creative joining of fact, hearsay, and fable, and in
his candid portrayal of himself, now courageous, now anx-
ious and afraid on his flight to safety at home, he shows his
gifts. His successors in the seven cities quest were not, however, interested in literature. They called him a liar.

Fray Marcos' "Relación del descubrimiento de las siete
ciudades" (written in 1539) provides the prelude to the
seven cities cycle. Francisco Vásquez de Coronado, the most
famous of its leaders, himself wrote a "relation" of the beginning of his journey as a report to the Viceroy in Mexico,
in August 1540. Forthright, concise, and energetic, Coronado as a writer adds nothing to the usual form of the report or letter. His best chronicler is one of his soldiers, Pedro
de Castañeda, who makes an effort, though an incomplete
one, to shape a story and to use devices for the engagement
of his readers.

From the opening pages of Castañeda's "Relación de la

jornada de Cibola . . ." or "Account of the Expedition to Cibola which took place in the year 1540" (written c. 1565?) the unfortunate outcome is foretold. Such and such were the happy expectations, he says, but the event turned out differently. He establishes Coronado as his central character, a hero, though a hero with a weakness. Coronado thinks too much of his fortune, and of the young and beautiful wife he has left behind him. If he had thought only of his responsibilities, he could have found success and uncountable treasure.

With the dramatic tone established, Castañeda turns to the physical conflict—the defeat of the resisting Indians and the investment of Cibola, which is not the rich and marvelous city of Fray Marcos, nor are the surrounding cities the wished-for seven. The seven cities are still farther away, according to the Indians, and particularly according to one of them, nicknamed the Turk, a Spanish slave.

In Castañeda's handling, the Turk becomes a figure of active malice, tricking his masters, holding before their greeds the seductions of his native city of Quivira. In the Turk's story, Quivira becomes the site of the seven, displacing Cibola. "There was a river in the level country," he said, "which was two leagues wide, in which there were fishes as big as horses, and large numbers of very big canoes with more than twenty rowers on a side, and that they carried sails; and that their lords sat on the poop under awnings, and on the prow they had a great golden eagle. He said also that the lord of that country took his afternoon nap under a great tree on which were hung a great number of little gold bells, which put him to sleep as they swung in the air. He said also that everyone had their ordinary dishes made of wrought plate, and the jugs, plates, and bowls were of gold."

Castañeda misses the excitement he might have gained, for he lets his readers know that the Turk is lying, although

the outcome is suspended while Coronado "pacifies" the Cibola Indians, principally by massacre. When the Spaniards
turn to Quivira, their chronicler makes a certain play on
the Turk's mendacity or truthfulness, but he has lost impe-
tus and has to rely on Coronado's disappointment and the
strangling of the exposed deceiver. The tension falls off with
Coronado's retreats, first to Cibola and ultimately to New
Spain. Castañeda cannot retrieve it. He tries, by bringing in
an astrologer's prediction that Coronado must die by a fall
from his horse. The accident occurs. Coronado survives it,
but is frightened into giving up his expedition. If only he
had gone a little farther, Castañeda insists, the golden cities
would have been his to plunder.

The effort toward dramatization, however incomplete, is
evident. In still another effort, Castañeda shows his awareness of literary plotting. He announces a three part organi-
zation—the Coronado story, an account of the Indians and
of the animals and fruits of the country, and last "the return
of the army." He does keep to the plan, but loses all proportion in it, and it weakens rather than supports his narrative.
His inconsistently practiced skills remain, both in history
and fiction. Beyond them, he is one more witness to the dramatic quality of the American experience and its congenial-
ity to the imagination.

5 / *Hazards of New Fortunes*

The seven cities cycle, the extravagant hopes having been blunted, suspends itself for almost forty years, during which the deserts of Nueva México, whether fruitful or sterile, and their natives, however poor, however gold endowed, were left free of invaders. One intruder, Ibarra, may have crossed its southern border in the 1560s but probably did not. His chronicler, Baltasar de Obregón, renounces the claim—"we failed to carry out the undertaking and to reap the benefits and honor of the discovery"—as he recounts the later successes of other men. Yet Obregón supplies a clue to what was and had been going on which is missing elsewhere. Such early Spanish adventurers as Coronado, he says, had been looking not only for the seven cities, but also for the east-west water passage, which he calls the Salado River. This salty watercourse, known from the Atlantic as the Northwest Passage, has been sailed, he affirms, between Ireland and Quivira, and has carried English and French fleets to the South Sea. Obregón documents not merely his fancies and wishes, but the active intent of Spain (and of Drake for England) to discover the elusive Strait of Anian

Samford University Library

from the Pacific coast, the Atlantic attempts having so far failed.

The cycle of the Strait of Anian rounds out of the journals and reports of sea voyages. Francisco de Ulloa, under orders from Cortés, explored the gulf and seacoast of Lower California in 1539, to be followed in the upper reaches of the gulf by Hernando de Alarcón, Coronado's officer who was to take a parallel water route toward the north. In the attempt, Alarcón had himself dragged up the lower Colorado River. Forced at last to give up the toilsome effort, he recorded his defeat with an engaging directness of observation, contributing to geography new information but to literature no novelty.

Much the same comment applies to the other Spanish sea journals of the Straits of Anian group, except as they offer direct evidence of a literary process. Commonly called "diaries," they are not diaries or logs (even in the broadest sense) but narratives written off from such original day by day records. The diary or log originals must have existed, since the calendar sequence is too close and too exact for memory. Yet the so-called diary of the Cabrillo-Ferrelo expedition of 1542–1543 northward along the California coast is probably the rendering of still another man, Juan Paez, who commonly uses third-person pronouns—"they-them" rather than "we-us"—and adopts the tone of a writer working after, not during the event. Other, later "diarists" reveal a like method, by references backwards and forwards in time.

Like the inland voyages, the Spanish sea explorations underwent a mid-century pause, likely enough from consternation with the storms and hurts of the Cabrillo venture, under which Cabrillo himself—less lucky than Alarcón—died, to be succeeded by Ferrelo as commander. Occasional expeditions set forth, usually looking for a harbor of refuge for the Philippine galleons. Such disconnected, even desultory attempts bear witness to political differences in Spain and New Spain. A strong suggestion can be documented that Spain did not want a Strait of Anian to exist, because such a passage might allow England or Holland to challenge her in the Pacific. Later, the Drake and Cavendish piratical sweeps of 1578–1579 and 1586–1588 strengthened this unwillingness. They too looked for and failed to find the great passage through the continent or the treasures of fabled California, but had astounding success in their Spanish booty of gold, silver, and other valuables. Narratives of their voyages enriched Hakluyt and history, but contributed nothing to literary evolution beyond, in the Drake, a notable episode to be discussed later, in another connection.

The early 1600s brought the return of Spain to the search, which Sebastián Vizcaíno, a Basque, took over, adding to history another failure, and, to writing, various records including another "diary" (1602–1603) whose authorship is doubtful. The cosmographer of the voyage, Fray Antonio de la Ascensión, kept still another journal, and from it wrote off various accounts, among them the "Relación breve . . ." (1620). The former, "Vizcaíno's Diary," is deliberate and unfortunately successful in the author's effort to avoid any sort of effect. Death from thirst, hunger, scurvy, accident, cold, and storm becomes a commonplace. He gives an occasional descriptive comment to the sick, exhausted, and starving survivors, but none whatsoever to the fabulous inducements to their suffering.

His successor, Father Ascensión, provides a relation, written "with his original diary in hand," as realistically unreal. Among the realities of fantasy, he does explain with care the geographical existence of the Strait of Anian, which runs between the "Kingdom of Anian" on the north, and the "realm of Quivira" on the east; to the west he puts China, and to the south Japan. His mapping makes California an island again, endowed with silver and pearls, while the Rio

del Tizón (the Colorado) of the mainland leads to the La-
guna de Oro "and the pueblos of the Crowned King." Such
hints of men's motives and follies suffice him, however. He
celebrates these "lures" in God's plan for the conversion of
the natives, but even his energies and devotions are level in
tone. His California island is at best a trading post with a
pulpit, his "relación" already outdated in form, its purport
hidden rather than revealed. Other writers, more ambitious
and more gifted, had already passed him by.

Inland, with or without royal sanction, both exploration
and the recording of it resumed after 1580. If Obregón's
Historia, written in 1584 of Ibarra's attempt of the 1560s, be
regionally disqualified for failure to reach New Mexico,
then the documents of the Chamuscado-Rodríguez expedition of 1581 begin the new series. That highly daring incur-
sion into unknown country of nine soldiers and two priests
—the soldiers bent on booty and the priests on the gar-
nering of souls—included no writer worthy of the happenings. The *Relación* of Hernán Gallegos and the official
declarations of several soldiers, like Obregón's summary of
first-hand stories, are nearly ineffective. Yet Gallegos was a
good enough observer to present one scene of Indian ceremonial, and Obregón a good enough interpreter to understand the bearing of the heroic chronicle upon Spanish ven-
turers into new lands. His Cortés becomes successor to
Tamerlane as conqueror, and, as champion of the faith, dis-
places the Spanish kings who fought the Moors.

Such hints of social pattern and preconception, such
notations of antagonistic beliefs and contradictory motives,
reappear in the two extended accounts of the Espejo expedition of 1582–1583. Of the one, written in 1583, Antonio de
Espejo himself is the author; of the other, Diego Pérez de
Luxán, a soldier of the company. Their violences, whether
born of courage or fear, brought about bloody enough fights

with the Indians to start the tradition of the "Western," if it
had not already been started in the East and West also.
Now peaceful and on both parts benevolent, now angry and
on both parts vengeful, prone to many obscurer complexities, the battle between Indian and intruder shapes into
one of the persistent subjects and one of the pervading ex-
citements of American writing.

Far more fanciful than the Espejo who insists upon the
truth of his account, and far more exotic in interests than
the fighter Pérez de Luxán, the much later Father Geronimo Zárate-Salmerón undertook to present the whole history of Californian and New Mexican exploration by sea as
well as by land. His title, *Relaciones de Todas las cosas que en el
Nuevo Mexico se han visto y Savido, asi por mar como por tierra,
desde el año de 1538 hasta el de 1626* (written in 1626), testifies
to his ambition rather than his accuracies. But in a larger
sense the credulous and garrulous friar, however unreliable
his facts, conveys evidences which have escaped the more
veracious. In his version, the Strait of Anian, the seven cities
of Cibola or Quivira, the mines and lakes and islands of
gold and silver and precious jewels persuade the minds of
men. His adventurers meet not only Indians whose kings
ride golden litters but seafaring "mulatoes resembling
Moors or Chinamen"; they hear rumors of "the Hollanders
of New France" who are only ten days journey away and of
fishermen driven by storm from Newfoundland to the South
Sea by a strait on which they had seen a rich city, "well girt
with walls," whose people they found "courtly and well
mannered." His Vizcaíno learns about an island of Negroes,
who are the Indians' friends, and sees an island whose
mountain is wholly bare, showing "from afar" veins of silver
and gold, of great richness. At the other end of the fabulous
strait lies Labrador, where are "great forests; and in them
many blood-thirsty animals—griffins, bears, and lions."

Zárate-Salmerón is therein picking bits and scraps from

the third of the persuasive fables, that of the Island of the
Amazons, the vision of which turned Cortés northward from
Mexico. He was not the earliest to respond to this construct
of myth and courtly romance. Columbus had heard of it,
somewhere in the Indies. Like the seven cities, it migrated
both south and west, giving its name to a huge river, and—
helped along by the chivalric tale, *Las Sergas de Esplandián* of
García Rodríguez Ordóñes de Montalvo—to California.
Montalvo contributes the name itself, but puts the California island ruled by the Negro queen, Calafia, "on the right
hand of the Indies." Undeterred by geography, utterly de-
ceived by expectation, men "saw" the island and its wealth,
and suffered starvation, thirst, wounds, and death to find
the black queen and her women, gold-armored riders of
griffins, and warriors fierce in hostility to the male sex.

Negroes, Indians jewel-bedecked, kings, queens, pearls,
emeralds, gold, and silver alternate in Zárate-Salmerón's
narrative with poor natives who give gifts of jack-rabbits,
fruits, corn, and squash, and catch sardines of which there is
"great quantity" (or, toward the Atlantic, codfish); who
wear cotton "mantles" or nothing whatsoever or tanned
hides; who oblige their questioners with tales of yellow
metals, golden weapons, and gleaming plates, but cannot
produce "even a grain" of the valuable stuff. Negroes there
are—the Negro slaves the Spaniards took with them. But
the queen who could outshine Sheba, the king who could
shame Solomon and the lilies—these are heard of but never
met. The seekers carried home samples of ore and some discolored pearls, burned when the hungry natives cooked
their food. The rest was the accumulation of fable—a curious jumble out of Pliny, Herodotus, Strabo, perhaps gilded
by Moorish fantasies, perhaps regilt and adorned out of
Marco Polo and Sir John Mandeville, and certainly glossed
by the actualities of Mexico and Peru.

Yet Zárate-Salmerón cannot wholly give himself over to

fancy. In all he spent eight years as missionary in New
Mexico, where, if his eyes corrected, his ears continued to
collect the legends he enjoyed. The lake of Copalla must
produce gold because its people wear armlets of it, and the
lake is only fourteen days journey away. To the west, another people have pots and bowls of silver, while those of the
island of Ziñogaba, all of them bald, build large boats with
sails and rudders, own huge pearls, and are ruled by a gi-
antess named Ciñacacohola. Then there are "prodigies of
nature" which the friar refuses to describe until they are
affirmed under oath. His implication is obvious—everything he has described has indeed been so affirmed.

Unluckily, as far as his standing as a writer is concerned,
Zárate-Salmerón is unconscious in his creativity. He is a
chatterer who offers his wonders not from aesthetic but from
what might be called politico-economic conviction. His tale
thereby falls short of a tall tale. Because of its insistence
upon actual metals and marvels rather than intoxicating
humors of the mind, his verbal rainbow sets its feet on real
estate, and arches to the clink of cash.

The early literature of the Southwest, then, presents a
variety of sea and land journeys, all of which claim accuracy and some of which achieve it. The experiences in the
narratives, by the freedoms inherent in the unknown, admit
the wished-for knowledges of hearsay, the figments of fancy
inherited from the past, and the translated motives of the
participants. Indigenous materials, handled for the most
part by inexpert writers, work upon the European voyage
form, and begin to change it. The ineptitudes of the scribes
contribute loosenesses (or flexibilities), contradictions (perhaps paradoxes) between preconception and actuality, and
conscious or unconscious ironies, of confidence expressed in
despair, power in weakness, and Christianity in cruelty. Admiration accompanies a fear-ridden hatred of the native

peoples. Theirs was a country wealthy to the imagination, where would-be raiders and evangelists starved for food and water, or lived to murder and be murdered for the treasures and souls they sought. Some few, lucky, straggled back from a land veined with ores, poorer than when they set out. The truth was itself a fantasy, while the fantasies held their truths.

Don Juan de Oñate (c. 1549–c. 1628), the *adelantado* of Zárate-Salmerón, under a vision of a princedom for himself and a new empire for his king, in 1598 led into New Mexico an expedition which totally impoverished him, while it enriched American letters. Conveniently enough and appropriately enough, the Oñate expedition offers three examples of belletristic writing, which employ European modes in an American context.

One of these is a play, perhaps the first dramatic effort to which the literature of the United States has a claim; the other, again appropriately enough, is a highly calculated political oration; the third is an epic poem, the appropriateness of which may be asserted or denied. Of these, the first two were parts of the ceremony below the Rio Grande by which Spain took possession of New Mexico, the whole observance being designed as a pageant in which the religious and imperial purposes of the expedition were portrayed.

This possibly first dramatic effort, called "una gran comedia," has survived in reference and even in epitome, though perhaps not in actual text. The likelihood that a draft of it exists is great; the likelihood of finding it is small. Bureaucratic Spain put everything on paper, every scrap of which got filed. Somewhere in Mexican or Spanish archives, perhaps in some Franciscan library in America or Europe, the "gran comedia" waits for the lucky explorer. Until he comes upon it, however, the historian has to be happy with the evidences that are available. It was per-

formed on April 30, 1598; it was written by Captain Marcos
Farfán de los Godos; it was in no modern sense a comedy,
but a religious drama of a well-established type—the "comedia divina" or "sacramentale." Its action portrayed the
coming of Christianity to pagan New Mexico.

A poet (of whom more later) made one of the audience,
and so described the play: "It showed New Mexico rejoicing in the coming of the Church, and offering a grateful
welcome. Reverently, knees bent to the earth, begging that
their guilt be washed away with the holy water of baptism,
many heathen received and were cleansed by the saving
sacrament." Presumably the friars, of whom Oñate had ten
in his company, took their own parts. Either Spaniards
acted as the "many heathen" Indians baptized, or many of
the savages who had come to the camp with gifts of fish
were pressed to serve. In the latter case, the perplexity of the
converts must have been as great as their pleasure, but since
the American Indians enjoyed pageantry when they were
not frightened, they would have made no difficulty.

Nor would such a theatrical piece have surprised Oñate's
men or strained their talents, since it was a simplification of
a form already established in Mexico and a remote outcome
of late medieval Spanish drama. By the end of the sixteenth
century, Mexico had seen many theatrical spectacles of various kinds, academic, sacramental, or secular—the last
being actually a mixed sort, notable for such liberalities
with fact as the showing of Cortés in the conquest of Jerusa-
lem, or the baptizing of Mexican Indians in the guise of
Moorish captives (this as the climax of the conventional
play of combat between Christians and Moors).

What eccentricities of its own the Oñate drama indulged
in must remain unknown until a text turns up. By the description, it remains a hopeful prophecy, a piece of pious
magic, as much to do with happening as with entertainment, as though the first northern American dramatist

knew by necessity that his play was an action in history as
well as an action of the stage. Nor is it fortuitous that it
was an act of piety, since the religious purpose of the invasion, by Oñate's own testimony, was as strong as the political.

The second literary effort, the Oñate "Act of Possession,"
is indeed as "highly important and curious" as the Mexican
historian, Riva Palacio, declares it to be. Probably a "first"
in literature can be claimed for it also—let it at least be
nominated as the first exemplar of European oratorical art
in the American canon.

Oñate presents two alternating theses, in making on the
one hand the imperial claim to the lands he proposes to occupy and govern, while on the other he pronounces the theological. Perhaps since the two show the same sublimation
of faith, both should be called theological, the more tenably
because the king's right is that of a Christian king: "I declare that in the voice and name of the most Christian king,
Don Philip our Lord, the single defender and fortifier of
Holy Mother Church and its veritable son; and for the
crown of Castile and the kings of its glorious line who come
to the throne thereof; and to the end and on behalf of the
prosperity of my governorship, I take and seize, once, twice,
and thrice, once, twice, and thrice, once, twice, and thrice,
and as many times as I can and should, the ownership and
possession real and actual, by law and by nature, in this
said River of the North, without exception of any thing and
without limitation, with the mountains, rivers, meadows,
valleys and their pasture grasses and springs; and the said
possession I take and seize by the power and authority
aforesaid, of the other lands, towns, cities, vills, castles, and
houses moated and without moat which are now built in the
said kingdoms and provinces of New Mexico and those

neighboring and bordering thereon and henceforth and forever in time to be established therein, with their mountains,
rivers, and fish ponds, waters, pastures, vales and glens,
springs and fountain-sources of gold, silver, copper, mer-
cury, tin, iron, precious stones, salt, minerals [?], mineral
salt, and all lodes of whatever sort, quality, and condition
which are or may be, with all the native Indians in each
and all of these places, and with civil and criminal jurisdic-
tion, high and low, as of the lord of the manor by gallows
and sword, *mero mixto imperio,* from the leaf of the forest tree
to the stone and sands of the river, and from the stone and
sands of the river to the forest leaf."

The tone of the claim is ecstatic even in its confusions—
closer to that of a man possessed by an idea than to that of a
bureaucrat asserting legalities. The same tone holds in the
religious declaration, with which Oñate begins and closes
his ritual, ending with these words: "O holy cross, divine
gate of heaven and altar of the only and essential sacrifice of
the blood and body of the Son of God, pathway of saints
and emblem of their glory, open the gates of heaven to these
infidels. Found churches and altars where the body and
blood of the Son of God may be offered in sacrifice; open to
us a way of peace and safety for their conversion, and give
to our king and to me, in his royal name, the peaceful possession of these kingdoms and provinces. Amen." The two
mysticisms merge and become one.

Oñate's art is a vocal one, the more impressive because of
the intensity of personal emotion which carries him to high
utterance, inspired beyond officialdom. Of the several versions of his "Act of Possession" which survive, that of the
Archivo General de Indias is the most polished and most
formal, while that of his poet-auditor, Villagrá, is the closest
to actual speech, the least manipulated, and the most
touching. Villagrá, who promises that he has not changed

"a single letter or phrase" of Oñate's, manages to transmit both the freshness and the quality, the fervor and the immediacy of the governor's prose hymn to the kings of heaven and earth.

6 / Epics of America

Oñate's poet, Gaspar Pérez de Villagrá (c. 1554–1620) contributes the third literary development of the New Mexican area. His effort in writing is ambitious, far beyond that of the dramatist Farfán or the orator Oñate. His opening lines unmistakably propose a Virgilian epic, which he carries through some thirty cantos.

> *Las armas y el varon heroico canto,*
> *El ser, valor, prudencia, y alto esfuerco,*
> *De aquel cuya paciencia no rendida . . .*

> The arms and the valorous hero I sing,
> The bravery, wisdom, and vigor in being,
> Of him whose fortitude never surrendered . . .

All the resonances of Rome and its imperial poet, after such a beginning, immediately accrue to the conquest and occupation of New Mexico. The huge land, to which no boundaries were set, might well sustain the comparison, but Villagrá, in challenging Virgil, rather strained his own case. His verses have been variously estimated. To one school of criticism, they are "crabbed," awkward, and contrived. Yet Pimentel, historian of Mexican poetry, praises Villagrá's integrity, his fidelity to the honest portrayal of event, finding him admirable in style also for his simplicity and naturalness. Pimentel names as his faults the prosaic or slack line, and fluency without strength or elevation, and quotes another critic who condemns the *Historia de la Nueva Mexico* (1610) for weakness of invention, a lack of creative artifice.

The English translation, in prose, of Villagrá's epic is not helpful to the study of his style, which is almost equally obscured in the original Spanish printing, with its contemporary and slovenly typography. Even a clear text, however, could hardly justify Villagrá's claim to eminence as a poet. He was a versifier with a purpose. His epic in its asserted kinship with the Greek and Roman classics is congenial enough for understanding, although he does not follow the Virgilian pattern in the unfolding of his story. His relationship to his nearer background of the Renaissance epic and the romances is unclear, and must be left to the study of experts. Superficially, he shows little knowledge of it, or of the contemporary Spanish-American epics of the southern continent.

His narrative, with its simple time sequence, remains within the scope of the general reader. The early action sweeps wide and fast. The Indian traditions of conquest, with their supernaturalisms, make the beginning, to be followed by the recounting of earlier Spanish explorations. The central plot comes out of the authorization (granted, hedged, thwarted, and at last confirmed) given to Oñate. His progress with his army and his colonists out of New Spain to the Rio Grande leads to the establishment of New Mexico, the Indians having made their submissions to him.

Thereafter, Villagrá condenses history in order to arrive at his dramatic crisis, the uprising of the Indians of Ácoma, who by Villagrá's account were led into the crime of treason against Spain by the malevolent warrior Zutacapán. Of this rebel, Villagrá writes, "O mortal glory, whose shifting

height swollen presumption and wicked arrogance struggle
to climb and seat! Tell me, damnable pride, how you ac-
cord the potent sceptre and the regal crown with an abject
savage, lost to virtue, begot of brutish dam and evil sire—
show how the high throne befits the barbarous pack, the un-
ruled place.

"O blind vanity, O empty pomp, sought after and pretended to, without prerogative or right or any sort of worth,
by the high, the mean, the low, and the worst, tell them how
this mad barbarian—engendered of so base a blood—seeks,
like Lucifer, to rebel and assume to himself the government
of all." In sententiousness and magniloquence, Villagrá outdoes his Roman master, but—more to the present point—
he grants his subject scope and significance as well as dramatic intensity. The Christian analogy to the war in
heaven, however dubious to the modern mind, is entirely
valid to the poet, who throughout his epic battle at Ácoma
sees it as a struggle between the powers of darkness and of
light.

In such a context, the satanic Zutacapán, however vil-
lainous, has dignity and stature. His first victory, his overthrow in the final battle, his punishment, and the burning
of the pueblo are in the heroic mode, and dramatically satisfying within the epic form and within the responses to be
assumed of the reader of Villagrá's own time. For the twentieth century, however, Villagrá's final reconciliation of his
theme, in the defeat of the Indians and the victory of Spain,
reverses itself. The response becomes one of sympathy for
the rebellious group, if not for the instigator. The speech of
the last of the rebels, two who were granted the privilege to
hang themselves rather than surrender, endows them with
valor and even greatness, rather than the detestation Villagrá should—in consideration of his thesis—have meant to
inspire.

"Soldiers, we now yield you our miserable bodies, hanged

from these unbending trees, as spoils of your strained-for, shining victory. Those unfortunates whom you brought to the rottenness of death lie huddled in their blood, their graves their quittance. So, damning fate destroys us with a crushing hand, and we are made an end of.

"This one grace you grant us, that we ourselves close the doors upon our lives, and go away, and leave you free on our once native earth. Be sure, then, that you may sleep here and dream lightly, without care, since no man turns back along the road which we now take. Yet of one other doom be sure—that if we could return to take revenge, no savage race in all the world would mourn more wretched sons than yours, o mothers of Spain!"

Perhaps the passage is not "invention," since Villagrá was a witness of these deaths and auditor of any speech the condemned men may have spoken, but—effort of the imagination or no—in it he gains his tragic climax. To repeat, in so doing he has to reverse his judgment and make his doers of evil heroic, a fact which points to the central weakness of his large attempt. Because he is committed to the timing and to the circumstances of history, he cannot manipulate his subject. Such changes of order as the Virgilian epic structure demanded of him may have been beyond his skill or even beyond his knowledge. They were most certainly denied him by circumstance. The "argument" of his poem was developing in history as he wrote. If he was to keep to his own experience and to Oñate's, he was committed to the narrative, not the epical form. The action, in historical terms, was continuing. So too, Villagrá's poem can arrive at no conclusion; he announced a continuation of it, but is not known to have written one.

If his plot ran counter to his literary design, his central character was no more helpful to him. After the impressive "Act of Possession," Oñate the hero fails him. The governor was not present at the battle of Ácoma, and after it and

after a ceremonial trial of the rebel Indians, he serves only
—in historic fact—as judge in sentencing the Ácomans to
horrifying punishment. Some six to eight hundred of them
having been killed, Oñate condemned the survivors to slavery for twenty years, the males over twenty-five to be further punished by having a foot cut off.

Such being the historic record, events rule the poet. Villagrá cannot introduce Oñate into the last nine cantos at
all. The governor fades into the background of authority
once he has decreed the destruction of Ácoma. Villagrá,
moreover, has to condone, if he does not approve, Oñate's
brutal measures.

The *Historia*, addressed to Philip III, was written and
published during the years when Oñate was officially scruti-
nized nearly to the point of disgrace, perhaps because of his
cruelty, certainly because of his failure to meet his promises
of wealth and rule. Once again, historic circumstance
breaks Villagrá's pattern and diminishes his tone. His poem
becomes a begging letter, asking the king for justice and
generosity to old soldiers, helpless, neglected, and abused by
idle, ease-loving hangers-on of courts. He hurries to explain
that he is not referring to the viceroy of New Spain, or deni-
grating the benevolence of the king himself, from both of
whom redress must come, but only such as are unworthy
governors. Even to reach these, he writes, to put before
them the pleas of misery and the just cause, the suppliant
must spend an eternity of haunted years, dying of hunger,
weary and afflicted, flattering the pages and the doorkeep-
ers, the servants and officers of their households. Because
Villagrá as well as Oñate, was under investigation, his com-
plaint is highly personal.

In the immediacy of his writing lies one of the answers to
his failure in the epic. Journalism, such as his own experience qualified him for, has to emphasize actuality. Villagrá may call Oñate a Spanish Achilles, but cannot show

his leader as such. He may claim an imperial conquest, but has to portray Spanish raiders robbing the Indians of their clothing. He may insist upon a land of immense wealth, but has to describe a sterile desert. Hunger and thirst, brutality and vengefulness, seen so close, lack nobility. Greece and Rome cannot be transplanted by mere naming to the American southwest. The structures of the classic mode cannot be made to fit a failed attempt to "pacify" pueblos.

Whatever the impossibilities, Villagrá unquestionably knew his epic materials and devices. Within the limits of his poetic gifts, he makes use of supernatural intervention, the pastoral interlude, the conflict, the death of the hero, the invocation, the eulogy, the moral reflection, the metaphor, and the rest. He shows no recognition of the inherent uncongeniality between the circumstances he deals in and the classic mode, between the uses of journalistic history and epical magniloquence. He simply carried the European genre to the new world, where realism destroyed it.

Much the same comment can be made about another effort to exercise the European conventions of the writer's art upon an American subject. Far to the east of New Mexico, in "Florida," the first native-born writer to be claimed by northern America found a subject for a courtly romance in prose. Garcilaso de la Vega (1539–1616) portrays in his De Soto a very different hero from the governor shown by the Gentleman of Elvas. Under Garcilaso's manipulation, De Soto the hunter of Indians becomes the courteous, valiant, magnificent Cid Campeador of the American wilderness, a role difficult to show even on the printed page, and impossible to play in forest swampland, as savage as its inhabitants.

His creator as such, called "el Inca," is himself an anomaly in early American letters. He was Peruvian by birth, son of a Spanish father and an Indian mother of noble family who was a niece of the last legitimate Inca emperor,

Huayna Capec. At twenty, the "Inca" made his migration, not westward but eastward to Spain, where he lived the rest of his life. Becoming first a soldier, he then made himself historian of Peru in his *Comentarios Reales* (1609, 1616/17). Between 1567 and 1599, apparently, he concerned himself as well with Florida and De Soto, although his *Historia del Adelantado Hernando de Soto, Governador y capitan general del Reyno de la Florida, y de otros heroicos cavalleros Españoles e Indios* was not published until 1605.

This early native American, chronicler of a voyage undertaken a year before his birth, by necessity plays the part of historian rather than diarist or journalist. He claims and has been conceded authority and authenticity, however, because he got his story directly from three men who served in De Soto's expedition, orally from an unnamed hidalgo, and in writing from two lesser men. According to Garcilaso, *La Florida del Ynca*—the short title by which the text is more conveniently known—is indebted to them alone. He pays no acknowledgments to the Gentleman of Elvas, nor to the brief De Soto narratives of Biedma and Ranjel.

In event, he traces much the same course. Again, De Soto makes his progress inland, exercising what one of his much later historians calls a cruelty not wanton but required by "strategical reason"; Garcilaso also justifies him, arguing necessity and the bad behavior of the Indians. Again, De Soto encounters Indians hostile and Indians friendly, and treats with, or enslaves, or slaughters them, or merely seizes the food upon which the Indians themselves depend for survival. His meetings with the Indian queen, his encounters with Indian kings, his obstinate search for gold and pearls, all are presumably side issues in the undertaking to which De Soto had in 1537 committed himself—to "conquer, pacify, and people" this new realm. Nevertheless the wandering of the soon forlorn but still merciless invaders seems to become a purpose in itself, in Garcilaso's rendering as in that

of the Gentleman of Elvas. The seeking out of Indian "kingdoms," the repeated conquests and subjugations of the natives, Indian revolts and attacks, victory in this encounter
and defeat in that, fatal accidents or lucky escapes, the sei-
zure of food or the failure to find it with starvation immi-
nent—all these make reasons to leave one place for the en-
ticements of another. The ultimate rational impulse was
always hunger, either for gold or food, but on the page the
actual motive becomes an irrational restlessness, trimmed
out with the familiar hopes of rich mines further on, the
passage to the South Sea just beyond the headwaters of
whatever river, the jeweled city no more than so many days
journey away. In these illusions some three hundred of De
Soto's men died. The death of De Soto himself and the final
flight homeward of the half of his men who still lived, make
the outcome of Garcilaso's romance as of the soberer earlier
narratives. The actual ending, which suggests that Garcilaso felt a need to restore his subject, brings in an anecdote
of chivalric loyalty, and an accounting of the Christian
martyrs of Florida, both lay and priestly. Exactly as in the
medieval romance, the holy battle lay between the true be-
liever and the "paynim" of whatever continent.

The *Florida del Ynca*, then, is an expression of a cultural
posture, that of the courtly romance, which earlier Spanish
writers either briefly defined, or implied or documented in
their narratives. Obregón's *History* explicitly joins to the
wars of "the old chroniclers" those of the conquerors of New
Spain, the Moors of the former giving over their roles to the
barbarians of the latter. Castañeda assumes the code for Coronado and his captains, in the name of "honor," while Cabeza de Vaca simply documents its required behaviors in
others, and on his own behalf abandons them in order to
live. Its economic aspects—the taking over of the treasures
of the conquered knights, their horses, suits of armor, castles, and so forth—could wishfully at least be practiced in

the regions of the "Golden Pole." The historic suitabilities
of the romantic pattern offer no trouble, since, as Garcilaso's editors point out, De Soto and his captains did in actuality follow a version of the formula Garcilaso describes and
subscribed to, so that the artificialities of the literary match
accepted social conventions. That these were invalid in the
new world is a judgment which emerges from the events, the
settings, and the characters of Garcilaso's portrayal.

In fidelity to the accounts of his three witnesses, he celebrates the honor, courage, magnificence, and nobility of
soul and behavior of both Spaniard and Indian, while at
the same time he documents the murderous pillage of the
Spanish intrusion. In one battle, he reports the killing of
eleven thousand Indian men and women by fire and sword.
Afterwards, in the nearby woods, the Spaniards found two
thousand wounded who "had not been able to reach their
homes. And it was pitiful to find them howling in the forests
with no remedy for their afflictions." No matter what the
exaggeration of numbers, as "pacification" such slaughter
was misnamed.

He blames a treacherous Indian chieftain for "all this unfortunate business" but finds no uncongeniality between the
action he presents and his earlier comment that De Soto
and his "ministers" always "regaled with great attention
and care those chieftains and their Indians who came to
them in peace." Furthermore, he declares, "they did no
damage to the towns or property of those who were rebellious other than to take from them the food they required,
and this they could not avoid doing." That the food was as
necessary to the Indians as to the Spaniards he may not
have known, although Cabeza de Vaca had repeatedly
shown, as he repeatedly shared in, the never resting struggle
of the tribes against famine.

He does not of course need to reconcile pillage and hon-
orifics, or massacre and magnanimity within the terms of

the romance of knighthood, in which booty rewards the vic-
tor, and in which the killing of thousands decorates the warrior hero, as does the observance of lavish hospitality, of the
rules of combat, of a generosity of praise granted to worthy
ally or adversary. The Inca, sensitive to the discriminations
of gallantry among the Spaniards, is equally aware (he was
half Indian himself, as his editors point out) of the nobilities
of the Americans. In regard to the latter, he speaks the language of feudalism, dividing them into lords and vassals.
One friendly cacique he describes as "very much a gentleman, as are most of the lords of that land. . . . In fact, he
appeared to have been brought up at court in an atmos-
phere of the best learning and culture."

In such a frame, the intrusion of realism is shocking. Yet
Garcilaso records again and again the fact that to Spaniards and Indians alike the death of a horse was more important than the death of a man. He must, as well, acknowledge that the Spaniards, deprived of medicines and
salves for their injured "occupied themselves in opening the
bodies of dead Indians and taking out the fat to use as un-
guents and oils for treating wounds."

He serves as accurate reporter for these actualities and
others like them, but in his context half-conceals their brutality. His tone prevails. His elevated interpretation turns
fact to fiction, sense to fantasy. His vocabulary is that of the
tournament and the palace, even in the setting of the cypress swamp. De Soto, in the exordium, he acclaims for "his
heroic feats and invincible spirit, his promptitude in battles
and attacks, his patience in hardship, his strength and courage in fighting, and his caution, counsel, and prudence in
both peace and war." Ranjel, De Soto's earlier journalist
and a member of his army, provides a comment in counter-
poise—"This governor was much given to the sport of
slaying Indians."

Garcilaso is generous, too, in the adornment of the natives, putting his emphasis upon the beauties of their persons, their courtesies, riches, and prides; their "strength and valor"; and the splendors of their costumes, their possessions, and their lands. His Indian cacique, giving audience "in his lodgings under a canopy," wears a "grave countenance," disdainful of the common Spanish soldiery. He refuses to rise to greet De Soto, but so arranges their meeting that "both of them sat down together on a seat which was under the Cloth of Estate," equal in honor. The Inca's Indian queen, hardly second in beauty to Queen Calafia of *Las Sergas de Esplandián*, is as richly endowed with pearls if not with other jewels. However, the Gentleman of Elvas reports that she made her escape from De Soto by taking to the woods "to ease herself."

So reality confronts romance, in this early phrasing of the American narrative by European literary modes. That Garcilaso, himself of American birth, should produce a work in the current of European literature rather than in that of a literature only beginning to find its forms, is an anomaly not unique in American letters. Emblematic in its countervailings, the stately, enchanting (and sadly ridiculous) progress of Garcilaso's knights-at-arms winds its bleeding way by deadly wilderness tracks and water courses, an anachronism in theme and style, costume and manners. That its author —half American by parentage—might be judged to be hardly an American writer at all merely accents the incongruities.

In its first century, then, the land voyage in its literary development follows much the same course as the voyage by sea. The early form of the journal or diary, largely objective but always colored, faintly or strongly, by the recorder, tends to admit to its truths highly doubtful speculations, interpretations, reports of reports, rerenderings of old fantasies, and ultimately enticing and entertaining distortions, more or less deliberate. This so to speak natural process, for the most part carried along by the nonliterary participator-author, undergoes a transformation when the conscious literary contriver undertakes to shape the new materials to an established design, whether that of argument or epic, or hoax, or moral essay, or history, or romance, or any combination of these. The two cultures, that of the wilderness and that of European architectural society, come to confrontation. In any orderly, reasonable growth, this should lead to a merging of inheritances, the expectation, supported by Villagrá and the Inca, being that the more highly formal structure will supersede the less formal and the unformed. This does not happen. Moreover, while the renderer of an epic or a heroic romance makes an appropriate ancestor for a Longfellow or a Washington Irving, he is not so appropriate a forebear for a Melville or a Poe or a Mark Twain. In fact, and in the immediate course of chronology, the looser forms of the journal or report or history prevail.

Indeed, the more representative writer in the area of the imagination (or "invention") is a much humbler fellow than either hidalgo. A common sailor, David Ingram more than likely could not use a pen at all. His only creative work is a deposition or interrogation or examination or report made to Sir Francis Walsingham, Sir George Peckham, and "diverse others" who were interested in the new world on behalf of Elizabethan England, and who questioned this returned mariner about his adventures there.

Ingram was one of a number of men whom Sir John Hawkins, having lost several of his ships to a Spanish attack, was forced to put ashore on the western curve of the Gulf of Mexico at the mouth of the Pánuco River. Most of the marooned were killed or enslaved by the Spaniards, but Ingram with two companions—beyond all credibility—managed to reach the east coast of Canada where they were picked up and brought home by a French ship. Such are the confirmed facts. According to Ingram's thirteen-years-later account, the three had walked northward and eastward a land distance of three thousand miles, give or take a few hundred according to their route, between their beaching in October 1568 and their rescue in an unnamed month of 1569.

Indians could have done it, of course, in much less time, knowing the trails and the rivers and the portages, but that three English sailors could have managed such a journey in the eleven months of Ingram's own statement, or in seventeen months—to give them the longest possible stretch of the calendar—is at least unlikely.

Even though they did so, Ingram's discourse of 1582 is still to be called a work of the imagination. If the fantasies are not his own, he remains their assembler. Guided by the questions asked him, he renders the Indians, the country, and the animals, doing all three more than justice.

For the suggestion of dialect and tone of voice in *A true discourse* . . . (1583), let the original typography stand. Therein, his Indian kings wear rubies "VI ynches long & 2 ynches broad," and are carried by their subjects in "A sumpteous Chaire of Silver or Cristall garnished about with sondrie sorts of precious stones." Even the common sort have pearls (as they probably did, but discolored) and wear bracelets "whereof Commonly one ys golde & two silver. And manie of the women also do weare great plate of gold covering ther bodies. . . ." After these informations, he breaks into more factual description—the Indians have tawny skins, often painted; they stand five feet tall; they are swift runners; in the south they are usually naked, and in the north wear furs.

He proceeds, alternating fiction and fact. The Indians use iron—Ingram's charitable commentators believe he is talking about metal got from the Spaniards—raise "kyne," make trumpets of "Elephants teeth." In their towns, "Ther

buildings are weake and of small form the howses are made
round like dove houses." Yet "some of them have ban-
quetting howses . . . builded with pillers of massie silver
and Cristall framed square whereof many of them are as
bigg as a boies legg of XV yeares of age and some les."

He "passed" many "great" towns and some "small," and
between them "diverse small villags," where "they have in
everie howse scowpes, buckets and diverse other vessells of
massie sylver wherewith they do throw out water and dust
otherwise do employ them to ther necessarie uses in ther
howses." To silver chamberpots and dust pans of his seeing,
he adds the finding of lumps of gold as big as a man's fist
and "great rocks of cristall . . . in quantitie sufficient to
load shipps."

The impression is inescapable that Ingram in making his
narration was having a thoroughly good time. Having dealt
lavishly with the people and their wealth, he goes on to
make an earthly paradise of Florida, filled with trees and
flowers and fruits—none of them forbidden—and roamed
by animals both familiar and strange, including "buffs"
twenty feet long, and sheep which sleep from five o'clock at
night till five in the morning and may easily be killed then
but are very "wylde" the other twelve hours. His most spectacular animal, however, he rightly calls a "monstrous
beast," twice as big as a horse and like a horse except for
"hinde parts" like a greyhound and "two teeth or hornes of
a foote long." Elephants, "ounces," parrots, flamingos,
Guinea hens, and penguins he mentions with comparatively
little attention, but pauses over a "straunge beast" whose
eyes and mouth were "in his breast . . . verie ougly to beholde" and pauses still longer over a "verie straunge byrde
. . . verie bewtifull to beholde," with feathers "more orient
than a peacocks feathers," eyes as "glistering as any hawks
eyes," and on its head "a crest or tufte of sondrie Colours."

Ingram does not name his "monstrous beast" a unicorn,

and indeed endows it with two horns, nor does he claim to have seen the phoenix, but wisely leaves the identifications to his hearers. Wisely also, in a dramatic sense, he provides himself with a climax. He presents the devil, called by the Indians "Collochio," first as judge and punisher of adultery, and then as an apparition. Of the devil's appearance, "He saith further that he and his two fellowes namely Rich. Browne and Rich. Twide went into a poore mans howse and ther they did see the said Collochio or divell with very great eyes like a black calfe uppon the sight thereof Browne said ther ys the divell and theruppon blessed himself in the name of the father the sonne and the holy ghost. And Twide said very vehemently I defie the and all thy works and presently the Collochio shank away in a stealing manner forthe of the dores and was sene no more unto them."

The rest of Ingram's relation is anticlimactic except for his affirmation by hearsay evidence of the existence of the Northwest Passage. He himself traveled "the span of 2 whole daies" along the "maine sea" of the North, where the people drew for him ships, sails, and flags "which thing especiallie proveth the passage of the Northwest." For additional support, he draws in Zárate-Salmerón's "shipp of China or Cataia uppon the Northwest of America."

His concluding anecdote of an island of five or six thousand Indians governed for the Spaniards by a single Negro slave is thrown in, without much coherence and for extra measure, to argue "the great obedience of theis people & how easily they may be governed when they be once conquered."

How much guile lies hidden in this last sentence of Ingram's is also arguable. Beyond any doubt lies his own willingness to interest and please his auditors, along with a shrewd idea of what would do so. For the rest, he may himself be gulled or gulling; he may be drawing upon experience embellished by wishes and sailors' stories and Indian fictions and even "sources" in the literary sense. Either he or his scribe refers to Coronado, and his "Collochio" is in sound a vague reminder of the "lesse" devil of Magellan's voyage, by name Cheleule. But there is no mention in Ingram of the "greate deuylle" of that earlier narrative, named Setebos.

For most if not all of Ingram's monsters or "verie straunge" creatures, bookish antecedents can be found, and parallels appear often enough in the writings of his contemporaries to sketch in the kind of anecdote he might have picked up by ear. Yet Ingram is alone in building, perhaps upon a frame of fact, the high, airy towers of the tall story, that kind of literary aspiration from small truth to large fantasy to the final captivation in unreason by the logic of sheer enjoyment.

7 / Episodes of America

A literature which of necessity accompanies and reflects a historic experience should show changes of form and subject as the experience changes. The literature of American settlement, then, might be expected to show another structure than that of the voyage, however interrupted for discourse about the Indians, about the wealth of the country or the lack of it, about the seen landscape with its plants and creatures, about the unseen and magical prospect of metals, jewels, and marvels. Since "settlement" must by definition be fixed, the sequence of narrative should cease to be linear, the subjects should be those of habitation and cultivation, the themes those of stability rather than "success."

So much for tidy theory, which in the course of more than a hundred years does actually work out. During the sixteenth century, however, the process of settlement follows a far from rational course, and the shapes and subjects of settlement writing veer with it, as defiant of reason and good government as "western planting" itself. However orderly, careful, and complete the scheme, however logical and provident the preparation, the outcome was always determined in confusion and overthrow.

Projects of colonization appear early. The expeditions of
Narváez, De Soto, and Coronado were by original intent
occupations as well as "entradas." Cartier's wintering-over
of 1535, though it led to Roberval's effort of six years later,
had no such specific intent, but because the voyagers were
held to one place its narrative hints at alterations of subject,
at new emphases, at closer conflicts both personal and elemental than those of the shifting journey. Cartier and his
men planned no conquest of the Indians, but survival in
their midst. Against the awfulness of the cold and the rottenness of scurvy, only God could provide, and all too often
God's help had to be invoked for travelers to still another
world. For the disemboweled Philip Rougemont, the narrator prays, "May God in his holy grace grant forgiveness to
his soul and to those of all the dead." A theme suggests itself, but is not developed. In the iron winter, with land and
water frozen motionless, men are impotent.

Such depths are only half-realized in the narrative. Nor
are the Indians fully understood, but are figures of playfulness, deceit, dignity, generosity, or need, as the case may be,
and finally of a hostility which is worked into an expectation of attack, aborted when the French escape by sailing
home.

As prophecies of the events and stresses of settlement literature, these suggestions are valid, but the wintering-over
made no claim to permanence, and remained an extended
episode within the broad pattern of the voyage.

The third voyage of Cartier (1541–1542) and, joined to it,
the Sieur de Roberval's venture in permanent settlement
contribute no evidence to the development of form and subject, perhaps because no more than fragmentary and incomplete accounts survive, and these in a few pages in
Hakluyt. Roberval, an aristocratic disciplinarian, does introduce one soon-to-be-familiar colonial subject, in the matter of punishment. Having had to recruit much of his com-

pany from the jails, he "used very good justice and punished every man according to his offense. One, whose name was Michael Gaillon, was hanged for his theft. John of Nantes was laid in irons and kept prisoner for his offense, and others were also put in irons, and divers were whipped, as well men as women, by which means they lived in quiet."

In spite of justice, the "colony" was so disastrous a failure that it endured only a year and for sixty years thereafter had no successor in Canada. It remains a quirk of history, which eventually contributes to belles lettres. Out of the Roberval experience, wonderloving André Thevet gained for France a doubtful story, which Marguerite of Navarre juggled in her *Heptameron* to produce a prototype of Hester Prynne. Therein, Roberval is said to have marooned his niece, guilty of having taken, in the one account, a lover, in the other, an offensive husband, on a savage island along with the man and her nurse. Of the three castaways, only the niece survived, feeding herself by shooting wild beasts, to be rescued nearly two years later by a French fisherman. Having been taken back to France, she turned to a life of piety and charity, becoming in fable an example of *extrème amour* and what is mildly termed *austerité*. As event, the tale is suspect on a number of counts; yet it is perhaps a fair example of the license to fancy afforded by the new, unknown world, and to the desire of consciously literary Europe to embellish American annals.

Such general testimonies as those of Cartier and Roberval are no more than indicative. Something closer to actual colonization, and the narrative of colonization which followed upon it, came not so much from their effort as from a motive ascribed to them by Spaniards, who believed that the French in Canada were trying to establish a raiding base from which to attack the Spanish treasure ships in the Bahama channel, far to the south. To protect their fleets against piracies official and unofficial, the Spanish under-

took a military-naval post of their own, a permanent, peopled installation. Earlier attempts at settlement having col-
lapsed into treasure hunts, the new undertaking aimed at
persistence. A preliminary exploration discovered harbors
on the north shore of the Gulf of Mexico, one of which
(Pensacola) offered a site. From there, by sea or land,
"Punta Santa Elena" was to be sought out and fortified,
Punta Santa Elena being a vaguely and variously identified
cape on the Florida-Georgia-South Carolina Atlantic coast.

Under Don Tristán de Luna y Arellano, in 1559, some
fifteen hundred persons took ship from New Spain, the men
being accompanied by women and children, the soldiers
being supported by laborers and slaves, Negro and Indian.
After a two months zigzag voyage, they made a landing. At
once, a hurricane struck, destroying most of their ships and
supplies.

It was less destructive than their own vagaries. A treasure
hunt—one more in the long series of golden fantasies—
capped expeditions into Indian towns and an Indian war.
Luna's officers quarreled among themselves and eventually
mutinied. Luna's own madness and the by now familiar but
still fearful history of starvation among his people provide
all the materials of drama and of melodrama.

The record of misfortune is full enough. Within the Spanish bureaucracy, paperwork held the highest importance.
No venture lacked a notary, and no event established itself
without his official rubric attached to the sworn statements
of witnesses. For Luna, the documents are many, the literary significances few. Among its penmen, the colony possessed only one writer, who composed only a few lines. His
single effort, anonymous in authorship and purportedly the
expression of a group rather than an individual, shows quality of expression. Driven to despair by famine, fear, and the
lack of shelter, the married soldiers petitioned Luna that

they, their wives, and their children be sent home to New Spain. Their scribe writes for them—

". . . we see very clearly that we ourselves, our children and wives and our estates, are suffering from the great hunger which we are at present enduring and we see that neither we nor your Lordship can remedy this situation, even though it be attempted with all the diligence in the world. And in order to provide relief for these wives and children we see the camp very much over-wrought and exhausted, which would not be the case if all the soldiers were single men. Wherefore, we pray and require of your Lordship, once, twice, and thrice, and as many times as we can in legal form ask it, that, in order that we may not see ourselves perish and our wives and children die, and before we see ourselves in greater necessity, your Lordship will send us to New Spain under whatever precaution may be proper. . . . And more than this, we say that whenever his Majesty or the viceroy in his name commands us to go and settle where the land may be suitably fertile and profitable, we will be ready with our persons and households to do it. And of your most illustrious lordship we ask justice."

Justice they hardly got, though some of the colonists were sent home and some survived to be rescued. The Luna "settlement" never grew beyond the camp the married soldiers called it, its story obscured in documentary fragments.

Two other offshoots in the Spanish record are deviations in the history of settlement as well as in literary history. The first of these, "The Relation of Florida . . . brought home by Brother Gregorio de Beteta" (1549), tells of an attempt by four Spanish friars to establish not a colony but a mission in Florida among Indians who had not been victimized by earlier invaders, and therefore might be persuaded to Christianity by these few men of good will and peace.

The heroic evangelists, led by Fray Luis Cancer, landed by chance among Indians who knew and hated the Spanish very well. Fray Luis, aware of the fatal landfall but undeterred in his apostleship, writes of the approach to shore, of the first apparently friendly greeting by the Indians, and of their carrying off one of the friars along with another Spaniard and the interpreter, a supposedly converted Indian woman. After an interval of doubt—are these three Christians dead? captive among friends? free, but not ready to return?—Fray Luis learns from a stranger, a deserter from the De Soto expedition enslaved among the Indians for many years, that the priest and the priest's companion have been killed. He sees with his own eyes the now naked interpreter, who has reverted to her people and tries to entice him ashore to his death.

He hesitates only for fear that the Spanish will avenge him. In the end he decides to die as the others have died, because he knows that their mission requires the blood of martyrs. He delays one day to write his relation, and then has himself taken to the beach where the Indians club him as he cries out to God. From the boat, the two surviving friars witness his death, ready to offer up their own lives, or to continue his effort. For lack of food and water, the sailors insist upon their return. One of the friars, Fray Gregorio Beteta, completes the narrative of Fray Luis, describing his death and the passage back to New Spain.

Such is the forthright account, the course of which is not, in the writing, direct. The first alteration of order Fray Luis himself makes as he writes his opening paragraphs, penning them while the small ship's boat takes him to the beach and the martyrdom he foresees. The outcome is, then, foregone. The succeeding episodes in the text, of the first arrival in Florida and the various encounters with the hostile savages, gain from the introduction a profound seriousness. The dramatic building to a climax has to by necessity stop short, since the description of the death of Fray Luis must be given by his companions. Fray Gregorio is the likely writer, who accomplishes his conclusion simply and effectively, after a confused overlapping with the narrative of Fray Luis.

The action itself is, of course, possessed of a high intensity. In part by planning, as Fray Luis opens his relation knowing and making known what his end must be, and in part by the imperatives of event, the intensity rises. The confused transition between the two writers makes for dramatic fault, but is perhaps lucky. Certainly unplanned, the disorder cuts off melodramatic excess, leaving to the murder its own peculiar horror. To the same restraint, the styles of both writers are direct and uncluttered, that of Fray Luis being notably quick, clear, and flexible. Once again, success comes not out of the effort to entertain, but to explain and report. Once again, a literary type shapes itself according to an action.

Where the martyrdom, this first deviation from the patterns of settlement, fulfills its literary purpose, the second deviation—an Indian captivity—fails. The "Memoria de las cosas . . ." of Hernando de Escalante Fontaneda should be but is not the account of a thirteen-year-old boy shipwrecked in 1551 and held in slavery by the Florida Indians for "many" years. Written down about 1575, and judged "unreliable" as a report, the text offers little except missed possibilities. Instead of his own experience, Fontaneda proffers political advices and moral condemnations. Only one somewhat theatrical scene between the Indian king and himself shows any skill, and that of a limited sort. The reminder is valuable that experience alone does not shape a subject or design a form. The writer, working against the material, can destroy its capabilities. Except for his early emergence in letters as Indian captive, Fontaneda could go unmentioned.

The survival of a young boy and the death of a devout priest are foreshadowings of narratives and of the shapes of narratives to come. They are variants from the main course of later sixteenth-century America. Settlement, not always for purposes of colonization, but still settlement, was central. The shores of the Bahama Channel, richer than El Dorado for those who could raid it, still demanded possession. French pirates and Indian wreckers had taken home fabulous cargoes of once Spanish gold. "Punta Santa Elena" was still out of colonial reach and unfortified. In Spain and France, Spanish ministers and their spies sniffed after evidences of French intentions, while, in Florida, Spanish sailors searched the coast, finding the site of a French "colony" set up in 1562 by Jean Ribaut under royal auspices, and named Charlesfort. It was a colony without colonists, its twenty or so starving settlers having already fled for home.

8 / The Peopling of Paradise

Beginning with the Ribaut venture, which established the northward post of Charlesfort (probably on Parris Island, South Carolina), the Florida story continues with a second French fort on the St. John's River, the Spanish attack upon it and massacre of its people, the Spanish founding of St. Augustine, and the French revenge in blood. The whole fearful tale is told, not by one individual, but by a number of writers in English, Latin, French, and Spanish, to make the first of the clusters of settlement narratives which were to become characteristic of habitation. The complex of St. Augustine, as it may be called, holds together by its historical subject. For literary evolution, the fact should be noticed that the unfolding of event, not the identity of a single writer, establishes the kinships of early American writing.

Among the French, four writers of significance present the history of their two settlements, Jean Ribaut, Jacques Le Moyne de Morgues, René de Laudonnière, and Nicolas Le Challeux. Three Spaniards, Francisco Lopéz de Mendoza Grajales, Gonzalo Solís de Merás, and Bartolomé Barrientos, for much the same happenings provide very different interpretations. A Frenchman, Dominique de Gourgues, contributes the epilogue in horror to a sequence which begins with an idyllic rhapsody.

Jean Ribaut (1520?–1565), author of the opening idyll, was a sailor of wide experience who, as commander of the French voyage of 1562, explored the southern Atlantic coast. By his own testimony, he followed an impulse in calling for volunteers to remain at "Charlesfort," and to hold the country for their king. The nature of the post is explicit in its name. It was a fort, and perhaps was to be a military-naval base, its position convenient for piracies upon the Spanish treasure fleets. Because Ribaut was a Huguenot, and Coligny had in mind a refuge in America for French Protestants, their plans were doubly offensive to Catholic Spain.

Whatever the French motives, the twenty-odd volunteers were left to hold half a continent for France, while Ribaut himself, with the rest of his company, returned home, there to be entrapped in the religious wars. A year later, he had to find asylum in England, where he undertook certain curious intrigues for the English settlement of Florida and published, in English, *The whole and true discoverye of Terra Florida (englished, the Florishing land.) Containing as well the wonderful strange Natures and Maners of the people, with the marvelous Commodities and Treasures of the Country; as also the pleasant Ports and Havens and Ways thereunto, Never founde out before the last year, 1562. Written in French, by Captain Ribaut, the first that wholly discovered the same, and now newly set forth in English, the XXX. of May, 1563.*

The Elysian tone of the title holds throughout the text, whose French original may never have existed. Ribaut, like other promoters of later colonies, portrayed a paradise. In it, while he wrote, his "colonists" were gold hunting, starving, quarreling, abusing, and even killing each other, until at last, in ultimate despair of rescue, they managed to build themselves a ramshackle ship to carry them back to Europe. Against all likelihood, it did, except for those who died at sea, and a man who was killed to be eaten by the others. One young boy, rather than undertake their crazed journey, chose to remain with the Indians, and was later picked up by Spanish rescuers.

The French narration broadens out with the second French attempt and in the recounting of it given by Laudonnière, which was not published until 1586, four years after his death. Laudonnière (?–1582) had the command of the new and ambitious settlement of 1564–1565, Fort Caroline on the St. John's River, which included women and children. This second attempt achieved a duration longer and even more distressed than that of Charlesfort, and an ending the most horrible in American annals.

As its leader, Laudonnière was either a victim of bad planning and bad men—as such he saw himself—or an administrator of fatally poor judgment and feckless act. His *Histoire Notable de la Floride*, for which one Martine Basanier edited and extended the French text of 1586 while Hakluyt translated it into English (1587), provides his self-justification in a chronicle of disaster. It is filled with action, some of it potentially heroic, some of it mean. It shows a range of human attributes from courage and energy to foolish violence and bravado to sly, futile trickery and treachery; from self-conceit and self-serving to high generosities and impossible endurances. One human quality is lacking throughout—that of wisdom; one capacity the action never has—that of effectiveness.

Laudonnière has no lack of events to describe, nor dearth of conflicts, and as far as the inherent confusions permit, he shows his experience clearly and energetically. The building of a fort, the alliance with the local Indians, repeated searchings out of gold, Indian warfare, mutinies and piracies on the part of the French, bitter hunger, Indian re-

venges, an incredible and temporary rescue by Sir John
Hawkins followed by the appearance of Ribaut with strong
reinforcements—the incidents succeed each other, in an alternation of hope and despair, of good and bad success, such
as might satisfy any writer looking for crisis and climax.

Dramatically, Laudonnière has one handicap. He has no
single hero. His weakness in recreating his adventures lies in
himself. Whatever his allowable excuses, he never controls
but is always controlled by circumstance. His compatriots
also, loyal or disloyal, possessed of or lacking in fortitude,
invariably lack stature. The heroes of his pages are the Indian chiefs, larger, simpler, and more generous in gifts and
behavior than their rowdy French invaders. The "para-
coussy," King Satourioua, and his eldest son, Athoré—in
Hakluyt's translation "a man . . . perfect in beauty, wisdom, and honest sobriety," of "modest gravity . . . gentle
and tractable"—exemplify the kingly rank which Laudonnière awards them. It is not an accident that the artist Le
Moyne de Morgues, in an original drawing which still survives, shows "Rex Athoré" taller than Laudonnière and the
French soldiers, while the caption describes him as "formo-
sus admodum, prudens, honestus, robustus et procerae admodum staturae . . . modesta quadam gravitate praeditus,
ut in eo majestas spectabilis reluceat."

Athoré personifies the early noble savage, that figure of
natural majesty, virtue, and grace which was to rule a much
later literary movement. Yet Laudonnière is no romantic.
Whatever the hieratic dignity in which he shows them, the
Indians are still to him little more than the human landscape within which he struggles to survive.

Nor can he, at the climax of catastrophe, portray himself
in a heroic part. Ready to escape his now hellish Eden, he is
stopped by the arrival of Ribaut with a large fleet and a
commission to supersede him, since he has been slandered
in France as mercilessly as he has been abused in Florida.

Into his story of bitter suffering comes a flavor of bitter comedy—he is accused not only of tyranny but also of misde-
meanor with his chambermaid, and of hoarding food and
wine, which he protests he kept for the sick. The mention of
the *fille de chambre* is one of the few reminders of the women
and children in the colony, whatever particular misery they
suffered earning them no special attention.

And so to the bloody end of this indeed "notable" history,
no hero manifests himself. Ribaut, scarcely arrived and already under pursuit by a Spanish fleet, sails off to be
wrecked not by Spaniards but by a hurricane; Laudonnière, left with no defenses and without effective men at
arms, suffers surprise in his "fort," saving himself by flight
from a massacre cruelly carried out by Spanish soldiers who
have marched against Fort Caroline from the just-estab-
lished Spanish post to the south, St. Augustine. Finding
safety on board French ships commanded by Ribaut's son,
Laudonnière and the terrified few survivors get back to Europe, the son refusing to stay in Florida to discover his father's fortunes, in death or life.

Laudonnière's is by far the most extended of the Charlesfort–Fort Caroline narratives. The much shorter *Discours*
(1566) of the carpenter Nicolas Le Challeux saves itself by
brevity from Laudonnière's confusions of text, but not from
bewilderments of understanding, or from fears and suffering. The first, common expectation of Florida as paradise
gives it poignancy—the land is one of sun and warmth, tempered by dews and the airs of night and the pleasant rains
which enrich the meadows; it is rich, too, in gold and all
sorts of creatures pastured in luxuriant fields; it has mountains and rivers marvelously delightful, and fragrant trees.
"Que tout cela consideré," Le Challeux adds without double meaning, "ne pouvait autrement advenir que l'homme
ne trouvast là grand plaisir et singuliere delectation." The
anticipation of inevitable pleasure and rare enjoyment in-

stantly meets the destroying reality. Le Challeux spends little time at Fort Caroline, among its miserable people, before he has to take flight from the Spanish assault,
witnessing the slaughter of his countrymen and barely
making his escape to the French ships through flooded forests and marshlands.

Jacques Le Moyne de Morgues, the artist-mapmaker
among the French, is less interesting as a writer than Laudonnière and Le Challeux, upon whom he depends, and
from whom he borrows. Whatever his original draft and its
vicissitudes—the evidences disagree—it was finally published in Latin by Theodor de Bry (1591). Le Moyne's story
moves fast; indeed, it reads like a recombination and con-
densation of earlier accounts. Its great interest lies in Le
Moyne's drawings, which de Bry engraved and published
with the text. Most of the original drawings have disappeared. One has recently surfaced, in a listing at auction.
Another has been identified for some time. This last suggests
if it does not substantiate (John White's drawings offer
firmer evidence) an intellectual process.

Le Moyne has placed in the center of his rather realistic
and simple sketch a column set up as an emblem of French
sovereignty. On the left, kneeling Indians worship the pil-
lar; on the right, the Indian king Athoré stands by, with a
French officer and his soldiers. The central pattern is that of
a formal and elaborate Renaissance still life, though the
figures which flank it are not notably stylized—the general
effect is that of reasonably accurate, modestly heightened
portraiture. In the far better known engraving of de Bry,
however, they are worked to excess. The anatomical development makes the naked Indian prince a Michelangelesque
Roman; the French officer and his men are touched up into
soldiers of the court, their clothing and arms enriched by
decoration. The figuration of the new world has then been
twice translated into European terms. Le Moyne himself,

first, with his derived design, and secondly de Bry with his baroque processing have brought savagery to terms with their own culture. The same transmutation appears, on close reading, in many a literary sequence, such as that of the Southwest from Alarcón to Villagrá.

To return to the literary record, the French narratives, in their confusions and doubts, their crossings of motives, their records of sins and miscalculations and fears, continually touch upon characterization, though they do not consciously aim for it. Laudonnière sketches himself when he insists upon his meticulous and fair counting out of the biscuit rations; so too, when he sets down with equal care his obtuse dealings with the Indians, while of his errors therein he remains oblivious. He gives himself no gallant part in resisting the Spanish. At the moment of attack, he was in his tent and says so, as honest as he was sick, weary, and resourceless. When Le Challeux, the elderly carpenter, pursued by a Spanish pikeman, manages to leap the eight- or nine-foot rampart of Fort Caroline—marveling at his feat—and get away still clutching the tool in his hand, he makes himself something more than the "poor old man" he said he was. And when, in the distresses of his flight, drenched, hungry, exhausted, scared, and hopeless of surviving, he utters to his equally miserable companions little, formal, Lutheran exhortations, he is so implausible that he gains both credit and character. Only one who had so behaved could have written of so behaving.

None of the French narrators witnessed the subsequent massacres by which the Spanish disposed of Ribaut and his soldiers and sailors, shipwrecked and stranded near Matanzas. The stories got back to France, however, through the few survivors and through the accounts of the Spanish themselves. The Spanish leader, Pedro Menéndez de Avilés, thereby becomes a monster of inhumanity, while in Spain his coreligionists and compatriots celebrate his slaughter of heretics and praise his conquests. The king, Philip II, applauds the bloodshed, and directs that the few prisoners Menéndez spared be sent to the galleys.

Indeed, if French Florida produced no actor of heroic stature, Spanish Florida finds one in Menéndez, who justifies the acclaim by acts and energies, clear judgment, and a temper which could be tolerant and even kindly and humorous when it was not coolly brutal. His eulogists do not excuse his exterminations of Huguenots; they share his lack of mercy, and explain his occasional exercise of it. For them the heretic has no right to life. He is a danger, in his doctrine capable of spreading a mortal disease. Menéndez doubles his glory as a soldier in his role as executioner for the faith. The three Spanish narrators who recount his victories, Francisco Lopéz de Mendoza Grajalas, Gonzalo Solís de Merás, and Bartolomé Barrientos, regard him as an emissary of God against the spawn of Satan.

Mendoza, his chaplain, proclaims the justice which Menéndez carried out upon the "Lutherans," those "maddened devils" who have lost their claim to Christianity and quarter. In the "Relación de la jornada de Pedro Menéndez de Avilés en la Florida," he exults in the killing of the Protestant French, a hundred and forty-two of them at Fort Caroline, surrender or no surrender, and one hundred and eleven unarmed prisoners from Ribaut's storm-wrecked fleet at Matanzas.

For some untold reason, he does not report the final, methodical butchery of prisoners, among them Ribaut himself, once again at Matanzas—the place was aptly named "the massacres"—near where the first shipwrecked group had been clubbed and cut down. There, in sight of the bodies of the earlier victims, some eighty more were tied, beaten, and stabbed to death. Those who professed and proved themselves to be Catholics were spared, and with them the musicians, a drummer, a fifer, and a fiddler, "kept alive to play for dancing."

Beyond those who escaped with Laudonnière and the younger Ribaut, fantastic chances led to the survival of a few who told their stories to French writers. Menéndez himself let live the women and the children under fifteen, so that there was no lack of accusing witness to the carnage. But French evidence was unnecessary. The Spanish provide the same testimony, not only Mendoza but also Solís de Merás, who was Menéndez' genial brother-in-law, and Barrientos, man of learning and studious biographer, whose main source may have been Menéndez' own narrative.

Historical moralities aside, the literary instruction of the Spanish texts is clear. In a transcript of action, the unequivocal statement lends trimness, speed, and force. The Spaniards did not qualify or confuse their issues. Menéndez himself offers the only suggestion that explanation of the slaughter was called for, in the statement (if indeed he made it), "I do this not as to Frenchmen, but as to Lutherans." Such terseness has power.

For further instruction, the Spanish narratives show the effectiveness of a strong and active central character. Solís de Merás and Barrientos—the two are closely related, even in phrasing—both profit by the personality of Menéndez, whom they find wholly admirable. Once their assumptions are granted, that the Huguenots are enemies of God and man, and that only the Spanish can rightfully hold Florida, Menéndez is transformed into a selfless patriot with a divine mission, a perfect officer of his king and a dedicated champion of the only true Christian faith.

The evidence is overwhelming. Within the flexible—and evocative—pattern of the historical chronicle, Menéndez becomes the ideal conquistador. First in the endurance of hardships and unhesitant in sacrificing his own fortunes, first in energy and daring, he shows himself as well to be an intelligent strategist, a canny persuader of less courageous followers, and a political, genial, and forceful dealer with the Indians, towards whom he is even capable of humor.

The Solís "Memorial" (written c. 1567) provides one of the rare passages of comedy in the sixteenth-century record, when Menéndez bends himself to court and indeed to take to wife the sister of the Indian cacique Carlos, in order that the heathen people should accept both Christianity and Spanish rule. Unlike most of the cavaliers, Menéndez—long married at home—was a reluctant suitor, who "showed much [desire] to try some other expedient [than marriage] but as none could be found, it was decided that thus it should be done.

"Then the Christian women who were there bathed and clothed her, and she appeared much better than before, when she was naked; and the captains praised her intentionally as being very beautiful and dignified; they gave her the name of Doña Antonia. . . . The supper, the music and the merriment took place on land, in some tents the Adelantado had had set up, near his ships, [and lasted] until two o'clock in the morning. The Adelantado had her seated next to him, and said many things to her through the interpreter which pleased her, and she answered so discreetly and in so few words, that we all of us marvelled at her. Her Indian women and the Christian women danced with the soldiers, and when that was ended, they conducted her to rest on a bed which the Adelantado ordered to be made, and he followed her; and in the morning she arose very joyful. . . ."

Menéndez, having withheld nothing in the service of his God and his king, kept to his courteous consideration of his unwanted bride, and when in Cuba she once more claimed her marital rights, he put her off with an excuse she could understand—a pretended rule of continence imposed upon a knight of Santiago for eight days after warfare. The apparently persuaded Doña Antonia was a woman of "good understanding" and a certain guile, however. Having tricked her way to Menéndez' room, she possessed herself of a lighted candle, "and looked to see if any woman were in bed with the Adelantado, and afterward she looked around the bed, and underneath it. . . .

"The Adelantado, with a gay and amused countenance, laughing greatly at this, told . . . Doña Antonia that he would be very glad if the 8 days were passed, so that she might lie there beside him." When he had given her presents to soothe her feelings, he got her to go away, and as soon as possible returned her to her brother.

Such is the episode in the "Memorial" by Solís de Merás (1567?). Its parallel in Barrientos' "Vida y hechos de Pero Menéndez de Auilés" (written 1568) is much stiffer and less amusing. Therefore Solís de Merás—one of the two Spanish officers who stabbed to death the unarmed Jean Ribaut— earns at least some of the credit for the good-natured, artful sketch. Throughout his text, he handles his actions and persons with singular ease, in contrast to Barrientos who in spite of cursive phrasing restricts his presentation, and in so doing loses flavor.

Both Spanish narrators add another episode to the military record, a fourth encounter between Menéndez and the French Lutherans. Friendly Indians having informed him of the last large group of survivors from Ribaut's wrecked fleet, eight days to the south of St. Augustine, Menéndez decided to leave no part of his work undone. Marching against the Frenchmen, he procured their surrender, and— astonishingly—promised them mercy. He not only kept his word, but gave them the same rations and the same treatment which he gave his own men. This one inconsistency of mercy to heretics the French documents do not mention; perhaps the commentators did not know of it, perhaps judged the mercy qualified, since the captives who did not recant or escape were destined for the galleys.

Menéndez, then, emerges in the Spanish estimation as an officer of remark and an individual of humane and even humorous bent, "much beloved, feared, and respected." The reconciliation between monster and hero has to come out of the passions of his era. Solís and Barrientos do not attempt it, but simply affirm the ideal man of arms and faith. Solís, of the two, in so doing draws not only the type but a personality—a rare effort and still rarer achievement in sixteenth-century writing.

The Solís manuscript, for unknown reasons, breaks off unfinished. The Barrientos, too, is in fact incomplete, Barrientos himself having died in 1568, while Menéndez lived six years after him. Both authors are using recognized patterns. Barrientos, a scholar, employs the biography with a measure of skill and more formality. Solís made the wiser choice of the historical chronicle, because the form helped to endow his Menéndez with the honors of earlier heroes.

The final episode of the St. Augustine sequence turns to the French again. Dominique de Gourgues, soldier and erstwhile captive and slave on Spanish galleys, noble and in all likelihood a Roman Catholic, undertook on his own account to avenge the massacres of his countrymen and the insult which the Spanish had "offered to the King and all France." Embarking in 1567 on a course which took him to Africa and the West Indies, he brought his ships and soldiers to Florida in 1568, where he visited upon the Spanish fort of San Mateo, which had replaced the French Fort Caroline, a justice as brutal and bloody as had been dealt out there by Spain.

"La Reprinse de la Floride par le Cappitaine Gourgue" (1586) appeared with the Laudonnière text in Basanier's *L'Histoire Notable* . . . Its authorship is in question, since the double meaning of the title allows of Gourgues himself, while Basanier and still a third person, scribe or copyist, named Prevost have claims. It is doubtful also as objective history, since the incidents are heightened extravagantly. The central event, the revengeful taking of San Mateo and the slaughter of the Spanish garrison there, is beyond doubt. Almost every other statement of the narrative has been challenged. Gourgues may have been a patriot, his only motive to restore his country's honor; he may, on the other hand, have been a slaver and a pirate. His version of the Fort Caroline story adds new frightfulness to the Spanish atrocities—bloody execution, the abuse of women, and the throat-cutting of children. According to him, Ribaut, having been murdered, is flayed and his skin sent to the king of Spain. French captives are starved, tortured, and mocked, and then hanged from trees. He accuses Menéndez of having left the message above their bodies—"I do this not as to Frenchmen but as to Lutherans." The accusation does not appear in the earlier Fort Caroline narratives.

Menéndez himself makes no mention of such dramatics, although in a letter he says that he hanged some of his French prisoners. In still another area of doubtful drama, the Indians are shown greeting Gourgues and his men as deliverers. Although at the time of the Menéndez massacres the Indians had come soundly to hate the French, and Satourioua (so Hakluyt spells his variously rendered name) had particular cause to resent bitterly their behavior to him, now he greets them lovingly, saying that since the French defeat "Florida has never had a single good day," and that the Spaniards have hunted them from their houses, violated their women, and killed their children.

If the enthusiasm of the Indians for the French is fictitious, their enthusaistic desire to attack the Spaniards is probably authentic, as is Gourgues's conquest of San Mateo and his subsequent slaughter of the Spanish, of whom he saved some few for formal execution. These he hanged, purportedly from the trees where Menéndez had hanged his captive French. In dramatic echo of Menéndez (or of the statement attributed to Menéndez by the drama-conscious French writer), Gourgues inscribed his message above them—"I do this not as to Spaniards and pigs, but as to traitors, thieves, and murderers."

The hideous reprisal completes a cycle. History, already bloody enough, has been manipulated into melodrama, and shaped to a well-made and planned conclusion. The writer is conscious enough of his effects to carry even the customary voyage ending—the return home, out of the strange to the familiar—over into a final twist of excitement and *blague.* The Spanish have tried to surprise Gourgues at La Rochelle, but he has already left there. Had he known of their coming, he would have awaited their arrival and given them such a response as would have offered them "great satisfaction."

The pun in French is sharper—"de s'en contenter"—but in any language the final flick of the pen betrays itself. So too the maneuverings of plot and temper. Nor does the Gourgues writer have to be taught what Laudonnière did not know—the requirement in a story of action of a central, energetic actor. His skills served him well; his machinery functions. Like his Spanish counterparts, however, he gains surface to the loss of depth. The muddling and muddled Laudonnière, and to a lesser degree the guileless Le Challeux do more for the minds and behaviors of men than their more adept rivals.

Whatever the final judgment of quality between them, the St. Augustine-Fort Caroline authors offer a juxtaposition of the loose-strung tale and the structured story, an early confrontation, in battle narratives, between a Stephen Crane and a Francis Parkman. Such comment can be made only by hindsight. Yet the texts support it, and the suggestion renews itself in the course of succeeding American centuries, during which the writers of confusion pose their theses against those of the writers of clarity.

9 / The Meeting Point
Between Savagery and Civilization

Whatever the literary accomplishment of sixteenth-century Florida, it produces no narrative of colonization. Menéndez managed to set up several little outposts and garrisons, occupied by soldiers who deserted at every chance, some few discontented, mutinous farmers, once zealous but soon martyred or disillusioned priests, and a scattering of unhappy "married residents" who earnestly wished to be elsewhere. These have left records for history, but to literature nothing, not even a sorrowful dirge of hunger and hazard, suffering and death. In the eighteenth-century Spanish *Chronological History of the Continent of Florida* (1723) by Andrés Barcia, attention shifts away from the peninsula of that name to other areas of the "continent"—New Mexico, the Northwest Passage, Virginia—and to such English personages as Hunfredo Gilbert, Ricardo Greinvile, Francisco Draque, Gualtero Raelig, and Rudolfo Lave, who, to Barcia's indignation, intrude upon the Spanish interest and challenge his king's dominion, most immediately to the north of Punta Santa Elena, at Roanoke.

Amusement aside, the distortion of familiar names serves as a reminder to the reader of English concentration that both Spanish claim and Spanish culture ruled a huge part of northern America. Yet the English Roanoke sets something of a limit to Spanish expansion on the Atlantic coast, Menéndez' plan to settle the Chesapeake having aborted, and the immeasurably courageous priests who set out to convert the northern Indians having met their deaths. For them there exists no parallel to the Beteta-Cancer martyrdom. A letter makes their only contemporary memorial.

Gilbert to the north, and Drake to the south and west gain written fame, but they are seafarers and their success goes into sea narratives. The landsman's tale of habitation, with its still-to-be-discovered shifts of subject, theme, and form, turns to Raleigh and Grenville as instigators, and Ralph Lane as governor and narrator of the first occupation of the northern Atlantic coast for England. Arthur Barlow, sea captain and enchanted explorer, writes the prelude for Lane, in the sense in which Ribaut opens the history of Laudonnière. Like Ribaut, Barlow sees a paradise in the new world. For Roanoke, as for Fort Caroline, the playing out of history lends the tension of tragedy to the first idyllic presentation.

Barlow's "The first voyage made to the coasts of America . . ." (1589) admits no doubts of a happy outcome. A "discourse" written from a sea journal, it develops as a voyage for a page or two, and returns to the voyage form at the end, but its center is a fable of utopia, its landscape the dwelling place of "such as live after the manner of the golden age." Barlow feels no apprehension of danger and admits of no uneasiness about the natives or the land he has taken formal possession of. He is entirely serene, except for the excitement of pleasure.

At the ship's approach to shore, he breaks into his minor rhapsody, smelling across the water "so sweet and so strong a smell, as if we had been in the midst of some delicate garden abounding with all kind of odoriferous flowers. . . ."

The green hills, the level ground, and even the trees are covered with grapes, whose vines cover the sandy beach so close to the water that "the very beating and surge of the sea overflowed them."

Fish, beasts, and birds the new country has in "incredible abundance." At the sound of a shot, "such a flock of cranes (the most part white) arose under us, with such a cry redoubled by many echoes, as if an army of men had shouted all together." "Deer, conies, hares, and fowl" crowd the forests of rich woods, fragrant gums, and spicy bark. "The goodliest and best fish" swarm in the sea, and in a mainland river, a "great store of mussels" offers pearls.

Perhaps of all the persuasions of the new earth, Barlow is most imaginatively captured by "the people of the country"—he does not call them Indians—whom he found "most gentle, loving, and faithful, void of all guile"; indeed, "a more kind and loving people there cannot be found in the world," and they welcome, respect, and wonder at the white-skinned Englishmen.

To display them, Barlow introduces three scenes, two brief and one extended. In the earliest, a native fisherman is invited to the English ship and given gifts. As a return of hospitality, he sets himself to catch a boatload of fish, making them a present to his hosts, and then "after he had (as much as he might) acquited the former benefits received, departed out of our sight."

The second scene is a formal audience with the king's brother, "accompanied by forty or fifty men, very handsome and goodly people, and in their behavior as mannerly and civil as any in Europe." Here Barlow emphasizes the natural dignity of the savages, their ceremonious behavior, and their reverence for rank, as well as their geniality. His later comment stresses the "difference between the noble men, and the governors of the countries, and the meaner sort"—

fitting differences, in the Elizabethan concept of social order.

He pays most of his dramatic attention, however, to the entertainment which the king's brother's wife offers the visitors. After greeting them "very cheerfully and friendly," she takes them into her house where she and her women wash and dry their clothes, and bathe their feet, and put food to cook for them "with as much bounty (after their manner)" as the hostess "could possibly devise." When men armed with bows and arrows frighten them, she punishes the offenders by having their weapons broken. When the English, still timid, refuse to stay in the houses and take refuge in their boat for the night, she grieves, and sends mats to cover them against the rain, and puts watchers on the beach to care for their safety. So sure is Barlow of the "love" and "familiarity" of the inhabitants that he apologizes for his precautions.

He takes precautions, however, and he speaks of the "cruel and bloody" wars which go on between the different native groups. Moreover, there is some reason to believe that he suppressed the mention of one encounter with an actively hostile "people of the country" who killed several of a landing party. Barlow's paradise thereby becomes a deliberate act of creation, obviously genuine in its beauties, joys, and affections, and as obviously directed to its Edenic effect.

Barlow was, of course—willingly enough by every evidence of tone—contributing to Raleigh's campaign for the confirmation of his royal letters patent for the discovery of new lands, a campaign in which Hakluyt took a personal and active part. The visionary eulogy was conceived to help along their practical aim. It is no less rhapsodic, and no less a vision, for all of that.

Barlow had three successors in the Roanoke group, two of whom—Ralph Lane and Thomas Harriot—report upon the first settlement of 1585–1586. The third, John White, gives the beginning of the last, "lost colony" of 1587, and his faithful seeking after survivors of it, whom he never found. The "fifteen men . . . furnished plentifully" whom Grenville left on Roanoke Island in 1586 had no chronicler and themselves vanished without trace, except for a single skeleton.

For the first attempt, there also survives a sea journal, perhaps by Barlow but showing no evidence of his style or skill, which is even less to the purpose in that it does not mention colonization except in a final list—"The names of those as well gentlemen as others that remained one whole year in Virginia under the government of Master Ralph Lane." It includes a brief, ominous incident ashore. The savages having stolen a silver cup and failing to return it, "we burned and spoiled their corn and town, all the people being fled."

The process of colonization, ignored in the sea journal, becomes the subject of Lane's later narrative, in which he relates what happened in the "one whole year" after the year had come to a sorry end. His "Account of the particularities of the imployments of the Englishmen left in Virginia . . ." (1589) is as cluttered as his title, although Lane was determined to "proceed with order" in his discourse. To that end, he divided it into two parts, the first devoted to the "particularities" of such areas of the country as he was able to discover, and the second to his reasons for abandoning the colony, "in the beginning whereof shall be declared the conspiracy of Pemisapan with the savages of the main to have cut us off. . . ."

He is reasonably faithful to his scheme, although his first part deals far more elaborately with what he would have done in explorations he dreamed of making than what he did in those he actually undertook. Secotan, the Chesapeake, "Chawanook" to the northwest—places he or his emissaries saw—fade out of interest in comparison with the magical lands he heard of. The kingdom of pearls, beyond Chawanook, so captured his fancy that he wrote down in detail his plan for getting there, utterly bemused with the discovery he never carried out. "I would have sent a small bark with two pinnaces about by sea to the northward . . . while I with all the small boats I could make, and with two hundred men would have gone up to the head of the river of Chawanook with the guides that Menatonon would have given me, which I would have been assured should have been of his best men, (for I had his best beloved son prisoner with me) who also should have kept me company. . . ."

Lane continues with his elaborate fantasy. He would have built forts to guard his route, he would have found the passage to the South Sea, he could have left boats for rescue along the way. . . . Then, with astonishing facility, he slips out of his unrealities into the very different narrative of a journey upriver, a suddenly clear story of risk, frustration, and a return to Roanoke with his nearly starved and exhausted men. The distinction between his two types of "meaning" is blurred, but the difference between the facts of his fancy and the facts of his experience is sharp.

Into this first part, devoted to "particularities" of the country, the savages inevitably intrude. Lane's early references to them are obscure. He holds Menatonon's "best beloved son" prisoner; he has released Menatonon himself "upon a ransom agreed for." Pemisapan, another "king," has turned hostile. Having persuaded the once friendly tribes of the interior that the English mean to destroy them, he has told Lane that these tribes "had the like meaning towards us." Such is the basis of his plot.

In bits and scraps of comment, disordered and sometimes contradictory, Lane sketches in the new, general enmity of the Indians toward the English. Lane's own precautions and procedures suggest much more than he admits—he is completely dependent upon the Indians for food; failing their friendship, he tries to take hostages; the Indians attack from ambush, while Lane's soldiers fire blindly into the woods.

The last instance might aptly enough be made into a metaphor of the meeting of the two cultures, their concepts of life and death divergent beyond reconciliation. Whatever the "cruelty and outrages" committed, according to Hakluyt, by some of Lane's company, the Indians were helpless to resist, as long as they believed the intruders to be maleficent spirits, not men. They were freed to attack the English only when they decided that the newcomers were not such supernatural beings, nor under the protection of omnipotence. With this change of conviction, "they grew not only into contempt of us, but also . . . now they began to blaspheme, and flatly to say that our Lord God was not God, since he suffered us to sustain much hunger, and also to be killed. . . ."

Out of their own belief in the hostility of the dead against the living, the Indians had in the beginning convinced themselves that the invaders "be dead men returned into the world again, and that we do not remain dead but for a certain time, and that then we return again." As dead spirits, or as such revived in human shape, the English were equally invincible—"we were not subject to be destroyed by them; but contrariwise that they amongst them that sought our destruction, should find their own, and not be able to work ours." Their wisest and their old men hold the opinion "that they have been in the night, being 100. miles from any of us, in the air shot at, and stroken by some men of ours, that by sickness had died among them."

This was the conviction which saved the settlement from massacre. By Lane's evidence, the Indians wavered in it. His second part, the story of Pemisapan's conspiracy, traces the chops and changes of that now credulous, now skeptical

king, ultimately beheaded by the English to the final settlement of his doubts, and of the now resistant, now submissive
fellow-kings whom he tried to unite against the possibly all-
powerful malignities of the "Fort at Roanoke."

Fort it always was, and had need to be. Not even the taking of Pemisapan's head could have saved it, had not Francis Drake come by with a fleet of ships and carried off its
garrison, beyond the reach of vengeance. Lane, his most
eminent passenger, bemoans the loss of charts, books, and
writings, which the impatient sailors threw overboard, but
took home in his mind, along with his failures and sufferings, fabulous tales of pearls and gold, those supernaturalisms to which the European was unwaveringly faithful.

These tales, along with the fantasies about the South Sea
or a "good mine," make the antiphony to Lane's griefs. In
the distant, never-seen country of "Chaunis Temoatan," the
Indians take from a river "a marvelous and most strange
mineral," paler and softer than copper, of which they have
so much that even their neighbors "beautify their houses
with great plates of the same." Three days journey by river,
and four days overland to the northeast, a certain king
holds an island in a great bay. "Out of this bay . . . this
king had so great a quantity of pearl . . . as that not only
his own skins that he weareth, and the better sort of his gentlemen and followers are full set with the said pearl, but also
his beds, and houses are garnished with them, and that he
hath such quantity of them, that it is a wonder to see."

Lane never saw that wonder but is nonetheless dazzled
by it, and thereby puts himself among the early visionaries.
He is also among the first to show the struggle between forest and fort, the wilderness adventure whose pattern recurs
in three centuries of American writing. His value as a writer
lies wholly in his subjects. For all of his insistence on order,
he can no more control the confusions of his pen than those
of his voyagings, and sounds as happy to be released from

the one as the other. His is no better than a bewildered, vague foreshadowing of later trials and terrors, more nobly expressed.

The true innovator in the Roanoke group is a very different person, Thomas Harriot (1560–1621), who, for reasons unknown, delayed the publication of his "Briefe and true report" of 1587 until 1588, after Raleigh's second group, which had orders to settle the Chesapeake, had sailed. Thereby he lost effectiveness as a propagandist; that he was nevertheless a propagandist for colonization remains obvious. He puts his attention and his insistence upon information essential to the colonist for habitation and survival in an unfamiliar country. He is ready to refute those who have "slandered" and maliciously "spoken ill" of Raleigh's first project with his own reasoned and orderly exposition of the "commodities" of Virginia. These will richly suffice for a man's own livelihood, and for his profit in trade. He hints at gold and jewels, to be sure, but makes his text upon humbler wealths and his own firm assurance of them.

This kind of emphasis is new and sensible and—superficially—self-evident. Yet no one before the scholarly and intelligent Harriot had made the recognition that food and what he calls "merchantable" produce, however simple as ideas, were as objects absolute necessities. Harriot understands that the gathering or cultivation of natural crops must be the first undertaking of the colonist. He had seen and might well have suffered the consequences of Lane's dependence upon supplies from home or those begged, bought, or taken from the Indians. He speaks with authority when by close implication he tells his planters to think first of their livelihood. Yet he is Raleigh's man, sent by Raleigh, to support Raleigh's plans. He never directly tells them that if they do not, they will die.

When, in another fashion, he blurs his importances, he may be forgiven. He writes as though "grass silk" and "worm silk" were as important to survival as Indian corn, or sassafras and civet cats and "walnut oil" as profitable as timber, tobacco, and furs. Even his year in Virginia under Lane could not endow him with powers of divination, though it put him among those early commentators who recognized not only the fertility but also the extent and value of the land itself.

His second contribution to new matter and new form is one of emphasis also. Other writers had reported upon the Indians as objects of curiosity, admiration, contempt, hostility, tolerance, fear, apprehension, incomprehension, or simple acceptance. Harriot touches upon the conventional in describing them, and then pays them much closer attention, examining especially their religious beliefs and their interpretations of Christianity. Because these concepts explained and governed what they said and did, Harriot takes care to be specific, enlarging upon Lane's evidences that the Indians "could not tell whether to think us gods or men. . . .

"Some therefore were of opinion that we were not born of women, and therefore not mortal, but that we were men of an old generation many years past, then risen again to immortality.

"Some would likewise seem to prophesy that there were more of our generation yet to come to kill theirs and take their places, as some thought the purpose was, by that which was already done. Those that were immediately to come after us they imagined to be in the air, yet invisible and without bodies, and that they by our entreaty and for the love of us, did make the people to die in that sort as they did, by shooting invisible bullets into them."

Harriot, who was a moderate and reasonable man, disapproving of violence, nevertheless sees the advantage to the

English of these superstitions. When the savages of "any town that had offended us" die without evident injury, so that the survivors believe such deaths "the special work of God for our sakes," he comments that the English "have cause in some sort to think no less." He will not use deceit, and he wants the Indians brought to know the "truth," but —once again by implication—he suggests that under these delusions this strange people "need nothing at all to be feared."

Throughout his discourse, Harriot is practicing the essay of persuasion. That fact, which makes him an innovator in form, also makes him disingenuous. A sharp observer who was capable of balanced judgment, he suppresses the happenings and the conclusions to be drawn therefrom which would have worked against Raleigh's plans. The near chance of starvation becomes in his text the stipulation that colonists be "reasonably provided for the first year," after which, with "diligence and care," they may plant and sow to feed and even to "enrich" themselves. He disposes of the increasing hostility of the Indians by admitting that "some of our company . . . showed themselves too fierce in slaying some of the people in some towns." He doubts however "the alteration of their [the Indians'] opinions generally."

He weakens himself as a writer, and dulls his effects, by acting as a pleader who pretends impartiality. His syllogistic argument is hidden, but reads, "Men of sense look to their profit, Virginia offers profit, therefore—" He nowhere plainly acknowledges that Virginia also offered hunger and danger, although his own body and mind must have afforded him that truth.

His treatise is a missed chance, thereby, and for all of its clarities and informations something of a bore. Whether he did better justice to his gifts in the "chronicle" he says he wrote, is a question which only the now vanished chronicle could meet.

The Roanoke cycle ends with the narratives of John White, Raleigh's governor of the last, "lost" colony of 1587. Its prospects shadowed by the failure of the first settlement and by the disappearance of the men left ashore by Grenville in the summer of 1586, the new venture has, in writing, a beginning and an end, but nothing more. John White kept a journal of the voyage out and of the first, unpromising month on shore. It is a bare record of mishaps and mistakes: the reestablishment of Roanoke instead of the new "City of Raleigh" further north on the Chesapeake, the disorders among the settlers, and the immediate attacks upon the Indians. White's relation of the "colony" ends with the insistence of the "colonists" that he return to England to make sure the supplies from home will meet their needs.

However unwillingly, White gave in. He could not get back to Virginia for three years because of the crises of the Spanish Armada. In 1590, he at last reached his settlement, to find nothing but the famous and mysterious message carved on tree trunks—CRO and the place name CROATOAN—without the agreed upon signal of distress.

The climax survives as an anecdote in White's sea journal of 1590. Whatever its place in the drama of history, it got no contemporary literary development. Like Lane, White lacked the gifts of a writer, though he amply possessed those of an artist.

His contribution to the complex of Roanoke is graphic rather than verbal. His drawings show him to have been a precise and delicate draughtsman, with a jeweler's fineness of design. Close observation of his subjects and fidelity to them served him well. Beyond techniques, he makes no translation of the Indians into European figures or patterns, such as Le Moyne seems to have practiced. When De Bry engraved the White sketches, however, he took them over into European mannerisms and embellishments. His boast that he copied them accurately is inaccurate. His most destructive changes are those of posture and expression, wherein he brings White's savages into a Graeco-Roman tradition.

White himself made no such mistake. His "people of the country" are indigenous to the New World, interpreted within their own culture, by expression, attitude, gesture, and activity. Detail illustrates the point. White's Indian fires burn indiscriminate pieces of wood, where De Bry's burn sawed logs, planks, and boards. White's Indians keep their necessary crudities and barbarisms, without loss of dignity and humor; their hair is rough, their tattoo marks are deep; their feet are large, spread by barefoot walking. De Bry and his engravers curl their hair and toes, and omit or lightly enchase their scars. White genially accepts their habits and practices in eating, dancing, making magic, or playing with their children, and leaves them the physical evidences thereof. His interpretations are those which he is entitled to make, always in good nature, of grossness or refinement, stupidity or wit, austerity or affability. His Indians possess the character, as individuals and as a group, appropriate to their environment and society.

De Bry's Europeanized renderings prevailed, however, perhaps because the original White drawings disappeared for some three hundred years. Perhaps, more significantly, the cultural translation was inevitable. Such modifications as De Bry's prevail in writing also. Only the occasional and rarely gifted writer may see and describe "the people of the country" without distortions. De Bry was not questioned, since he provided what his audience was already prepared to accept.

White closes the sixteenth-century English record, a "colonial" literature which never gained a right to the adjective. Rather, for France and Spain, as well as England, the record shows attempts at occupation—either failures or meager survivals of large plans. The building of forts and the contriving of missions mark the intent to control and convert rather than to colonize. However often the plan required permanent settlement by families, however often the planners called upon farmers and artisans to establish themselves in a true community, the realities governed.

The literature of the late sixteenth century in northern America is not one of colonization, then, but of confrontation. While there is no such frontier as Frederick Jackson Turner postulated and variously defined, his "meeting point between savagery and civilization" makes itself evident beyond the slightest doubt. A moralist, in discriminating, may question which side of the conflict earned which term. The conflict itself moves through every action and idea, whether of peace or war, idealization or contempt.

The narratives identify many other sorts of conflict and confrontation. The rivalries of Europe transplant themselves to the new, golden world, while men vie against each other, in utopia as at home. The elemental conflicts by sea and land, in which frail humanity struggles against wind, water, earth, and fire, offer another sort of opposition, differently resolved. The encounter of the two races and cultures, however, provides the inescapable, the inevitable collision, in history and in writing. The sixteenth century shows it, most clearly at Roanoke. The seventeenth century carries on and elaborates its dramatic violences and its philosophic discords.

10 / The Pathfinder, or, The Inland Sea

After a hundred years without true colonization in northern America, the voyage necessarily remains the dominant form in writing. Signs of modification appear. Harriot writes an essay, in which he omits the description of the voyage, its occurrence being understood. Barlow keeps to the voyage, as does Ribaut, but both are travelers to utopia. Solís de Merás, along with lesser Spanish writers, fits his voyage to the tradition of the chronicle history. These and other shifts illustrate the flexibilities of the voyage form, while they testify to its persistence. It is hardly surprising then to discover it dominant in the writing of the early seventeenth century, where such writers as John Smith and Champlain use it, as they must, and eventually carry it beyond its earlier limits. Indeed, these are not in any strict sense "colonial" writers, but voyagers who at the end of a century of narratives, relations, and "true discoveries," have both their own travels to give account of and those of other men. Finally, therefore, each takes the form over into the writing of history, by the imperative of time as well as experience. Neither time nor experience, but individual talent and energy and creative impulse led them to still wider and more fertile variation, so

that, while they round off the antecedent decades, they
bring about the decades to come. In the early 1600s, Champlain and Smith reshape "sixteenth-century" writing to its
culmination. Joined at that time by their unjustly obscurer
compeer, Marc Lescarbot, they achieve, in their different
manners, the beginnings of a different era.

By date, Samuel de Champlain (c. 1567–1635) can claim
to be the first of the early seventeenth-century writers to
provide the transition from the sixteenth-century sea and
land discoveries and relations to the later, very different
narratives of the voyageur and the *coureur de bois.* A soldier
and a sailor in the French civil wars, he first served in the
New World under the Spanish, astonishingly enough, and
wrote his first book about a voyage which he made to their
Caribbean island and mainland domains. This *Brief Discours
des Choses plus remarquables . . . aux Indes* of 1601, along with
his sailor's skills, earned Champlain a part in the new
French attempt to occupy the "terre des Bretons," or New
France, as the French entitled the Atlantic coast, while
Spaniards continued to call it Florida, and the English, Vir-
ginia.

Champlain's first northern journey took him on a six
months voyage to Canada in 1603. The voyage prospered
by the trade in furs along the shores of the St. Lawrence.
For himself, Champlain gained repute by his account of it,
*Des Sauvages: ou Voyages de Samuel Champlain . . . faict en la
France Nouvelle . . .* (1604).

Lacking in innovation, *Des Sauvages* might well have been
written in the era of Jacques Cartier, whose routes in the
Gulf of St. Lawrence and upriver it follows. Though clearer
and more precise than earlier texts, it remains a navigator's
report, based on a sea journal, giving instructions for other
navigators to follow. "On Monday . . . we departed from
Quebec, where the river begins to grow broad sometimes

one league, then a league and a half or two leagues at most.
. . . The north coast is full of rocks and banks of sand: you
must take the south side, about some half league from the
shore."

Moreover, like his predecessors, Champlain is looking for
a passage to the South Sea, and getting very encouraging
news about it. Three different sets of witnesses tell him
about a chain of great lakes, tending to the south, in their
last reaches "brackish" or even "exceeding salt." "Which,"
he comments, "makes me believe that this is the South
Sea"; but he adds moderately, "so much credit" he may not
give without "apparent reasons," the stories he has gathered
providing merely "some small show thereof."

A river leading to Florida, mines, the diamonds of Quebec—Champlain echoes Cartier's interest in all of these,
and so too in observing the savages, but with them Champlain pauses and becomes thoughtful. As other men had
done, he reflects upon their ways of living and housing
themselves, upon their beliefs, their clothing, their feasts,
their sins, and then, still more closely, thinks about that de-
ceptively simple Indian tool, the canoe. The French boats
will not do for river travel, because of the rapids. "But with
the canoes of the savages a man may travel freely and readily into all countries, as well in the small as in the great rivers: so that directing himself by the means of the said savages and their canoes, a man may see all that is to be seen,
good and bad, within the space of a year or two." His timing was off, but he had made a discovery more valuable and
more important than a mine of gold. In history, it was to
open a continent; in literature, it would help to open the
new way to feel and see and celebrate which goes by the
name of romanticism.

Champlain did not at once turn thought into act. The
voyage of 1603, in which he was an officer, looked for a site
for a "colony," its support dependent upon a monopoly of

the fur trade. The voyage of 1604 established it, not in the
St. Lawrence but in the Bay of Fundy on St. Croix (or Do-
chet's) Island in the state of Maine. There, the king's pat-
entee for Acadia, the Sieur de Monts, committed himself to
colonization. Yet De Monts chose his site because it was de-
fensible and accessible, because the Indians would bring
their furs there, because mines had been seen thereabouts,
and because summer was going by—indeed, for almost any
reason except its suitability for living. With little land and
inadequate water it could be no more than a fort, a base for
shipping and exploration, and a trading post.

Champlain devotes a few pages to the wintering-over at
St. Croix in his second account of New France. He spends a
few more on the settlement at Port Royal, across the bay,
for which St. Croix was abandoned. From both places he
undertook to explore the shores of Maine and Massachusetts as far as the southern coast of Cape Cod. Again, of
these ventures he writes sea journals, in the familiar pattern.
His virtues are accuracy, brevity, and speed. His structure
remains that of the voyage. Such relations make up the first
book of *Les Voyages du Sieur de Champlain* . . . *ou Journal tres-
fidele des observations* . . . *de la nouvelle France* . . . (1613).

The later "observations" which conclude the volume are
far more significant for literature, since Champlain devotes
them to the establishment of trading posts, and—still more
important—to the new kind of voyage, in the Indian
"canoa," which he undertook on the rivers of Canada. His
purposes were three: the winning of alliances with the Indians, the development of the fur trade, and the discovery of
the waterway to China.

On the voyage of 1608, he went beyond the usual base at
Tadoussac, familiar to traders legal and illegal and once before the site of a hut "colony" in which sixteen men wintered over miserably. His landing farther upriver at Quebec, there to establish a factory, furthered all his intentions

because the Indians had an encampment nearby. By help-
ing and protecting them, he gained their friendship.
Through a winter of bitter cold and snow, with the usual
fearful mortality among his company, he observed the savages, earned their confidence, and got their promise to
guide him. In early summer, he was ready. At Quebec, he
writes, "I had a shallop fitted out with all that was necessary for making explorations in the country of the Iroquois,
where I was to go with our allies, the Montagnais." At
Chambly Rapids, on the Richelieu River, he had to abandon the shallop. "Accordingly," he continues, "I embarked
with the savages in their canoes." In the act, he was following out his old idea, and bringing to birth a new breed of
men. As the historian Brebner puts it, Champlain "invented, as it were, the *coureurs de bois* and the *voyageurs*." He
did so, not only by becoming the first of them, but also by
sending out his young men along the rivers with the Indians, to live in their villages, and to entice them to French
trading posts.

Thenceforth, in his narratives, the factory-fort at Quebec,
except as a necessary supply camp, recedes from attention.
The river journeys and the Indian experiences take over. In
these, Champlain achieves new stature as a writer. Beyond
speed, accuracy, and brevity, he acquires the enrichment of
a fresh understanding. He not only observes but takes part
in the Indian play and pageantry of war. His friends, the
Montagnais, having made every effort to surprise their enemies, the Iroquois, blunder into an encounter and arrange
the terms of battle. "We were out upon the water, within
arrow range of their barricades. When they were armed and
in array, they dispatched two canoes by themselves to the
enemy to inquire if they wished to fight, to which the latter
replied that they wanted nothing else: but they said that, at
present, there was not much light, and that it would be necessary to wait for daylight, so as to be able to recognize each

other; and that, as soon as the sun rose, they would offer us battle. This was agreed to by our side. Meanwhile the entire night was spent in dancing and singing, on both sides, with endless insults and other talk; as, how little courage we had, how feeble a resistance we should make against their arms, and that, when day came, we should realize it to our ruin. Ours also were not slow in retorting, telling them they would see such execution of arms as never before. . . ." He shows a certain grim humor in the boasting, since he and the Frenchmen with him were about to use their arque-buses, and thereby to change Indian warfare from a cere-monial sport, bloody but sacrificial, to the far bloodier fights of extermination made possible by guns.

Champlain, no idealist of the primitive, reports the tor-turing and dismemberment of captives, which, however frightful to him, he cannot control and must eventually con-done. When the victorious Montagnais give him, "as if it were something very precious," the head of one of their pris-oners along with "a pair of arms taken from their enemies, to keep and show to the king," he can only comment, "This, for the sake of gratifying them, I promised to do." Beyond such forced acceptance of barbarism, he did not go. When, in France, he was summoned to the royal presence, he took along a "very pretty" girdle of porcupine quills, two small, bright scarlet birds, and the head of a fish.

For the following year, 1610, Champlain has another war foray to present; for 1611, he describes his meetings with the Indians, their councils, and their reasonings in negotiating with him. Again, the "old trading-station" at Tadoussac, and the post at Quebec offer little to his pen, except for his attempts at the latter to plant gardens, invariably neglected by the servants there.

Time at last brought him his opportunity. In 1613 he was able to embark on his long-planned journey by canoe to the "North Sea," where Hudson had already met his death and where a young Frenchman who had wintered with the Algonquin Indians claimed to have gone. With four Frenchmen and a single Indian, Champlain made his way up the Ottawa River, by day struggling to drag his canoes through the rapids or by land at the carrying places, at night putting up such barricades and shelters as the Indians had taught him to make. Forced to lighten the loads by leaving his supplies behind, he and his companions fished and hunted to keep from starving. Of one portage, he writes, "We had much difficulty in going this distance overland. I, for my part, was loaded only with three arquebuses, as many oars, my cloak, and some small articles. I cheered on our men, who were somewhat more heavily loaded, but more troubled by the mosquitoes than by their loads. Thus after passing four small ponds and having gone a distance of two and a half leagues [five miles], we were so wearied that it was impossible to go farther, not having eaten for twenty-four hours anything but a little broiled fish without seasoning, for we had left provisions behind, as I mentioned before. Accordingly we rested on the border of a pond, which was very pleasant, and made a fire to drive away the mosquitoes, which annoyed us greatly, whose persistence is so marvellous that one cannot describe it. Here we cast out lines to catch some fish."

The passage is a good example of his usual narrative technique. He consistently underwrites, moving fast. Translation makes his verbal style stiff and succinct to a fault; in the original, he is brisk but achieves an agreeably fluent rhythm. His statement is his abiding concern; he is indifferent to elaboration. When, after this difficult, perilous, and exhausting journey, he finds that his young Frenchman has lied to him, and has never seen or even gone near the "North Sea," his comment reads ". . . without any hope of seeing the sea in this direction, except in imagination, I felt a regret that I should not have employed my time better, and that I should have had to endure the difficulties and hardships, which however I was obliged patiently to submit to. If I had gone in another direction, according to the report of the savages, I should have made a beginning in a thing which must be postponed to another time."

Champlain never did make the river journey to the "North Sea," soon to be named Hudson's Bay, but he had made more of a beginning than he gave himself credit for. His later *Voyages and Discoveries in New France from . . . 1615 to . . . 1618* (1619) takes him as far west as Lake Huron. From there he doubled back south of Lake Ontario with a war party and, disappointed in his wish to return to Quebec, wintered among the savages. The best-known passage from Champlain's writings occurs here, in an attack upon the Iroquois town, during which Champlain introduced into Indian warfare the European military machinery of the cavelier and the mantelet. The first, a high, movable platform to be pushed up to a palisade, allowed the French arquebusiers to fire down upon the town's defenders; the second, a large shield of boards, protected an assaulting force. He reports the enthusiasm of the savages for these, and then their inability or unwillingness to submit themselves to any kind of rational order or discipline. "In vain did I shout in their ears and remonstrate to my utmost with them as to the danger to which they exposed themselves by their bad behavior, but on account of the great noise they made they heard nothing." Even in retrospect, Champlain finds no humor in this conflict, as much between cultures as hostile Indian tribes.

Apart from warfare, Champlain the writer shows his best gifts in describing the Indian towns, the banquets, the councils, the ceremonies of the Pilotois or witch doctors, and the masquerades and dances. His devout Christian beliefs keep him from understanding the social and religious significance of these, but not from the careful, exact development of the scenes which appear at intervals throughout his narratives. In the upshot, he judges the savages to be intelligent, capable of training, and on the whole, though unpredictable, faithful to their proven friends. Their sins of thievery, vengefulness, and cruelty he ascribes to their ignorance of Christian truth. The dividing line cuts the heathen off from full humanity. Yet he is convinced that they can be brought to cross it. At his insistence, Franciscan missionaries—Recollects—came to the St. Lawrence to offer the teaching without which this people must suffer damnation. Yet for all their spiritual darkness, and for all the poverty and danger of their lives, he judges them to be happy. "Their life is a miserable one in comparison with our own; but they are happy among themselves. . . ." With a kind of puzzlement, he repeats himself, "Yet with all their drawbacks they seem to me to live happily among themselves. . . ." In the second instance, he is drawing a contrast in contentment between the more settled Indians and the completely nomadic, but the essential contrast is always, here as elsewhere, between the civilized and the primitive man.

Champlain's effectiveness does not show itself in separable passages, or even—fully—in his scenes. It is cumulative. He does not polish, nor does he decorate. He never develops beyond short comment the philosophic theme of natural happiness. At his worst he is dull and limited; at his best, he is vigorous, firm, economical, incisive. Consistently, he is a writer, as he was an individual, of integrity.

His inland voyages over in 1616, Champlain became administrator of the fur trade and lieutenant over the "colony" of Quebec, which owned one family of settlers in 1617 and two by 1627. Others either refused to enlist, or were not recruited by the various trading companies, or, like two butchers and their wives who were sent home after a year, "did nothing but enjoy themselves hunting, fishing, sleep-

ing, and getting drunk with those who gave them the where-
withall."

The record of these years appears in Champlain's final
volume, his "history," whose eighty-word title has by economic necessity to be reduced to *Les Voyages de la Nouvelle
France Occidentale* (1632). The text is essentially a statement
of the French right to Canada and the St. Lawrence, by virtue of early exploration. To this purpose, it provides a brief
résumé of French ventures, beginning in 1504. The greater
part of the book goes over Champlain's own achievements,
repeating with cuts and changes the narratives he had already published. In a "Second Part," he carries through the
history of Quebec as a fort and a colony, to its surrender to
the English in 1629, under the piratical attack of the brothers Kirke.

The history, though his most ambitious work, does little
credit to Champlain as a writer. An anonymous editor is
probably guilty of shortening and altering Champlain's already published texts, and of doing both faultily. Modern
editors believe him to have been a Jesuit or a partisan of the
Jesuits, because the rival order of Recollects—the first and
some of the boldest missionaries to Canada—goes almost
unnoticed while the Jesuit achievement claims all praise.

The notable fact remains that Champlain assembles his
history out of voyage narratives, using his materials for argument—largely an argument for French imperialism. He
is using the past to serve the purposes of the future, to establish a right by virtue of such men as Cartier and Ribaut to
the vast and rich country of his own adventures. By the final
date of publication, the treaty returning Canada to France
had been signed, and the way to colonization opened again.
The final paragraph of the history, far from accidentally,
celebrates the possibilities for the French, predicting
"grands progrez à l'advenir." The movement is toward time
to come.

11 / *The Evangelist of Fish*

Hundreds of miles to the south of Canada, the Spanish having failed to occupy Chesapeake Bay or proselytize its natives, the English had come in, some twenty-five years before Champlain's history denied them their right to be there. With Raleigh's planters gone forever from Roanoke, and his "City of Raleigh" in Virginia never more than a name, the freshly organized "Virginia Company of London" had taken over his project. Its Jamestown venture—one misguided academic proposed to call the settlement "Jacobopolis"—had not only survived adversity, but from 1607 on had accumulated a history of its own, recorded in a sizable body of writing.

Through the early decades of the seventeenth century, a number of persons undertook narratives of the settlement, or argued in its support, or entered into the many controversies over its government, attacking or defending the proposals of the company which controlled it, blaming or praising its officers and servants. Foremost among them stands Captain John Smith (1579/80–1631), variously celebrated as hero or mutineer, leader or traitor, redeemer of a cause nearly lost or loser of the cause, man of knowledge and experience, boaster, liar, only truth-teller—the list of plaudits and pejoratives could be lengthened, but to no great use. Smith himself took part in controversy, and has become a controversy. This makes for liveliness, and he was lively, but also makes for confusion. It is sensible, therefore, to present at once the generally accepted facts of his life and writing.

An orphan, Smith came of farming stock, and inherited a small patrimony. When he was about sixteen, he took off from England to follow a soldier-sailor-adventurer's career of fortune in Europe, at the climax of which he served against the Turks. On his return to England in 1604, or perhaps 1606, he enlisted for Virginia. Having by his then age of twenty-six gained experience and repute, he was appointed a member of the governing council there, but on a charge of mutiny during the voyage across the Atlantic, found himself excluded from it by his fellow-councilors. Allowed his office after a month or so, he turned explorer, traded with the Indians for food to keep the settlers from starving, and—not least of achievements—counted as one of thirty-eight survivors out of the hundred and forty-four who sailed from England. Hunger, disease, Indian fights, and faction and punishment among the planters accounted for the rest. From September 1608 until July 1609, Smith served as President of the settlement, but was then officially displaced, and, desperately wounded as well, went home. He never got back to Jamestown, but voyaged to New England, where he explored and mapped the coast. In spite of his efforts to return to the New World, he spent most of the last ten or fifteen years of his life in England, writing the pamphlets and books which have made for no fewer disagreements than the "facts" of his biography.

Smith's first account of Virginia (to what extent his or another's?) he entitled *A True Relation* . . . (1608); his second, of which the first half is his while the last is ascribed to

a number of other writers, *A Map of Virginia* . . . (1612). For
some years thereafter, Smith abandoned Virginia as a subject, in favor of New England. His *Description of New England*
(1616), *New England's Trials* (1620, 1622), and *Advertisements
For the unexperienced Planters of New-England or anywhere* (1631)
record his mapping of the northern coast, his hopes for settlement there, and his advice to those who proposed to colonize it. His *Generall Historie of Virginia, New-England, and the
Summer Isles* (1624) brings his earlier works together, with
embellishments, and adds an account of the Bermudas. *The
True Travels, Adventures, and Observations of Captaine John Smith*
(1630) provides a hero for the prose epic of the *General Historie*. Indeed, in time of composition the two must have been
contemporary, since the largest part of the *True Travels* was
first printed by Purchas in 1625. If the epical term be
doubted (a modern authority makes the epic-hero point in
connection with the second part of the *Map of Virginia*),
an earlier critical understatement may be substituted—
". . . the historical writings of Captain John Smith were
conceived in an expansive spirit." Smith's bitterest opponent can hardly deny that modest truth.

For purposes of clarity in the given list of Smith's writings, the chronology has been altered. The acute reader will
already have noticed this, and the informed reader will also
have noticed that the few titles of Smith's which do not concern America have been omitted.

Quite understandably, Smith's course in American authorship offers a parallel to Champlain's. Like *Des Sauvages*,
Smith's first venture, *A True Relation of such occurrences and accidents of noate as hath hapned in Virginia* . . . (1608), is a conventional, journalistic account of the explorations, adventures, conflicts, and sufferings of Jamestown's first year. If
Des Sauvages might have been written by Cartier, *A True Relation* might have been composed by a less distracted Ralph
Lane. Smith's subjects are much like Lane's—the building

of the fort, the search for the passage to the South Sea, relations with the Indians good and bad, quarrels and threats of
mutiny among the settlers, sickness and starvation, and the
uncontrollable wanderings through the woods after mines of
jewels and gold. Yet now and again, unlike either Champlain or Lane, Smith suggests by implication the impassioned themes of his later texts, the relief and redemption of
the poor in the new world by the cultivation of the wilderness, and the heroic ennoblement of industrious men in
making a savage, sterile landscape fruitful for their posterity.

What he sees is antithesis to any such utopianism; reality
shows "most of our chiefest men either sick or discontented,
the rest being in such despair, as they would rather starve
and rot with idleness, than be persuaded to do anything for
their own relief without constraint." The land itself is, however, "exceeding good ground," bearing an abundance of
fish and fowl. In sum, he calls it a "thorough desert"—that
is to say, entirely uncultivated—"yet exceeding fertile." For
the spring of 1608, he reports that the English who have
planned but been thwarted in an expedition to discover the
South Sea have turned "husbandmen, to fell trees and set
corn," activities which even Smith suggests are a come-
down.

Smith's second publication, *A Map of Virginia. With a description of the Countrey* . . . by Captaine Smith . . . "whereunto is annexed the proceedings of those Colonies . . .
taken faithfully as they were written out of the writings of
. . . diligent observers . . ." (1612), carries the initials of
an editor, "W. S.," also. The wordy title, abbreviated
above, introduces many questions of authorship. Whoever
may have composed the annexed "proceedings," whether
the signers of the various segments, or Smith himself, or another, the first part of the text—*A Map of Virginia* proper—is
without question Smith's own. If, as has been suggested, it is

an expansion of a draft which Smith wrote in Virginia in 1608, then Smith must have carried out his elaboration after his return to England in October 1609.

In the *Map*, Smith writes another sound, energetic, and conventional relation, describing in considerable detail and color the "commodities" of the country, its native people, and their activities and ceremonials. Above all, he urges the possibilities. Virginia offers "great plenty by the industry of men." This prediction he begins to build up into a theme, while he spends little attention upon the search for the Northwest Passage and for mines. In his conclusion he speaks out against the "bad natures" of those planters who slander the country because of their ignorance of and failures in it, who "because they found not English cities, nor such fair houses, nor at their own wishes any of their accustomed dainties, with feather beds and down pillows, taverns and alehouses in every breathing place, neither such plenty of gold and silver and dissolute liberty as they expected, had little or no care of anything, but to pamper their bellies, to fly away with our pinnaces, or procure their means to return for England. For the country was to them a misery, a ruin, a death, a hell."

Smith offers nothing but scorn to such, and warns those who listen to the boasters and falsifiers and pretenders. The lying tales of these "ingenious verbalists" have raised up the "disasters that spring in Virginia," where "the labor of thirty of the best only, preserved in Christianity, by their industry, the idle livers of near two hundred of the rest. . . ."

Surely, if Champlain invented the voyageur, Smith invented the true colonist and the true colony. For his time in Virginia, and for perhaps another ten years, Jamestown was an exploitative, not a colonial, settlement. The historian defines it as trading post first, and then plantation, and somewhere between 1616 and 1619 at last a colony. Smith, unpossessed of such terms and discriminations, nevertheless by experience and the contemplation of experience gradually shows an understanding of the necessary process.

The testimonies of his adherents, in the second part of *A Map of Virginia* (their pens were perhaps Smith's own), shift Smith's early willingness to look for the South Sea into an effort "to search the country for trade" and for corn to feed the starving; early delvings after ores become a questioning of "golden inventions" and a rejection of the "gilded refiners" and their "dirty skill." For a ship's lading, cedar wood takes over from the "gilded dirt," for the gathering of which "all necessary business" must be neglected, and men die because "There was no talk, no hope, nor work, but dig gold, wash gold, refine gold, load gold."

In protest, writing at home with passionate indignation, Smith makes himself the evangelist of fish. His subject becomes New England. In a voyage of 1614, he succeeded in exploring that coast, from which he brought back his preachment, along with the knowledge upon which he built his best formulated and most closely developed book, *A Description of New England* (1616). Smith does not formulate his text so well, however, that he clearly defines his subject, which is actually not single but double. He does indeed describe New England and its commodities, but to this first concern he adds another, in his insistence upon the character of its colonists.

For New England itself, he gives assurance of the "goodness" of sea and land, and of its size and "greatness," to which he responds with wonder and admiration. From such high terms, he returns again and again to the "base" commodity, fish. Here is the true source of wealth, he declares. Fish caught and marketed may buy gold, silver, and pearls. Fish may subserve armies and navies, build fortresses, towns, and cities, and draw in all the commerce of the world. Fish proffer an affluence taken without harm to the weak and innocent, and in the taking a light labor to enrich the poor, to feed the hungry, and to give sport to gentlemen. Such are the true mines of the sea, as the true mines of the earth are the crops of its soil.

These are the promises of New England, in all practicality. To such promises, gained by his own experience, he adds—out of knowledge, again—an even more valuable statement of ignorance. Of the two thousand miles of the Atlantic coast, he points out that "more than half is yet unknown to any purpose: no, not so much as the borders of the sea are yet certainly discovered." For the mainland, he confesses to a deeper obscurity—"only here and there we touched or have seen a little the edges of those large dominions, which do stretch . . . God doth know how many thousand miles."

With equally inspired discernment, Smith sketches in his ideal colonist, rejecting "silvered idle golden Pharisees" and celebrating "industrious iron-steeled publicans." He speaks for the man who works and makes provision for his offspring. Let the heirs of such men follow their example, and "imitate their virtues to be worthily their successors."

"Who can desire more content, that hath small means; or but only his merit to advance his fortune, than to tread, and plant that ground he hath purchased by the hazard of his life? If he have but the taste of virtue and magnanimity, what to such a mind can be more pleasant, than planting and building a foundation for his posterity, got from the rude earth, by God's blessing and his own industry, without prejudice to any? If he have any grain of faith or zeal in religion, what can he do less hurtful to any: or more agreeable to God, than to seek to convert those poor savages to know Christ, and humanity, whose labors with discretion will triple requite thy charge and pains? What so truly suits with honor and honesty, as the discovering things unknown? erecting towns, peopling countries, informing the ignorant, reforming things unjust, teaching virtue; and gain to our native mother-country a kingdom to attend her: find employment for those that are idle, because they know not what to do: so far from wronging any, as to cause posterity to remember thee; and remembering thee, ever honor that remembrance with praise?"

Here is Smith's colonist—the man who plants and builds, and by his own effort arrives at virtuous greatness. The colonist becomes what he has not been. He gains his entitlement to remembrance, and to the praise of his children, and beyond them to the praise of that wider posterity of the redeemed poor. He earns the thanks of his birth country in raising her up another kingdom. He teaches; he informs; he reforms. In changing his own condition, he acts to bring about the betterment of all men. He works under a noble ambition. He dies a greater man than ever he was born, his monuments the newly peopled countries which had been "thorough desert," and the towns erected "by the industry of men."

Smith drew his splendid concept out of harsh and ugly reality. He had given his story of disease, starvation, and killing. He knew the hazards of the woods and waters, of storm, sucking marsh, ice, lightning, and the secret wraths of enemies. He knew that no such vision as he had sketched could come about at any one man's hand, but only through some group as yet unshaped. At the end of his life, he told the planters of the Massachusetts Bay Colony how they should and should not demean themselves, to build their kingdom from their small beginnings.

Smith's colony is formulated in his last book, *Advertisements For the unexperienced Planters of New-England, or anywhere* (1631), whose subtitle gives his method of thinking. It reads, "The Path-way to experience to erect a Plantation." If, to the twentieth-century reader, his mention of experience seems mild and reasonable, in the literary context of his own and earlier times it is subversive. Throughout the sixteenth and well along into the seventeenth century, the approach to colonization is *a priori*. Only rarely, in forced response to crisis, or in afterthought, does the writer-planner look for objective evidence from which to draw his ideas. Smith says first to his "unexperienced planters": do not fall into the traps your predecessors have been caught in. The bane of Virginia has been "the strange misprisions of wise men." Most of these "misprisions," though Smith does not directly say so, go back to the original certainty that America was Asia, with all the immediate wealths and splendors of the Orient—the gold, the silks, the spices, and the jewels. Smith's doctrine of experience eventually overthrew that illusion, to substitute for it such illusions as reality might in time justify. His warning of the moment is clear. The "wise men" of Virginia, "so doating of mines of gold, and the South Sea; that all the world could not have devised better courses to bring us to ruin" have shown how *not* to erect a plantation.

After that rejection, Smith turns to his affirmative "advertisements." The foundation of the colony is land, to be generously and freely distributed, its produce lightly and little taxed, so that an industrious man may profit from his work in the forests and meadows, and gain by the increase of his cattle and the harvesting of fish. Let the government over him be simple, commonly supported for the common good, with few officers and few fees, and clear, just laws, "for as the laws corrupt, the state consumes." In religion, Smith was an establishment man. Avoid schism, he advised his planters of New England, who did not listen to him. In trade, he was heterodox—"use all comers with that respect, courtesy, and liberty [that] is fitting"—here his New Englanders did listen, assuming certain liberties Smith might not have yielded them, but, as he promised, they gained from their freedoms.

Smith's scheme for a colony is modest, or, as he puts it,

"small in conceit" compared to fantasies of golden cities—Cibola, Manoa, El Dorado. Yet he sees it also as a "great work," a kingdom to be built, not merely invaded, a wealth to be created, not seized. "It is much better to help to plant a country than unplant it and then replant it." Once again he lays his stress upon the hazard—the effort or hardship or danger—which promises honest reward. "Truly there is no pleasure comparable to a generous spirit; as good employment in noble actions . . . it is a happy thing to be born to strength, wealth and honor; but that which is got by prowess and magnanimity is the truest lustre: and those can the best distinguish content that have escaped most honorable dangers; as if, out of every extremity, he found himself now born to a new life, to learn how to amend and maintain his age."

Smith's eloquences are many, occurring often enough in his narratives and his arguments to earn him both praise and remembrance. Yet he can be a stiff, dull, confused stylist also. Perhaps his least commendable, though his largest, work is his *Generall Historie of Virginia, New-England, and the Summer Isles* (1624). Like Champlain, Smith makes the collection and joining of earlier voyage narratives serve his historical purposes. He is satisfied to bring together the accounts of Roanoke, his own relations of Virginia and New England, and those of others later there than he, and to reprint some of the voyages to the Bermudas. Throughout the text he acknowledges his originals with reasonable thoroughness, except for his own writings which he unmercifully plagiarizes and often simply repeats. The result is a clutter beyond his control, although (or because) his aim here is definitely ambitious. He wishes to be literary, embellishing his text with tags of verse (generously borrowed) and carrying out (or permitting) the expansion of passages from his earlier books. The *Generall Historie* thereby brings to an issue the tangled subject of Smith's authorship of certain passages reprinted from or added to the early books, but ascribed by him there and in the *Generall Historie* to other colonist writers. The most famous of these, though by no means the only elaboration of earlier materials, is the story of Pocahontas' rescue of the captive, about-to-be-executed Smith, a story which has become a part of American tradition, as firm a fact (or fancy) as Plymouth Rock.

The case against the authenticity of the tale rests upon the undeniable truth that neither Smith nor his collaborators mention it in their immediately contemporary writings. As "event" it occurred in 1608. Smith's earliest reference to it he may have made in 1616, though he did not print that reference until 1624, as part of the *Generall Historie*. There the full episode also appears, being ascribed not to Smith but to three of the "diligent observers" of the second part of the *Map*. At least two of these had died before the occurrence, and by the time of the printing Pocahontas herself had been dead for eight years. As history, the account which Smith sponsored is indeed suspect.

There are two flaws in this logical conclusion. The first is the assumption that the story would inevitably have been printed at once. Actually, until the small Indian princess became a figure of the English court and of American legend, it was not to Smith's credit, nor did it help the reputation of the Jamestown settlement, that the Indians had Smith at their mercy. The second, more genial truth lies in the recognition that the modern concept of accuracy in history did not exist for such as Smith. As Hakluyt agreeably remarks, no sensible reader needs to believe everything he finds on paper; he can question what he wishes, and still be entertained.

Late nineteenth- and early twentieth-century critics tend to discard the tale; more recent commentators admit it, as possible or even probable. In either case, it stands on its merits, by the strongest power of evidence—its general acceptance. No critical condemnation could remove it from American annals. Here, without cavil, when Smith is the captive of the Indian king Powhatan, his daughter the princess Pocahontas will always save Smith's life at the risk of her own. The scene of the *Generall Historie* is brief; its few lines read, "two great stones were brought before Powhatan: then as many as could laid hands on him, dragged him to them, and thereon laid his head, and being ready with their clubs, to beat out his brains, Pocahontas the King's dearest daughter, when no entreaty could prevail, got his head in her arms, and laid her own upon his to save him from death."

Fact or fiction, whether written by Smith or by its purported authors, dead-long-since "Thomas Studley" and the rest, the anecdote is for dramatic purposes true. The validities of history cannot destroy its validity as literature. So too, the beautiful little scene in which Smith presents the dying girl for the last time, in England in 1616.

"Being about this time preparing to sail for New-England, I could not stay to do her that service I desired, and she well deserved; but hearing she was at Branford with divers of my friends, I went to see her. After a modest salutation, without any word, she turned about, obscured her face, as not seeming well contented; and in that humor her husband, with divers others, we all left her two or three hours, repenting myself to have writ she could speak English. But not long after she began to talk, and remembered me well what courtesies she had done: saying

> You did promise Powhatan what was yours should be his, and he the like to you; you called him father being in his land a stranger, and by the same reason so must I do you:

which though I would have excused, I durst not allow of that title, because she was a king's daughter; with a well set countenance she said,

Were you not afraid to come into my father's country, and
caused fear in him and all his people (but me), and fear you
here I should call you father; I tell you then I will, and you
shall call me child, and so I will be for ever and ever your countryman."

Fiction or history? The speeches are certainly contrived,
and the effect is deliberately planned. The likelihood that
the meeting occurred is high. This is fictive history, then,
and one more evidence that the voyage readily goes over
into imaginative writing; as readily as it goes over into annals.

In this context, Smith's much debated *True Travels* (1630)
may have a good deal to contribute to an understanding of
his methods. The first problem in dealing with that so-
called autobiography is one of confusion. To repeat, Smith
published the *True Travels* independently, with new introductory and concluding matter, the year before he died.
Five years earlier, in 1625, Purchas had printed a few pages
of introduction and conclusion, to frame the main narrative
of Smith's exploits in the Transylvanian wars against the
Turks. This narrative, according to Purchas and to Smith,
was not written by Smith but by "Francisco Ferneza a
learned Italian" as part of "a book entitled, The Warres of
Transilvania, Wallachi, and Moldavia." Smith says that
Purchas himself translated the text from the Italian. Yet,
unfortunately for authentication, no such text is known, and
no such historian as Farnese, or Ferneza, learned or un-
learned, has ever been identified.

The tale is no less enjoyable for that; nor has it failed to
gain defenders. Commentators of the 1960s and 1970s in-
cline to support Smith's claims to have gone to the wars
against the infidel, to have distinguished himself there only
to be captured and enslaved—all this capped by his escape
into Russia, travels in Europe, and at last the voyages to the

New World. The claims, insofar as they concern "Transyl-
vania, Wallachi, and Moldavia," are, of course, not Smith's
but Farnese's, if the text is to be believed.

The debate is irrelevant here. The more mendacious the
historian John Smith, the more inventive John Smith the
creative writer. Since much of the literary criticism of
Smith's work is moralistic—some of it reads as though
Smith were being considered for the gold star in Sunday
School—it blurs or ignores his methods. Of these, his outstanding device is the use of other writers to build his own
personality, to support his actions and arguments, and to
color his narratives with excitement and emotion. So "Farnese" presents his Captain Smith as partaker in "many a
bloody sally, strange stratagems and valiant exploits." So
one "diligent observer" of the second part of the *Map of Virginia* writes of Smith, "what shall I say? but thus we lost him
that, in all his proceedings, made justice his first guide, and
experience his second; ever hating baseness, sloth, pride,
and indignity more than any dangers; that never allowed
more for himself than his soldiers with him; that upon no
danger, would send them where he would not lead them
himself; that would never see us want what he either had,
or could by any means get us; that would rather want than
borrow, or starve than not pay; that loved actions more
than words, and hated falsehood and cozenage worse than
death; whose adventures were our lives, and whose loss our
deaths."

If another hand wrote the passage, Smith is merely quoting the praises of his partisan. If Smith himself wrote it, he
becomes, before Defoe and before Swift, a wearer of the
literary mask, a maker of the "persona." If Smith composed
the Farnese "history," did both he and Purchas accept the
trick as a literary flourish? If the Pocahontas story is a slow
growth of the imagination, then Smith is entitled to his act
of creation. If he merely wakens late to its possibilities, then

his credit is less. Yet even in that case, it is high, and the school of history as fact should yield to the genialities of a Hakluyt.

In the history of American letters, the evidence of Smith's writing supports the dominance of the voyage as form, while it indicates new directions. It provides, in essay and argument, the long-awaited shift to themes and shapes appropriate to the colony. Whatever the decisions about authenticities, it takes the pattern of the journey further along towards dramatic presentation, in scene and speech as well as in confrontation and crisis. It offers little that is new in reshaping a series of voyages into historical exposition, except in emphasis. The exception is important. Even more notably than Champlain, Smith turns the record of the past to the purposes of the future. Time present cannot be said to exist for him. Time past ushers in time future. Events, places, and men take part in a process of becoming. Smith's colonist must catch more fish, build higher, break more sod, carry on a wider trade, and improve his estate. The heir is posterity.

12 / The American Is a New Man

Neither Smith nor Champlain was a mystic. It was not given them to see the world in a grain of sand, or the universe in a snowflake. They were visionaries of practical bent. Champlain saw an empire in the forest, and Smith good success in the crops of field and ocean. To their new worlds, the impalpable contributed little, nor did they look for help to bookmen and philosophers.

The third historian of northern America, their contemporary, though no more a mystic than they, differed from them in reading much from books, and in interpreting his voyages by the guidance of the classics and of social criticism in his native France. Marc Lescarbot (c. 1565–?), lawyer and humanist, could quote Aristotle, Pliny, Ovid, Herodotus, Tacitus, and the rest, as easily as he summoned in the Bible. He knew the work of French historians. His studies in the ancients and moderns had made him something of a student of human races. Learning and his own experience—he was a victim of legal injustice, according to his belief—had made him both a scholar and a rebel against society. He took ship for America "to flee a corrupt world." There he spent the year between July 1606 and July 1607

as a member of Mont's settlement at Port Royal, along with
Champlain. When the settlement had to be abandoned, he
made his "Adieu à la Nouvelle France" in genial rhyme,
and a year later turned to equally genial prose. Much of his
prose history is library work. To the texts of his study, he
added his own account of life in the wilderness, and of the
American savages.

The first issue of his *Histoire de la Nouvelle France* (1609) begins as a compilation of earlier French voyages, turns to his
own twelve months experience, and ends with a study of the
Indians, for the illumination of whose origins and customs
Lescarbot refers to the Bible sometimes, but more often to
the writers of Greece and Rome. A second edition of 1611
brings the narrative of New France up to date, and consid-
erably expands his discourse. His final version of 1617 further extends and enlarges it, and defines his methods and
his purposes. His book of poems, *Les Muses de la Nouvelle
France,* accompanies all three issues of the history, with new
verses added as the poet-historian saw fit.

Like Smith and Champlain, Lescarbot puts his first emphasis upon the voyage, summarizing or quoting the relations of Verrazzano for the Atlantic seaboard, of Ribaut,
Laudonnière, and Gourgues for Florida, of Léry and even—
by reference—the inventive André Thevet for Brazil, and,
most importantly, those of Cartier and Champlain for Canada. With Canada, he enters the area of his own knowledge
and experience, and begins to break the pattern of the
"recueil general" of the "traitez" and "memoires" of his
reading. Champlain's claim to have been the first discoverer
of the St. Lawrence had offended him, and by matching
passages from Cartier with their equivalents in Champlain's
discoveries, he proves Cartier's right. He and Champlain,
fellow officers in the Port Royal establishment, were obviously not congenial, though Lescarbot is fair in giving
Champlain all due credit for his true discoveries.

Lescarbot's innovation in form lies in the fact that he ultimately writes history as an essay rather than as a compilation. In Europe he had predecessors in the technique,
though he may not have known their work. The affable
Peter Martyr (1455–1526), friend of Columbus and Sebastian Cabot and many another explorer, had undertaken his
"Ocean Decades," more formally entitled *De Orbe Novo*, a
century before the young Frenchman undertook the history
of New France. Though Peter Martyr wrote in Latin, and
adopted or, better, adapted the Ciceronian letter to a revelation of American discoveries, the necessarily unplanned
sequence of disclosure forbade him any strict or logical or-
ganization. Like Lescarbot, he enjoys his freedoms, and indeed sets a looser pattern, with cheerful, lively inconse-
quence, presenting as he heard it the news that came to
him, sure of its excitement and of the amazed interest of the
intellectual world. If Lescarbot did not read the "Decades,"
he must have shared something of their author's enthusiasm
and energy. Both men were historians endowed with personality as well as erudition.

During the sixteenth century, Spanish writers long before
Lescarbot had taken the history of America beyond the simple collection of voyages into the pattern of connected exposition, towards an argument or propaganda or perhaps only
a narrative of action. Herrera, Oviedo, Gómara, Las Casas,
and—for the Portuguese—Antonio Galvano either had
firsthand experience of some part of the events they wrote
about, or like Peter Martyr got their information and misin-
formation at close secondhand. They concern themselves
not only with the sequence of events by which Europeans
came to the knowledge and the conquest of America, but
also with the natural wealth of the new continents and with
its peoples and its geography.

Description early sharpened into controversy. Mere naming could lead to huge consequences. What the Spanish

"rightfully" owned as Florida, the French might not claim. But the "Terre des Bretons" was undeniably New France. At the extremes of north and south, such namings might not lead to trouble, but where they met and overlapped, whatever the latitude, a Menéndez was bound to slaughter his French heretics and a Gourgues to avenge them. Historians, like geographers, put politics on paper.

Lescarbot knew this, whether or not he knew his Iberian forerunners. He assumes the French right with no hesitation at all. In another kind of controversy, he shows his horror at the Spanish extermination of the island natives, against which their own Bartolomé de Las Casas had long ago written his impassioned outcry. For continental writers about America, history was as much opinion as narrative or record. The wars of religion, Catholic against Protestant, were early and late fought out in chronicle. The humane Lescarbot, as devout in his convictions as the fanatical Barrientos, is nearly alone in his toleration of difference.

He is quite alone in his use of American history for large social criticism. True offspring of Montaigne, though not a doubter who loved the doubt, he finds European society wholly vicious and contemptible. The European is vain, ostentatious, uncharitable, quarrelsome, and cruel. Covetous of property, he erects governments and courts to protect his substance, only to find it wasted. Ridiculous in ostentation, he will cover himself and his women with useless ornaments and extravagant fashions, for no purpose but display. In his appetites unrestrained, unchristian in his sins, his foolish satisfactions deny him happiness.

Yet even in castigation, Lescarbot is good-tempered, exercising as much compassion as anger. "Those men are indeed to be pitied," he writes, "who . . . pass their lives in cities, bowing and scraping to each other, seeking excuses to go to law, worrying over this and that, endeavouring to get the better of their neighbors, racking their brains until the day of their death how to pay the rent, how to dress in silk, and how to buy rich furniture; in short, how to cut a figure and feast on a little vanity. . . . 'Poor fools,' says Hesiod, 'who little realize that half of these things possessed in peace and quietness is worth all of them together accompanied by so much vexation of spirit.' "

Lescarbot is not, however, wholly a Thoreau. He does not admit his austerities to the dinner table. On the contrary, he is a social rebel who emotionally enjoys a lavish meal. What Paris cookshop, he demands to know, will provide for no price but the taking the abundant delicacies of the American wilderness? In poetry and prose, he celebrates the banquet of plenty—succulent venison, bear, and beaver; roast duck, goose, pigeon, and bustard; oysters, lobsters, crab, salmon, shad, sturgeon, and cod. His forest trees are trellises for wine grapes, while in every patch of clear ground he envisions green salads and ripening grains.

Probably, feasting aside, Lescarbot's revolt against Europe has its firmest basis in the classics rather than in the writings of his contemporaries. His golden mean is Hesiod's and Aristotle's rather than Montaigne's; his satiric bent is shaped by Horace rather than Rabelais. Beyond all influences upon him, his complexities of thinking come from his experience, rather than from an innate subtlety. He is not a man of balances and hesitations but of forthright questions. If his answers, forthright also, oversimplify, oversimplification like his was to become important indeed in France and America both. His formulation, vague and loose though it is, of a new social order to come out of America is the first to be elaborated, however many scattered hints of social reflection preceded it.

The base of his triangular scheme is land. Upon that foundation, he builds and shapes a new community of two human kinds. The native Indian, refined and chastened by Christianity, and the Frenchman, once poor and discarded

at home but reborn in America, together will cultivate the
soil. In France, Lescarbot sees troubled men in every station
in life, even the highest. He tells them that the earth of the
new world will never betray them if they embrace her in
good understanding—"la terre ne nous trompe jamais si
nous la voulons caresser à bon escient."

He and Smith, whom he preceded as historian by some
fifteen years, have the ground in common. Indeed Smith
may have come to his awarenesses through Lescarbot, and
such passages as Lescarbot's "Let us return to our tillage;
for to that must we apply ourselves; it is the first mine that
must be sought for, which is more worth than the [Peru-
vian] treasures of Atabalipa: and he that hath corn, wine,
cattle, woolen and linen, leather, iron, and afterward
codfish, he needeth no other treasures for the necessaries of
life."

The advice, which Smith could have known through Purchas, may well have generated Smith's own colonial inventions, as to fishing as well as farming, and so to his idea of a
colony. Lescarbot invents a colony too, though his, unlike
Smith's, comes out to be a pastoral utopia, rich not only in
the true wealths of the soil and the sea, but also in the kind-
nesses of peoples towards each other. He makes the Indians
a fair and equal half of his hopeful commune, understanding their flaws and faults of cruelty and revenge, their heed-
lessness, childish deceits, and instability, but understanding
also their freedom from meanness and vice.

Again and again, he speaks of them as a race of the
golden age, whose avoidance of quarrels and litigations lets
them rejoice "in the happiness of the first of times, when As-
trea the beautiful dwelt among men." He praises their liberality and charity towards each other and towards their
French visitors; their love of children, their sense of honor,
their lack of greed, their braveries and endurances, their
uncorrupted natures. Even in paganism he sees them as rea-

sonable beings, formed in the divine image; now in spiritual infancy they can be brought up to the maturity of Christian knowledge, having already within themselves the attributes of the "golden mean, which is the very seat of virtue."

Of the four Aristotelian "cardinal" or "natural" virtues, he finds the Indians possessed of fortitude, wisely sobered by the fear of dishonor and death; temperance, only excepting a gluttony in eating; liberality, praiseworthy even though they expect generosity in return; and finally the sense of justice which provides simple, fair redress or a punishment usually mild but, if harsh, quick.

Yet he does not pretty up his subject. In an anecdote, he describes the horrible playfulness of the execution of a female prisoner-thief, put to death by Micmac women. "Kinibech'-coech', a young maid of eighteen years of age, plump and fair, gave her the first stroke in the throat, which was with a knife. Another maid of the same age, handsome enough . . . followed on, and the daughter of Membertou . . . made an end of her." When the French reproved their cruelty, "they were all ashamed, and durst not show themselves any more."

He admits, as well, another failing. His Indians are not industrious. Like most Europeans, he underestimates the rigors and endurances of their lives as hunters and fishermen. To him, hunting and fishing are sports. He ignores the often sore necessity of such activities to the Indians, though he calls them "no bad thing."

His slip here is minor. On the whole he studies the savages (whom he refused to call by that term in any philosophic sense) more closely, and with more comprehension than any of his contemporaries. His "sagamo" Membertou who appears both in his prose and in his verses is one of the few Indians to emerge from the page as a viable personage, not because Lescarbot makes an effort to characterize him, but because Membertou takes his part in the life of his peo-

ple and in their intercourse with the French. Only in Lescarbot's mock epic does he become a literary figure, given
heroic stature in fun rather than derision. Now and again,
even the fun yields to honest applause for his craftiness and
courage in war, a shift which seems no more than reasonable since he was over a hundred years of age. Friendly,
loyal, and honest (Champlain says he was a thief), he is at
last baptized, and proposes thereafter open war against all
who refuse Christianity, moved, as Lescarbot comments,
"with a religious zeal (but without knowledge)." When the
French leave Port Royal, Membertou and his people weep
at the parting.

Lescarbot understands more about the Indians than men
had understood before him, but he is not complete in understanding. The complexities of Membertou's sorrow—not to
deny him the sincerity of grief—Lescarbot does not mention. Aspects of power and prestige, refuge against hunger,
access to tools and knickknacks, and above all to the magical forces the French brought with them—all these escape
him. He is particularly heedless of Indian magicalities,
among which he recognizes no more than the usual per-
formances of "sorcerers." He does record, without comprehension, a play battle between men and women before the
men go to war, which is clearly a rehearsal to insure victory,
and a ceremony on a return from war in which the principal hero is disguised from the vengeance of the spirit of the
man he has killed. "They have still another custom concerning any individual who brings in an enemy's scalp.
They make great feasts, dances, and songs for many days;
and whilst these are going on, they strip the conqueror, and
give him but some dirty rag to cover himself withal. But at
the end of eight days or thereabout, after the feast, everyone
presents him with something to honor him for his valor."

Among the fables told of the Indians, he disbelieves most,
accepts a few, and hesitates over others for want of evidence.

He jeers at Champlain for relating the story of the "gougou," the monster which devours men, and explains the prodigy as a projection of human fear and guilt—a theory curiously modern in an age of the marvelous. As for the gorgeous city of Norumbega, he flatly states that it does not exist. Of the Armouchiquois, reputedly so long-legged that when they sit their knees poke up higher than their heads, he says, no such thing—they are well-shaped men. On the other hand, there may be pygmies in the Iroquois mountains; he does not know. Nor does he know whether the Indians have tamed bears to carry them up trees "à faute d'eschelles." Bear-ladders, a two-footed beast reported by Cartier, diamonds which may not be "fine" but are very pretty—such possibilities cannot be denied in a landscape of nearly limitless possibility. His guiding motto reads, "Believe, but don't believe everything"—in his own words, "Il faut croire, mais non pas toutes choses."

Tending on the whole to skepticism, and demanding proof, Lescarbot has come a long distance beyond his fellow countryman and predecessor, André Thevet, who, never having seen Canada, can report of it what he wishes. His *Singularitez de la France Antarctique* (1557) can happily claim, through the eyewitness of others, a realm of Amazonian women, and perhaps men with fur, whose geographical whereabouts are vague, to whom he does not commit himself but whose interest he brings in to embellish New France, both south and north. Eventually claiming a visit to Canada which he never made, Thevet edges himself out of history into free fancy, for which Lescarbot could have nothing but scorn.

Lescarbot's imagination is of a different order. Sometimes weakened by his discursiveness, he is as often enriched by it. His imagery, classical and Biblical, places the Indian in the great scale of being, in a kinship of thought and behavior with other families of the human race. They are not "logs of wood," nor citizens of "a republic of Plato." They have customs in marriage and family life; they love their children; they bury their dead with reverence and ceremonials. Indian hunting, planting, war, feasts, dances; their religious beliefs and practices, the honoring of parents by their children, and the estimation of virtue—the acts, thoughts, and emotions of the new people cross his pages in a kind of pageant conducted against the backdrop of "the ancient Romans, Tartars, Muscovites, Getulians, Germans, Ethiopians . . . Gauls . . . Turks . . . Phrygians . . . Hebrews. . . ." It is hardly surprising that he sometimes loses control of his discussion; it is perhaps more surprising that however loosely he treats his immediate subject for purposes of illustration and comparison, he rarely obscures it. With information and wit, he exemplifies his thesis, and restates it. Here in a fresh world, free of the depravity of Europe, two sorts of men may join together and, each contributing its endowment, make a society as nearly perfect as imperfect beings can conceive.

At his most serious, Lescarbot is irrepressibly happy in his new-gained surroundings. He enjoys digging and planting his garden, wandering in the woods and hunting, sailing along a dangerous shore looking for a mythical mine, or simply contemplating the magnificence of the land where he hoped to spend his years. However cruel the weather, he can take pleasure in the life of the Indians or the life of the French fort. Champlain's "Ordre de Bon Temps" delighted him. Each member of a "table" or mess, by the rules of the "Order of Mirth," took his turn in supplying "some dainty thing" and as "Governor of the feast" marched "with his napkin on his shoulder, and his staff of office in his hand, with the color of the order about his neck . . . and all of them of the order following him, bearing each one a dish." The small display, he reports, served "to keep us merry and cleanly concerning victuals." Such practices, he insists, helped to hold off or cure the frightful scurvy, of which only four men died in Lescarbot's winter at Port Royal.

His own contribution to merriment was a masque, by which he and the Indians and the French settlers greeted Champlain and the governor, Poutrincourt, on their return from a voyage of exploration. Lescarbot's *Le Theatre de Neptune* shows the god of the sea with his tritons saluting the hero of New France, while the Indians give him gifts. Second in time to Captain Farfán de los Godos' *auto sacramentale* of the Spanish expedition to New Mexico, Lescarbot's small drama is the first—as of today—for which a text survives. It earns him the credit of grace and humor and vitality, though he has no better claim to the first rank in the theatre than he has in poetry.

Here is his "Second Savage" who offers his tribute "holding his bow and arrow in his hand," and makes "a present of beaver skins":

> *Voici la main, l'arc, & la fleche*
> *Qui ont fait la mortele breche*
> *En l'animal de qui la peau*
> *Pourra servir d'un bon manteau*
> *(Grand* Sagamos*) à ta hautesse.*
> *Reçoy donc de ma petitesse*
> *Cette offrande qu'à ta grandeur*
> *J'offre du meilleur de mon coeur.*

> Behold the hand, the arrow, and the bow
> Which did bring low
> This beast whose furry skin
> Will make a cloak to warm you in
> If now your Eminence give grace
> To lowly huntsman. Then embrace,
> Great Lord, this gift in all good part,
> Which I do give in all good heart.

The verses are jingling and light, simple and charming, wholly without pretentiousness.

In his masque, Lescarbot has no better luck than Villagrá as a transplanter of European literary forms to an American scene, but he is conscious of the incongruity, and of the inherent joke. An agreeable artificer, graceful and good-natured, he makes his absurdity a part of his entertainment.

He is equally amusing in his mock epic, "The Defeat of the Armouchiquois by the Sachem Membertou and his savage allies, in New France, in the month of July, 1607." Therein he becomes not only a poet-satirist but also a historian again, as he is careful to point out.

> *Je ne chante l'orgueil du geant Briarée*
> *Ni du fier Rodomont la fureur enivrée*
> *Du sang dont il a teint préque tout l'Univers*
> *Ni comme il a forcé les pivot des enfers.*
> *Je chante* Membertou, *et l'heureuse victoire*
> *Qui lui acquit naguere une immortelle gloire*
> *Quand il joncha de morts les champs* Armouchiquois
> *Pour la cause venger du peuple* Souriquois.

I sing not the pride of giant Briareus,
Nor the rage of proud Rodomont, made furious
By blood with which he dyed the universe;
Nor how he made the gates of hell reverse.
Rather, I sing of Membertou—his happy story
Of a great victory; his immortal glory,
In flowering the fields with dead Armouchiquois
To avenge their abuse of his nation Souriquois.

These opening lines are introduced by a prose sentence: "Here are shown the ambuscades at war of the said savages, their funeral rites, the names of several of them, and their ways of healing their wounded." And to the passage Lescarbot adds a note—"The author wishes to say that this history is not in the least fabulous."

He is right in stressing history, because he shows his highest bent as historian, and all his wit serves that end, to the further end of utopianism. The fruitfulness of a land en-

riched by nature, and cultivated by men who are true children of nature, makes the vision which enchants him—the
spectacle of virtue allied with virtue, of barbarism tamed by
the worship of God, of vice healed by the good health of
earth.

For himself, he planned to spend his years where he could
satisfy his pleasure, "so great a desire had I to know the soil
by personal experience. So much so that the summer days
were too short for me, and very often in the spring I was still
at work in the moonlight . . . whatever I did, I did joyfully,
wishing that if God prospered our voyages, I might there
end my life."

Beyond himself he reminds other men that "the promises
made by God to the patriarchs Abraham, Isaac, and Jacob,
and afterwards to the people of Israel, by the mouth of
Moses and of the Psalmist, are, that they shall possess the
land, as a certain heritage that cannot perish, whereon a
man hath wherewith to sustain his family, to make himself
strong and to live in innocency; according to the word of
Cato the Elder, who was wont to say, that the sons of husbandmen are usually valiant and strong and think no evil."

His new American is prophetic, as far as literature is concerned. Crèvecoeur, his fellow countryman, was to echo
him, and among others Thomas Jefferson. Still later writers
of the nineteenth and twentieth centuries were to show
giants in the American earth.

13 / Narrative and Action

The record of early American writing establishes beyond questioning the prime importance within it of the voyage as both subject and pattern. Aside from a few essays, and these dependent upon the voyage, the literature is made up of voyages. If such a statement suggests that either the action or the pattern is rigid, forbidding development and change, the literature itself disproves the suggestion.

Champlain, Smith, and Lescarbot practice an obvious form of elaboration by joining one voyage to another in order to construct a history. They could have claimed predecessors. George Best's *A true discourse of the late voyages . . . of Martin Frobisher* (1578) illustrates an early exercise of the kind, and a rather elaborate one. Best not only puts his three voyages in sequence, but provides an introductory essay, the "two fold discourse," and a conclusion separately entitled "A generall and brief description of the Countrey, and condition of the people . . ." Another example of the same sort of arrangement appears in Basanier's *Histoire notable de la Floride . . .* (1586), in which the Laudonnière narratives are joined with the Gourgues "Reprinse."

Oddly enough, no one—not even Lescarbot—took the

simple collection of voyages over into a fully assimilated history of the north. In spite of the example of the Spanish historians, in spite of an equivalent tradition in the historical chronicle, the northern historians remained faithful to the method of assemblage. It may be that the collections of voyages by Richard Eden, Ramusio, Hakluyt, De Bry, and Purchas established a precedent in structure from which they had difficulty in breaking away.

The compilation is not, however, the most creative bequest of the voyage form to American letters. Rather, it contains within itself as wide a range of possibility as the experience. Since the experience and the report of it are inseparable, and the former can be roughed in as the gradual disclosure of a strange land to travelers on sea and shore, the latter in its structure has to derive from their progress. Cartier's prologuist, who made his tribute to Aristotle in the quotation, "Experience is the teacher of things," could for the world of his description have made it read, "Experience is the writer's teacher."

Because the voyage, as well in complex as in rudimentary development, makes both the subject and the method of presentation, the same outline works for both—we left a familiar place, arrived at an outlandish destination, met with such and such opposition, achieved such and such success, and returned home. The only intrinsic reversal is a reversal of course. The progress of the voyage moves forward with the prow of the ship, in space as in time. Movement and change are inherent. Even the safe anchorage is no more than a temporary port where the vessel refits for another course or another voyage.

So an Ishmael might have described the hunt for Moby Dick. The possibility is a valuable reminder that only the baldest of voyage narratives actually fits within such a limited scheme. Once again the reference has to be to experience. That the crisis is one of encounter and conflict does not make for sameness but for the unexpected, for variety, and for all the uncertainties of outcome in danger, death, bare survival, or rich return. The landscape is always new, its inhabitants marvelous creatures, dangerous and unpredictable in their novelty, perhaps of limitless powers for destruction and evil, perhaps endowed with goods and virtues. Everything seen, every stress undergone, every act undertaken calls for interpretation, response, or speculation on the voyager's part. His art like his errand is that of discovery, his materials being things unknown. His boast and pride in writing, or perhaps his excuse in defeat and his plea for understanding are that he has beheld "what no man has seen before." This makes the great action of his text. Within it certain kinds of conflict become conventions—though not conventionalities—dramatically inherent in the adventure of lives by sea and land.

Of such are shipwreck and disaster, the lot of Gilbert's *Delight*, "whom we saw cast away, without power to give the men succor, neither could we espy any of the men that leaped overboard to save themselves . . . yet all that day, and part of the next we beat up and down as near unto the wrack as was possible for us, looking out, if by good hap we might espy any of them." That there were survivors, Hayes knew as he wrote. After a deliberate suspension of the episode, he adds the story of their hardships and the rescue of most of them. Turning Hayes's episode into an independent relation, their "Master," Richard Clarke, to defend himself from the guilt of losing the ship, writes a separate, short narrative of considerable effectiveness.

Stories of the sort, as parts of longer developments, are many. Cabeza de Vaca in 1528 outlives the storms in which most of his companions die, only to find himself a castaway, dependent upon the charity of the savages. Cabrillo, Ribaut, Fontaneda, Frobisher, and John White are only a few of the many whose voyages suffered checks and overthrows. The classic of the shipwreck dramatizations, William Strachey's "Letter to a Noble Lady" (written 1610), offers a studied, eloquent, and sometimes overwritten, presentation of the type.

In this "true reportory," Strachey multiplies the possible conflicts of the sea voyage. Rescued from drowning on the way to Virginia, but marooned on their island, the wicked of his ship's company turn to mutiny, piracy, and murder; the good, to the gathering of food, the building of ships in which to continue the voyage, and the making of huts for shelter. Thus, the latter uphold civility and decent lawfulness in the reputedly demonic Bermudas, islands "given over to devils and wicked spirits." Strachey denies this reputation, to stress the human within the elemental conflicts. "For surely (Noble Lady)," he writes, "as death comes not so sudden nor apparent, so he comes not so elvish and painful (to men especially even then in health and perfect habitudes of body) as at sea." The twentieth-century writer, in history as in fiction, still subscribes to his recognition.

The sea fight, as inherently dramatic as storm and shipwreck, appears rather rarely in the sixteenth-century literature directly related to northern America. The reasons for this may well have been political, according as France, England, and Spain were officially at war or at peace with one another. Certainly the occurrence was common enough, under the generally observed dictum that beyond Pope Alexander's imaginary demarcation line "there is no peace."

Hawkins and Drake obeyed it in the Caribbean and along the coasts of South America, whatever the relationship between the governments of England and Spain. The Spanish, for their part, were as ready to fight when they believed their ships the stronger. Menéndez as well as Ribaut expected an engagement by sea until the fatal hurricane

gave the French the defeat on the water, while Menéndez
took Fort Caroline by land. At home, friendly countries
traded accusations of piracy; abroad, their citizens carried
out such forays as opportunity permitted.

Yet the written record is thin. In 1589, released from cen-
sorship by the Armada, Hakluyt was free to print his few
privateering narratives, with their raids on Spanish colonial
towns and their attacks on Spanish shipping. Hawkins, attacked and defeated by the Spanish at St. John de Ulloa
during his voyage of 1567–1568, writes his own history of
the conflict, which comes close to the concerns of American
writing because David Ingram had thereafter to be put
ashore. The various Drake relations printed by Hakluyt either in 1589 or 1600 endow the Caribbean and South
America with fights by sea and land, but beyond the raiding of St. Augustine do not show violent conflict in the
north, probably because the booty there was not worth the
price of blood. Above the Bahama Channel, there was little
prospect of capturing gold and jewels, silks and spices.

At the fishing stages of Newfoundland, Spanish, French,
and English scuffled and tricked each other, taking to pillage whenever the chances seemed good. At sea, the larger,
better-armed ship robbed the smaller and weaker. Only the
protesting victims found such skirmishing worthy of record.
Along the Atlantic coast, the schemes of English and French
to establish privateering bases actually came to nothing.
Outright piracy, common enough in casual reference, made
a subject perhaps too touchy for larger developments. Nevertheless, in spite of politics and latitudes, patriot privateers
like Hawkins and Drake got taken over, with questionable
geographic right, into the literary tradition of the north.

The trading voyage, however, which is not ostensibly
aimed at physical conflict, is seldom without its forceful aspects. Since its ship has to come to land, it thereby becomes
a hybrid, joining the exploits of ocean and coast. Verraz-

zano recounts the suspicious approaches of the Indians of
the north Atlantic. The Northwest Passage cycle offers
many an anecdote of barter with the Indians, or attempts at
it. A few of these encounters are friendly exchanges of gifts,
one of the favorite offerings to the savages being the "babe,"
the small, elaborately dressed doll, which the Indians seem
particularly to have liked. John Davis goes so far as to give
a party for the natives, at which his musicians play and everyone dances. Less fortunate meetings may turn to horror.
Hudson's trading on his third voyage of 1609 up the Hudson River, at first peaceful, eventually became violent. In
retaliation for pilfering, the "Masters Mate" killed the
thief; one Indian who tried to overturn the ship's boat had
his hand cut off "and he was drowned." Thereafter the crew
shot and killed some ten or a dozen savages who looked for
revenge. "Success" might go the other way, with the crew
tempted ashore and then ambushed.

Like the sea fight, the trading encounter does not yet develop beyond the episode within the longer narrative. In
mid-sixteenth century, however, it brought in a new subject,
that of the slaving voyage, which on the part of English and
Spanish led not to moral considerations but frequently to
"certain words of displeasure" and to the show, at least, of
fighting. John Sparke's narrative of Hawkins's voyage of
1564 takes its course to Madeira, the Canaries, and the west
coast of Africa, there to meet the friendships, the tricks, and
the threats of the Portuguese; the crews attack and capture
their African victims who sometimes defeat them; and so on
to the Spanish towns of the Caribbean, to sell the cargo, al-
ternately entertaining and threatening the buyers; and so to
Florida and the Bahama Channel, and eventually home
with the profits. Into his accretion of actions, Sparke inter-
polates descriptions of the countries, the peoples, the plants,
and the animals. In the upshot, he writes as full an example, unluckily peripheral to the north, of what might be

called the conglomerate voyage narrative as the literature offers.

He even manages, no doubt properly enough, to suggest the by then common "action" of the marooned man, instanced much earlier by the celebrated marooned woman, Roberval's niece, who so valiantly sustained herself on her island. The high tone of her story suggests that she may be a fiction which enters history, while David Ingram, her English male counterpart of the next generation, illustrates a history which moves into fiction. In any event, accident or punishment, sometimes as a consequence of mutiny, made the case common enough. Crusoe was merely, of many, the one who was most fortunate in his penman.

In the voyage by land, the encounter with the Indians is the predominant subject. Peaceful or warlike, it is the one action which the narrative must provide, and the one which is most likely to achieve dramatization through dialogue, the shaping of the scene, the description of the setting, and an approach to characterization. The Gentleman of Elvas provides meeting after meeting between the Floridian caciques and De Soto, each with its ceremonial staging, its formal speech of submission, De Soto's response, and the upshot in the exchange of gifts and food and courtesies, or bait, deceit, and battle. Cartier at Hochelaga provides a friendly northern counterpart to such a scene, in his case even more elaborate. The Indians welcome him with dancing and singing; on the morning of official greeting, "one of the principal lords" leads his retinue to greet the godlike visitors. Within the Indian town, the savage audience shapes itself as though to watch a play, with Cartier and his men as actors and—in the Indian expectation—miraclemakers. Sick and crippled having been brought to him for healing by touch, he carries out his part as best he can, and reads the Bible. The giving of gifts, the Indian response in food and information, the departure at last after the vision from Mount Royal of the long waterway to China—these rituals complete the pattern of the meeting in peace and confidence.

In the Southwest, the Spaniards provide the drama when they make their *entrada* under Oñate, putting on their small play of baptism, and otherwise entertaining the native inhabitants. Much earlier Fray Marcos had reported his idyllic entertainment by his Indian hosts, but had to end in the disaster of bloodshed. So too Laudonnière, in Florida, with the grave and regal Athoré.

Menéndez, received by the cacique Carlos and his sister Doña Antonia, Coronado's lieutenant met by Cibola's ambassadors with promises of food and intentions of ambush, Champlain at the solemn feast in the northern woods—the list could be extended to show the variations of handling, in the portrayal of trust and the lack of it, of understanding and misunderstanding through speech and answer, gesture, and ceremonial. The comedy of manners is serious, though its possibilities as literature remain unfulfilled.

The entirely hostile encounter is still more frequent. From Columbus, Cabeza de Vaca, the Gentleman of Elvas, and Castañeda, throughout the roll of voyages to Champlain and John Smith, whether between Indian and Indian or between Indian and European, the Indian fight occurs and gets its record, usually as an extended episode in the journey by land or the attempt at settlement. In this period, it does not stand by itself, although in many instances it makes a discrete, readily excerpted part within the narrative. Champlain's forays with the Algonquins against the Iroquois, like the swamp battle of Narváez briefly given in Cabeza de Vaca, or like the Ácoma fight in the Oñate relations, can stand alone. So immediately does the Indian war shape itself in history that it seems ready-born to literature.

Two other events either arrive at or prepare for distinct

literary types—the martyrdom and the Indian captivity. Because the Luis Cancer–Beteta narrative has no parallel, the martyrdom in most instances either is an anecdote or takes the form of a verbal report such as that of the boy Alonso who survived the Spanish priestly martyrs of the Chesapeake. The Indian captivity, unless Cabeza de Vaca's relation is forced into that category, remains episodic, although the occurrence was frequent. The evidence of the boy Guillaume Rouffi of the first Ribaut group, and the Fontaneda account—in itself confused beyond any sort of shape—along with the mentions of sailors, soldiers, and priests who outlived calamities to become slaves among the savages, move towards, rather than establish, the later convention. John Smith's captivity, in its different versions, at last comes close to the emerging pattern.

In a final category of action in the land voyage lie the encounters between European rivals for possession of territory, or control of the sea. The Menéndez-Ribaut-Laudonnière group of relations is, of course, the example and prototype, with its religious as well as political and military hostilities. In the Gourgues relation, the missing characters appear—the Indians whom the avenging captain enlisted by the promise of their revenge also. The narrative is a direct forerunner of the historic and literary future.

14 / *Narrative and Fiction*

In the literary evolution of the voyage, one of the most significant appearances is that of fiction, which—notably—does not always occur where it might be expected. Villagrá's epic and Garcilaso's courtly romance are dramatizations, no doubt, but they use the tools of imaginative writing to embellish the actualities of history. The early writer of fiction in the American scheme reverses the process, using the tools of history to support the actualities of the imagination. However framed in dates, names, places, and other realisms, the fully achieved work of fiction must establish its own reality, not that of its origins and materials. By this definition, needless to say, the greater part of sixteenth-century writing does not belong to fiction, and there is no reason why it should. Indeed, the remarkable evidence is that fiction, and fiction of a particular type, quite different from the contemporary European tale, appears at all.

Not merely dramatizations, but valid achievements in fiction appear reasonably often in episodes within longer narratives. An instance, which also serves to illustrate differences in handling, occurs in the several renderings of the death and burial of De Soto. Among these, the Gentleman of Elvas presents his leader's final end according to the dictates of literary tradition as to the death of the hero. De Soto makes his farewell speech, and his peace with man and God, and gets his epitaph—he becomes the man "whom fortune advanced . . . that he might have the higher fall."

Whereupon, De Soto's successor, Moscoso, conceals his death from the Indians and buries him secretly, but the savages become suspicious "and passing by the place where he was buried, seeing the earth moved, they looked and spoke one to another." Therefore Moscoso has De Soto's body dug up, weighted with sand, and thrown into the river. A cacique tries to trick Moscoso into admitting De Soto's death, but fails. De Soto's "goods," four slaves, three horses, and seven hundred hogs, are raffled off. After that—so the Gentleman makes his conclusion—almost everyone has swine to eat, and after that, having meat ordinarily, obeys the rules of fastdays, which have been disregarded. The romantic death of the hero has found its culmination in the disposal of a corpse, its result in the eating or not eating of the hero's pigs. The "high fall" is accomplished.

The development no doubt issues from the facts. Equally beyond doubt, the Gentleman was deliberate in his selection of facts, and in his ordering of them. His sequence makes his statement—the hero has been brought low. A realist and recorder, he has taken his materials halfway toward fiction and the ironies of the imagination. He has not gone all the way. He seems rather to scant than to exploit his possibilities. He is perhaps unaware of his chances, perhaps unskillful, perhaps hesitant to give offense.

Of the other writers who describe the same event, Purchas paraphrases the Gentleman of Elvas, including the "higher fall" theme, and omitting the pigs and thereby the sharpest point. In the particular instance, he is an expositor, denying his episode its ultimate interpretation. Still a third De Soto narrator, Garcilaso de la Vega, goes to the opposite extreme by straining for dramatic effect within the cliché metaphors of the romance. Like Purchas, he puts apart the realisms and their ironies, preferring to keep within the heroic mode, being moved to compare De Soto's river burial with that of King Alaric of the Goths. Garcilaso presents in some detail the Goths' diversion of a river from its bed, their building of a sepulchre for their king in its channel, and the final return of the river to its course—a story particularly appropriate to the circumstances, the more so because he holds the Goths to be the ancestors of the kings, the nobility, and the people of Spain. By the time he gets through all this, he has of course buried De Soto not twice but thrice, and put any possible achievement in imaginative writing out of the way as well.

The suggestion seems to be that the illusions of American fiction will come out of realities, and not from any overlay of stereotyped effects and literary analogy. It is a suggestion merely, which finds the most of its support in episodes which go no further in achievement than the De Soto of the Gentleman of Elvas. Some few, and these often very short, arrive at completeness, in that they are controlled and disposed towards preconceived effects. Such are David Ingram's encounter with the devil, Smith's rescue by Pocahontas, and the marriage of Doña Antonia and Menéndez.

A much more complex event, the trial and execution of Thomas Doughty during Drake's voyage of 1577–1580 around the Americas and the world, shows in the various versions which survive the range from factual mention to anecdote to expanded episode. Moreover, it undergoes three different interpretations, the most explicit of which comes close to the short-story form.

Two narrators handle the incident with the utmost brevity, suggesting that Doughty, one of Drake's captains, was guilty of vague and various crimes, and therefore deserved death. Hakluyt provides a more detailed but still brief account, in which Drake begins "to enquire diligently" into Doughty's actions and finds them "tending rather to contention or mutiny or some other disorder" and threatening the outcome of the voyage. Brought to trial, "the cause being thoroughly heard . . ." Doughty is found guilty and accepts the death penalty. Before his execution, he takes communion and having "embraced" Drake "in quiet sort laid his head to the block, where he ended his life."

In this passage, the conflict shapes up, though it is impersonal and loose still, with Doughty a curiously passive victim, and Drake a far from ruthless prosecutor.

The Doughty story also survives in three elaborations, only one of them printed before the mid-nineteenth century. This published text, of 1628, Drake's nephew "carefully collected" out of the notes of Drake's chaplain, Francis Fletcher. The term covers an indeed careful piece of editing, by which Fletcher's notes were changed and cut. Drake emerges as a fulsomely generous leader, who indulges Doughty far beyond reason, until he finds his own life and the achievement of the voyage in jeopardy. Only then does he bring Doughty to trial, whereupon Doughty, overwhelmed by his own iniquity, "acknowledged himself to have deserved death, yea many deaths; for that he conspired, not only the overthrow of the action, but of the principal actor also, who was not a stranger or ill-willer, but a dear and true friend unto him; and therefore in a great assembly openly besought them, in whose hands justice rested, to take some order for him, that he might not be compelled to enforce his own hands against his own bowels, or otherwise to become his own executioner."

This is melodrama of a most florid sort, as is the rest of the account—Doughty's condemnation by his judges, his refusal of the escapes offered him by Drake (a return to England for trial, a marooning ashore in which he would have at least a small chance of survival), and his two requests, that he receive communion with his leader and that he die a gentleman's death. In a theatrical culmination, he and Drake take communion and thereafter dine together "as cheerfully in sobriety, as ever in their lives they had done aforetime: each cheering up the other, and taking their leave, by drinking each to other, as if some journey only had been in hand."

So runs—most certainly in the high embellishment of fact—the Drake rendering of the episode. Counter to it, Francis Fletcher's own notes tell a briefer and more moving, though less astonishing story. Fletcher suggests that Doughty was the victim of jealous men, who maligned him to Drake as a thief and a traitor to their voyage. Doughty himself, Fletcher insists, maintained his innocence during the taking of the sacrament and "at the hour and moment of his death." He accepts death not as a guilty man but as a Christian mystic—"long before his death he seemed to be mortified and to be ravished with the desire of God's kingdom; yea to be dissolved and to be with Christ. . . ."

Still a third writer, a certain John Cooke of whom nothing is known, presents Doughty as a victim if not a saint, and Drake as a satanic anti-hero. Offended by Doughty, Drake pretends to forget the offense, but "daily sought matter against Master Doughty, seeking at every man's hands what they could inveigh against him." Drake at last finds a pretext to disgrace him and brings against him the accusation of witchcraft and the conjuring up of storms. Doughty is helpless to defend himself, so that Drake can embark on a series of tyrannical abuses of him, with no other motive than an insane malevolence. Drake's self-revelation—it is he who is revealed rather than Doughty—occurs in a series of scenes, developed in dialogue, through the rising course of which Drake exercises his irrational hatred. Lesser men of the company feed it out of their own jealousies and malices; the honest are impotent to stand against it; the weak yield to Drake's bribe of a rich voyage ahead of them, if Doughty's treachery does not prevent.

For his part, Doughty is far from confessing any sort of serious guilt, and asks to be returned to England for trial. Refused, on Drake's protest that the voyage would then be overthrown, and refused survival in the custody of a friendly captain who speaks for him, Doughty finds himself doomed. His heroic recourse lies in the death of a Christian gentleman, which he plays out in the forgiving of Drake and his accusers, "his only trust in God . . . himself so valiant in this extremity as the world might wonder at; he seemed to have conquered death itself, and it was not seen that of all this day before his death that ever he altered one jot his countenance, but kept it as staid and firm as if he had had some message to deliver to some noble man."

The historian can resolve some of the perplexities of this action, not only by reference to Christian virtue but also to the contemporary social stricture of the "good end." A man of the Elizabethan period, of Doughty's position, was obliged to die gallantly and, so to speak, with style. Therefore Doughty's attendance with Drake at communion, and at the "banquet" whereafter each reassumes his opposite role. The drama depends in part upon these acts, but far more upon the conflict of motive, the confrontation of spiritual and physical strengths. The three versions, in quality, run from the fluent stereotype to the outline of dramatic implication to the acted and spoken narrative of Cooke, in which the oppositions are shown as well as implied, and the whole is carried near to full effectiveness. Cooke does not entirely understand the short story form, which was long years away from its recognized shape, nor is he skilled enough as a writer to polish his text and give a final definition to his subject. Herman Melville, had he come across the nineteenth-century printing, would have found it to his purposes, and could have made from it the sea tragedy it deserves to be.

Whatever Cooke's limitations, he is a practitioner of fiction, and a beginner in a new shape. As a redactor of the episode, he develops it to a new literary validity, to which history contributes, but in which truth is dramatic, not reportorial.

However incomplete the development of the short story as a form, the complete short story makes its appearance twice in pre-colonial American literature. The Gourgues "Reprinse de la Floride" and the Pricket "Larger Discourse" show a wide difference in quality, but each achieves a finished structure. The "Reprinse" makes a simple and forthright short story of physical action, with planned stages of event, worked to a climax and a resolution. It is fitted out with a strong central character—Gourgues himself—and subsidiary heroes and villains, the latter off-stage until punishment overtakes them, so that the massacre which Menéndez had perpetrated against the French in Florida is avenged. Its statement is an affirmation of justice accomplished and honor redeemed, asserted loudly enough to hush the historic truth that merely another slaughter has been carried out. Its use of the tag line puts it in the category of the well-made short story, even. The taunt here ascribed to Menéndez—"I do this not as to Frenchmen but as to Lutherans"—gets its match in Gourgues's answer—"I do this not as to Spaniards" but as to "murderers." The "reprinse" could hardly be more thorough or more succinct.

Pricket gains the same finality, on a much higher moral plane, in much sharper intensity of emotion. The fact that he was pleading a cause, and that he himself might be among those condemned for the mutiny and the virtual murder of Hudson, may partly explain this, but cannot ex-

plain his ordering of his presentation and his use of specific
detail, for effectiveness. Whatever actual provocation
brought about the mutiny against Hudson, Pricket is deliberate in choosing and placing the incidents which show its
rising course in his story. Whatever part the person Henry
Greene may have taken in it, Pricket's "gray cloth gown"
and his character Henry Greene establish the emotional
truth. The many themes of human endurance or veniality
or virtue which the events could be made to justify, he puts
aside. These "many devices in the heart of man" are less
fitting to his issue than the larger and profounder statement,
"but the counsel of the Lord shall stand."

The relatively simple voyage structure is entirely appropriate to his dramatic action, in the gradual passage out of
known courses and customs into the unpredictable, where
new currents in the sea and the new dangers of wild coasts
test and break the tempers of men, until Hudson himself
yields to insane rages and violences, and murder becomes
by stages possible, probable, and inevitable. Not until God's
judgment and punishment are complete can the voyage
turn back to customary places, and men return to normal
demeanor as they return to the familiar landscapes of their
lives.

15 / *The Imaginary Voyage*

Of the many early American narratives, almost all concern themselves with actualities, however embroidered or developed or reshaped or interpreted. Hudson did make a voyage into a great northern bay, in which his crew mutinied and cast him adrift. Dominique de Gourgues did seek and get revenge upon the Spaniards in Florida. John Smith did go to Virginia and there encounter Pocahontas. Imagination recreates such voyages, but does not bring them to pass.

However, one of the notable types of American fiction—the imaginary voyage—has the whole job to do. By definition, it must portray that which has not happened, and does so either in the terms of a fantasy shared with the reader or in the terms of a purportedly true relation which throughout its essential falsity appeals for belief. America provides the setting for both types. Rabelais practiced the former kind, in the travels of Pantagruel, drawing upon Peter Martyr and Jacques Cartier for his fabulous new world. For the latter sort, the mid-sixteenth century also contains an American example, fully worked out and astonishingly accurate in its recognition of the voyage form. Known as the Zeno "Discoverie," it has its own complex record, having been accepted both as history and as geography when it was published and—however sharply questioned—defended by one or another authority for three and a half centuries thereafter.

The "Discoverie" got its first publication in Venice, as the second part of a small volume entitled *De i Commentarii del Viaggio in Persia de M. Caterino Zeno . . . Et dello scoprimento dell'Isole Frislanda, Eslanda, Engrouelanda, Estotilanda, & Icaria, fatto sotto il Polo Artico, da due fratelli zeni . . .* (1558). The first part of this unassuming book is indeed devoted to the travels in Persia of Caterino Zeno, member of an illustrious Venetian family. There Caterino Zeno had indeed led an embassy and carried out important negotiations. The "discovery," which makes up the second part of the text, of the attractively named and variously spelled islands of Frislanda, Eslanda, Engrouelanda, Estotilanda, and Icaria by two other Zenos deals with very different matters, notably the existence of unknown (and nonexistent) countries to the northwest of Scotland and Norway.

This second narrative, later included in the Ramusio volume of 1574, long after Ramusio's death, got picked up and reprinted by Hakluyt in his *Divers Voyages, touching the Discoverie of America, and the Ilands adjacent . . .* (1582). Whether or not Hakluyt later questioned the authenticity of the Zeno relation—however shored up by the undoubted authenticity of the Caterino Zeno embassy—he omitted the Zeno "Discoverie" from his later, larger collections. If he did move from acceptance to rejection, he was among the first of the skeptics. For generations, mapmakers of the highest repute put some or all of the Zeno islands on their charts. As late as the nineteenth century, Icaria kept a place in intellectual history at least, when the French socialist Étienne Cabet made it the kingdom of his utopian fantasy. He was right in so doing. The original Zeno island is as imaginary as Cabet's ideal realm.

Both are intimately concerned with northern America and its voyage literature, but only the Icaria of the sixteenth century illustrates the complete shift of the voyage into fantasy, and the strong likelihood of the revelation of wonders as yet unknown to become the revelation of wonders never to be known except on the printed page.

Useful and interesting in these respects, the Zeno "Discoverie" offers still other insights to the student of American writing, who is once again required to make his way through confusions. The story is far from simple. It begins with a recital of the Zeno ancestry, which itself begins "In the year of our Lord 1200, there was in the city of Venice a famous gentleman, named M. Marino Zeno. . . ." The mention of this historical personage, along with some twelve generations of his offspring, assures the credibility of the Zeno claims to a pre-Columbian finding of the new world, which was actually ascribed not to M. Marino Zeno but to two descendants of his, "M. Nicolo the knight" and Nicolo's brother, Antonio, and begins not in 1200 but in 1380, still well before Columbus.

So ratified by its introduction, the Zeno voyage takes off with Messer Nicolo's "wonderful great desire . . . to travel and to acquaint himself with the manners of sundry nations." He sets forth by ship to satisfy that desire, is "assaulted by a storm on his way to England and Flanders" and "so tossed for the space of many days with the sea and wind" that he has no idea where he may be until his ship is wrecked on the "Isle of Frisland." The whereabouts of that island (it is nowhere) are not given.

The inhabitants of Frisland attack Messer Nicolo, but the noble Zichmni, Prince of Porland and Duke of Zorani, rescues him. Zichmni is invading the island, and with Messer Nicolo's help conquers it and other neighboring places. Thereafter the prince shows Nicolo such favor that Nicolo summons his brother Antonio to the prince's service. The

brothers carry on the voyages of conquest, usually success-
fully, but "Iseland" is too strong for them (here the author
had to be careful, because Iceland does exist).

From one of his forts, Messer Nicolo starts a voyage of discovery to the northward, and reaches Engroueland (Greenland), upon which he finds what no one else has ever found
there—a volcano "like Vesuvius and Etna," and a monas-
tery heated by "a fountain of hot burning water" which
cooks the friars' food and warms a covered winter garden so
that they grow "flowers and fruits and herbs" during the
nine months season of "extreme" frost and snow. So great is
the flow from the fountain that it keeps a "haven" in the sea
from freezing, in which fish and fowl abound.

Stone and lime from the mountain for building, a large
trade in fish carried by ships to Europe, in sum, "the greatest commodities that may be wished" spring from this Arctic Eden, so that "these friars employ all their travail and
study for the most part in trimming their gardens, and in
making fair and beautiful buildings. . . ."

M. Nicolo completes the description of utopian Engroueland, but cannot go further because he dies. M. Antonio, his
brother, takes over as narrator, writing in letters the relation of a voyage made by fishermen to Estotiland, an island
a thousand miles west of Frisland. There another shipwreck
reveals "a very rich country, abounding with all the commodities of the world . . . having in the middle thereof a
very high mountain, from which there riseth four rivers,
that pass through the whole country."

Whether or not these are the four rivers of the Earthly
Paradise which Columbus expected to find further south,
Estotiland is highly favored, not only in its landscape, but in
its people, who are "witty," whose king has a library which
contains books in Latin, whose mines provide "all manner
of metals, but especially they abound with gold." And to the
southward, the fishermen hear of another country "very

rich of gold," but when they explore this land of Drogeo, they find cannibal savages who eat "the most part of them." The survivors are rescued by a "Lord" and go through a series of adventures. One of them eventually escapes to Estotiland, becomes rich, and returns to Frisland to tell his tale, in consequence of which Prince Zichmni and M. Antonio set out for Estotiland but arrive instead in Icaria. Refused a landing in this kingdom whose first ruler had been the as yet undrowned "Icarius," son of "Dedalus, king of Scotland," Zichmni finds another country, builds a city, and demeans himself (presumably) as should a prince "as worthy of immortal memory as any that even lived, for his great valiancy and singular humanity."

There is no reason, of course, why the Zeno narrative should ever end. The shipwreck, discovery, exploration, conquest, habitation chain can be extended until the writer's energies wear out. The particular instance stops with the statement that the contemporary author, a sixteenth-century Nicolo Zeno, has as a child played with his ancestors' manuscripts—"a particular book" and letters and "divers other writings"—and carelessly destroyed the most of them. As a grown man, he says, in repentance he put together his "discourse" out of "whatsoever I could get of this matter" in honor of the great discoveries of the time and in praise of his forefathers.

In the age-old tradition of the imaginary voyage, the "Discoverie" occupies a minor place, but one of especial interest. Certain aspects of its significance can best be seen by what it is not. It is not a minor *Odyssey*, nor is it, like Lucian's *True History*, a deliberately fantastic and satiric excursion to the moon or wherever. Nor is it another *Utopia*—Sir Thomas More's imaginary voyager brings back from his American travels a Platonic realm, for the contemplation of philosophers rather than of seafarer-conquerors. Nor is it an offspring of the medieval tradition of the voyage; except in its sequence of islands, and in its monkish community, it shows no parallels to the voyage of St. Brandan to paradise —indeed, it is entirely secular. All of these—imaginary voyages in every sense—make their appeal to the imagination. The Zenos, however imaginative, make their appeal to the sense of fact. Their fiction is a work of realism; they establish their illusion by removing or trying to remove all possible doubt of its truth.

Could the Zenos, men of eminent place and historic distinction, lend themselves or even their names to a deceit? From his opening genealogy to his closing excuse for his destructiveness as a child, Nicolo Zeno the writer strains to establish his authenticities. In passing, it is amusing to notice that he uses the ancient manuscript device to confirm his story much as Hawthorne uses it in *The Scarlet Letter* to gain his reader's acquiescence. Other devices—the provision of a map, the geographical echoes of such place names as Frisland and Icaria, the careful pilferings from valid sources for local color—support the Zeno realities.

The naming of Dedalus as king of Scotland, however, most certainly does not seem to do so. Why Dedalus? Once that name comes in, then a revived Icarus or Icarius can follow, in the text of a writer like Zeno whose scholarship in mythology was uncertain, to say the least. But even though Icarus be admitted, why Dedalus?

The probability is that this choice, which now seems wholly fanciful, was part of the Zeno effort for authenticity. Hector Boyce (or Boece or Boetius) had published his *History of Scotland* in Latin in 1527. Translated by John Bellenden into Scots, it could be read in manuscript by the 1530s and in black-letter print as well. Boyce and Bellenden, most eminent of authorities, give not Dedalus but another Greek, Gathelus, as the first king of Scotland. A reader uncertain of his lettering can easily confuse the "G" and the "D" in either manuscript or black letter; in manuscript, he could as readily read "d" for "th" if he did not take the substitution for granted. Nicolo Zeno, no scholar, was all too likely to read a somewhat familiar name in place of one strange to him. In so doing, of course, he would in his own estimation be calling to his help a source of unquestioned competence.

Scholar he was not, but he was widely enough read in the literature of the Atlantic to pick up detail and color from Columbus, Olaus Magnus, Peter Martyr, and the reports of Mexico and Peru. A true writer of fiction, he uses his materials as he pleases, but always in the climate of fact. In structure, action, landscapes, and persons he shows his understanding of the voyage, reading its themes of empire, wealth, and wonder with far greater accuracy than he read his alphabet. He got the first acknowledgment of his skill in being believed as a geographer. He is better entitled to an acceptance in literature, as a creator and adapter in a form which travelers of the seventeenth and eighteenth centuries were to practice, and Poe and Melville and Cooper to carry forward during the nineteenth century.

No other sixteenth-century imaginary voyage compares with the Zeno "Discoverie" in completeness or in understanding. False claims to have gone this place or that show up as parts of longer narratives. André Thevet, intent upon genial amusement, reports upon journeys he never took and sights he never saw. David Ingram is free to embroider into an actual journey fantasies of golden cities he might have visited but did not. A wandering Greek, Apostolos Valerianos, otherwise known as Juan de Fuca, tells the Englishman Michael Lok about his journey through the Straits of Anian in 1592 from the Pacific to the Atlantic. Lok shapes up the story to persuade investors to back him in finding the golden waterway; Purchas prints it, although the investors were not persuaded and although Lok fell short of literary quality.

Still another individual, Captain Lorenzo Ferrer Maldonado, leaves a record of a voyage which he claims to have made in 1588. His narrative, apparently written in the early 1600s, aims to lead Atlantic navigators by the north and west of Labrador to a waterway between Asia on the north and America on the south, and finally to a short "Strait of Anian" into the Pacific. Maldonado outdoes even the Zenos in factuality, but gains for his entirely imaginary "true" course no greater interest than if he were plotting a known route. Like Valerianos-Fuca, he merely attests to the strength and persistence of fables, and to the congenialities of the imaginary voyage to the American experience.

Maldonado gives the name of his pilot as Juan Martinez, suggestively enough if he knew of that Juan Martinez of the early 1500s who made perhaps the most notable of imaginary voyages, to the rich city of Manoa in the magnificent country of gold, El Dorado. A castaway, Martinez claimed to have been rescued by the Guiana Indians, and carried far into the country "until he came to the great city of Manoa, the seat and residence of Inga the emperor. . . . He lived seven months in Manoa, but was not suffered to wander into the country anywhere. He was also brought thither all the way blindfold, led by the Indians . . . and was fourteen or fifteen days in the passage. He avowed at his death that he entered the city at noon, and then they uncovered his face, and that he traveled all that day till night through the city, and the next day from sun rising to sun setting. . . ."

So reads Sir Walter Raleigh's account of Martinez' fabulous travels; he has found the original relation, or rather a copy of it, in Porto Rico. There too he has heard why Martinez gave the country of his discovery its golden name. The people of that kingdom, Raleigh writes, are "marvellous great drunkards." For their solemn feasts, the emperor's courtiers are stripped naked, anointed with a balm, and gilded all over with a fine gold dust to become golden men. Martinez comes honestly by his "Dorado," seeing them, and seeing "an abundance of gold" in the city, the "images of gold" in the temples, and plates, armor, and shields of gold for warfare.

In the true convention of treasure trove, Martinez is robbed as, laden with golden gifts, he leaves the country. Raleigh, in a literary sense, gives them back to him and more too, by reminding the audience of the comparable riches of Cuzco, "because we may judge of the one [Guiana] by the other [Peru]." The trick gains for Guiana's golden man the wealth of the Inca, "all the vessels" of whose house, table, and kitchen, Raleigh says in paraphrase of the Spanish historian Gómara, "were of gold and silver, and the meanest of silver and copper for strength and hardness of metal. He had in his wardrobe hollow statues of gold which seemed giants, and the figures in proportion and bigness of all the beasts, birds, trees, and herbs, that the earth bringeth forth: and of all the fishes that the sea or waters of his kingdom breedeth. He had also ropes, budgets, chests and troughs of gold and silver, heaps of billets of gold, that seemed marked out to burn." Moreover, the Inca enjoyed a "garden of pleasure . . . which had all kind of garden-herbs, flowers and trees of gold and silver."

So Raleigh, in a discourse of the year 1595, fortifies his hopes of Guiana by the example of Pizarro. The fallacy lies in the assumption, "we may judge the one by the other." The fallacy itself agreeably illustrates the leaping logic of the imaginary voyager. Indeed the literature of El Dorado, in Raleigh's connection with it, takes the process the whole way. By 1617, a member of Raleigh's last expedition threw out all idea of comparison, and transferred the Peruvian treasures to Guiana forthwith. "Newes of Sr. Walter Rauleigh. With The true Description of Guiana . . . Sent from a Gentleman of his Fleet" (1617) repeats the passage which

Raleigh himself had properly attached to Peru, but turns it over outright to El Dorado. "For as all the springs and rivers in the world have but one head, namely, the sea: so it is thought all the wealthy mines in the world have but one sovereign, which is an empire placed in these parts, and that is the great empire of Guiana, ruled by the great Emperor Inga: of the great wealth and riches whereof Francisco Lopez [Gómara] and others thus report; that all the vessels of the emperor's house, tables, and kitchen were of silver and gold. . . ." And so, through the original list of statues, figures, trees, ropes, and so forth, to the "billets of gold, which seemed wood marked out to burn" and the "garden of pleasure" with its precious growth, the Gentleman gilds Guiana and no other place. Thus he affords to the student of the fabulous a nice instance of its manner of increase, and to the imagination of Juan Martinez an affirmation. Pity was that Martinez, like most imaginary voyagers, was long dead before fame took him in.

El Dorado survived him into still later centuries, and indeed still survives, never having gained more than a fragmentary dramatization. A theme perhaps too compelling for any but the greatest of geniuses to master, it keeps its power over men's acts and minds, regardless.

16 / Ptolemy's America

Action, of whatever sort, must have its setting, so that the voyage to an unknown world categorically includes a "description of the country." Through such descriptions, the continents of America were to be created, so to speak; were to be built, piece by piece and decade by decade before valid outlines emerged. Three centuries had to pass before one large outline took firm, if not final, shape.

The sixteenth-century traveler in northern America, giving his whereabouts, was likely to state that he was so many leagues or miles from Tartary, or so many from Ania or Tierra Firma or Meta Incognita, or (with a nearer chance of being right) so many from his starting point. Even about the last, he was guessing well or badly, and his readers had to guess well or badly what his guess might mean. His educated readers would know that he could not possibly be boxing a continent or continents because on the authority of the great geographer Ptolemy there were no such lands to box. Yet there was undeniably something. The question was what the shape of that something might be.

Early in the sixteenth century, an Englishman who was probably John Rastell, Sir Thomas More's brother-in-law, tried to describe the new world in a small play, "A new interlude and a mery of the nature of the iiii.elements &c" (c. 1519). His difficulties with the four elements are compounded by his awe and his honest ignorance of the lands just discovered, still unportrayed.

At first he is sure only of their size—

> And that country is so large of room,
> Much longer than all Christendom
> Without fable or guile,
> For divers mariners have it tried
> And sailed straight by the coast side
> Above five thousand mile . . .

The character named *Experience* is speaking. He continues, describing as he can the people and the fruits of this "so far a ground," while his companion *Studious Desire* urges him on, so that he expatiates upon his "matter of cosmography." Showing Europe and Africa and, to the east, India, he explains that the new shore is called America, and lies little more than a thousand miles across the "great east sea" from Cathay.

> But whether that sea go thither directly
> Or if any wilderness between them do lie
> No man knoweth for certain . . .

At last sure only of ignorance, he begins to waver, to "know nothing at all . . ."

> Nor whether the most part be land or sea . . .
> Of this we know nothing . . .

In posing the huge uncertainty, *Experience* foreordains one of the large commitments of early American writing, which must provide a landscape or a seascape, the disclosure of which is the purpose of the voyage and its setting as well. The writer must not only visit but describe his arctic or antarctic, his tropics, and his habitable "climates." As a pilot, he will give the seamarks by which he steers. On land too, the traveler will take his bearings, and send home such facts as he gathers along with his description of its mountains, plains, and valleys, its rivers and lakes, its deserts of sand and ice. These make the pictorial parts of the large design, the outline map which they illuminate, or perhaps change or even destroy.

Since by the era of colonization—1625, say, give or take five years—much of the northern continent had been traversed, and since both coasts had been repeatedly scanned, some more or less accurate, more or less accepted geographical entity might be expected to emerge for a beginning of representation. The maps of the first hundred years of exploration show that this expectation is false. On paper and in men's minds, the continent was protean. Even Rastell's "large of room" did not hold. The land above Mexico could shrink. Ocean, or Asia, or even a polar extension of Europe might take its place. Or it could simply disappear into the blankness of the "unknown." There is no consistent cartographical evidence of a continuity of knowledge or the broad acceptance of such knowledge as had been gained by observation. Probably the most accurate general statement to be made about the continental American maps of the sixteenth and early seventeenth centuries is that no accurate general statement can be made about them.

Geographers provide the technical reason why this should be so. Exploration, with its gathering of evidence, was going on, to be sure, but the influence of authority was as strong or stronger. According to the Ptolemaic scheme, as the Renaissance developed it, the part of the world's sphere not occupied by Europe, Asia, and Africa was covered by water. Scattered islands—Japan, Antilia, St. Brandan's, the Moluccas—broke the surface. Any uninterrupted continental coastline must be that of Asia.

Thereby Claudius Ptolemy, an Alexandrian Greek of the second century, profoundly influenced not only American cartography but also early American literature. Long after circumnavigation had put Asia far to the west, across a second ocean from the Americas, both mapmakers and men's minds could bring it back to extend over the north of a truncated continent which, above Mexico, is likely to contain "Laborador," Nova Francia, Florida, Quivira, and Cibola, the last two being bordered at the north by the "Sierra Nevada" and beyond these mountains by a clear east-west waterway and finally Marco Polo's "Mangi" and "Anian." Such is the plan of Sir Humphrey Gilbert's schematic map of 1576. George Best's of 1578 follows much the same plan, but above the passage which he names Frobisher's "Straight" he extends a "Terra Septentrionalis" which balances his "Terra Australis" at the southern pole. His "Strait of Anian" is vaguely in the position of Bering Strait. By 1582, Michael Lok has reverted to Ptolemy; above the "Sierra Nevada," for the west, and beyond a miniature "Canada" and "Saguenay," for the east, he admits of no land. His ocean is open to the Orient. The mapmaker Hondius, illustrating Francis Drake's voyage around the world, finds a different solution to the Asian-American geographical relationship. He extends northern Asia over the pole and draws a strait above North America; another strait separates an Asian "Mongol" peninsula from an "Anian" which he has moved to western America. Implicit in all these designs is the Ptolemaic doctrine that Europe can reach Asia by water.

The same conviction explains the tendency of both mapmakers and writers to break up the northern continent into islands. On the Atlantic coast, Labrador, "Norumbega" (vaguely, New England and the Maritimes), "Canada" (a small area not always identical with New France), "Cuba" (not the actual island but mainland), and other areas can become insular. South America fairly soon takes continental size; if it can be called an island, it appears as a very large one. Of North America, this is not true. "Terra Nova" (Newfoundland) may be an Asian peninsula, or a clutch of islands, while farther south the continental coast disappears and an island takes its place. To the west, Coronado's men had proved that California belonged to the mainland, and that Lower California was a peninsula. The intrusions of the Strait of Anian had made both into an island by the early seventeenth century. Thereafter, the wandering waterway was to cut through the continent according to various designs, making islands large and small across the prairies. Well into the seventeenth century, Father Zárate-Salmerón—himself highly imaginative and entirely capable of geographical fantasies of his own—had to protest "against the incredulous who are unwilling to believe that Florida is mainland with [New Spain] and with New Mexico." He offered the plain fact "that men have come overland from there," but had no confidence that his readers would believe him.

Zárate-Salmerón was right in his protest and his doubts. The "incredulous" continued to disbelieve, no matter how clear the testimony of Cabeza de Vaca, or of Coronado and De Soto, who had come within two hundred miles of meeting. Or the flight of the "tatooed woman," otherwise known as "Zaldivar's Indian woman," who had run away from Coronado's soldiery and crossed Texas, eventually to reach Moscoso's men to the east. Or, for another dimension of the continent, the late sixteenth-century Spanish marauding expedition which ended in murder and massacre, but in spite of that climax got as far north as the River Platte. The records show that only the northern Mississippi basin and the Northwest remained entirely untrodden by Europeans. Yet a patriotic Englishman could claim that the whole idea of a continent was a Spanish plot to keep Englishmen from sailing west to China from Hudson's Bay.

For this geographer, the Oxford mathematician Henry

Briggs, Hudson's Bay is not a bay but an open sea to the west. Upper and Lower California must, of course, be an island. Since Briggs wants to go to the Orient by water, he protests against the theories which prevent him. Those who give "too much credit to our usual globes and maps, do dream of a large continent extending itself far westward to the imagined Strait of Anian, where are seated (as they fable) the large kingdoms of Cebola and Quivira, having great and populous cities of civil people; whose houses are said to be five stories high, and to have some pillars of turquoises." These fables, he concludes, are deliberate deceits, "cunningly set down by some upon set purpose to put us out of the right way, and to discourage such as otherwise might be desirous to search a passage . . . into those seas." So, without fear of contradiction, and as good a right to belief as any, Briggs can make solid land disappear.

Other men spoke for its existence. To this side of the argument, more or less qualified persons offered estimates of vast extent and huge distances. Verrazzano provides the measurement of North and South America, finding the two new continents "manifestly larger than our Europe together with Africa, and perhaps Asia. . . ." Cartier passes along the Indian statement that the St. Lawrence River is navigable for "three moons." For Coronado, Hakluyt estimates "2850" miles "passed" between Mexico and the southern California coast. For the land beyond New Mexico, the Spaniard Rio de Losa reports to the viceroy in 1602 that it is "very vast, both in latitude and longitude, for it is 2,485 leagues from east to west, and 1,435 in crossing the land." With better than two and a half miles to the Spanish league, his figure gives a continent some sixty-two hundred miles in breadth. This is the distance, he explains, from "Point Cod [Newfoundland] to the end of the Strait of Anian." To the confusion of geography and the encouragement of fable, he provides other figures:

"From New Mexico to the end of the Strait of Anian across from Tartary, the distance is 1,435 leagues.

"From New Mexico to the sea and lake of Caribas in the region of Tartary, the distance is 415 leagues. . . .

"From New Mexico to Santa Elena on the Bahama channel, the distance is 577 leagues."

No terrestrial globe could allow for his measurements, except the last. He has gone over into the cosmography of the marvelous, obscurely knows it, and gives the gist of what he is saying in unarithmetical terms. "We may well believe that in a country of such vast proportions where it is said that there are people who bear a metal crown like our kings, there are walled towns and houses of five, six, or seven storeys, fruits as good as in Spain, large numbers of people, and cattle like those of Tartary and Germany, for our Lord did not deny it abundance and sustenance, and silver and gold, as in other lands and in the Indies."

His faith is not troubled by the fact that in his next paragraph he has to describe New Mexico as a "land sandy and lacking in wood and water . . . people and silver," most of whose settlers have had to abandon it. "Some arrived here in the province of your lordship in a pitiful condition, and it was grievous to hear those who came back tell of the plight of those who stayed behind."

In Rio de Losa, Ptolemaic science and the actualities of experience meet in open conflict. His and Ptolemy's Asia is not however the only encroacher upon the American scene. The pre-Columbian ocean, be it remembered, had admitted of certain islands, now called imaginary. Plato's Atlantis, long since swallowed up by the sea, was not charted, but remained in mind. Antilia, whether one island of Seven Cities or a group of islands, seven or nine, endowed the Caribbean with a name, and then, as an idea, migrated to the continent. Established on the mainland, and indeed well in the interior, Antilia gains reality as a force in history, under the name of Cibola or Quivira or Copal. Elsewhere in the western sea the Welsh Prince Madoc had found a new and pleasant country, and named one of its islands Penguin Island. On a far more significant voyage, the Irish St. Brandan had found the island of devils and the island of the earthly paradise, the latter being named for him on many maps.

These and other islands of less literary importance adorn the Atlantic Ocean, with neither more nor less reality than the Zenos' Frisland and Icaria. Only two important imaginary islands of significance are left to the sea between America and Asia, the Island of the Amazons and the Island of California. The former had evidently more interest for writers than mapmakers, while the latter fairly soon sheds its identification with the realm of Queen Calafia, and may even appear in full reality as mainland.

For the most part, these oceanic realms are utopian, by one definition or another, be it beauty, or virtue, or wealth, or happiness, or sanctity, or a combination of these and other high qualities whose brightness accrues to the American landscape. Either by association or outright identification with them, America takes on the splendors and refulgences of the ideal.

Sir Humphrey Gilbert, who in his "Discourse" makes the firm statement that America is Atlantis, is singly concerned with an argument to prove the existence of a Northwest Passage. Nevertheless he provides for America the connotations of that island kingdom of divine origin and—before its degeneracy and downfall—perfect rule and justice. Plato's imaginary country, which Gilbert took to be real, endows a different land with riches, power, grace, ease, and order.

Where Atlantis represents the classical landscape, Antilia shows forth the medieval, in a combination of holiness and

oriental embellishment and—above all—wealth. Islands
whose very beaches are of golden sand glitter with something other than sanctity, however certainly discovered by
seven bishops in flight before invading infidels. By the time
Antilia establishes itself on the Strait of Anian in the American mid-continent, the bishops and their congregations are
forgotten. Gold and jewels color the scene. The long-sought,
never-to-be-found strait takes the place of the ocean, while
in the new Antilia Indian lords ride the waters in boats
rowed by twenty rowers, with sails and awnings, and a
golden eagle at the prow. Castañeda's retelling of the Turk's
story, which in turn must have got its decor from the Spanish themselves, gilds Quivira almost as richly as Manoa,
while the Indian prince sleeping to the music of little golden
bells outdoes the Gilded Man as a poetic figure. At still a
further remove, he is Marco Polo's Golden King, translated
out of an Asian into an American setting.

David Ingram, all unaware of his sources, is highly aware
of the enchantments of an Asian panoply. His progress
across an America he actually saw is vague in comparison
with the magical America he induced himself and his hearers to see. A single paragraph describing Florida as a paradise of real natural beauty yields before twenty paragraphs
which present a supernatural country, whose kings are Solo-
mons in their glory, whose peoples are regal by virtue of
precious metals and gems. Ingram's is not a landscape so
much as a Tom Tiddler's ground of imagined delights.

St. Brandan's Island possesses the same magicality, in a
very different sense. Whatever its wealth in "fair and precious" stones it is far richer in holiness.

> So clear and so light it was, that joy there was enow,
> Trees there were full of fruit well thick on every bough . . .
> It was evermore day, they found never night,
> Wayfaring they found nowhere so much clear light.
> The air was ever in one state, neither hot nor cold,
> But the joy that they found may not ever be told.

In all its phrasing (the quoted passage has been translated into modern usage), the journey of the saint and his followers over the ocean to the Earthly Paradise belongs far more to an eastern than to a western tradition. Brandan is a godly Sinbad, and the mapmaker Martin Behaim shows a sound literary sensitivity in placing his island off the coast of Japan, with the island of the Seven Cities to the north and east. So, for 1492. After Columbus, St. Brandan's Eden moves to the mid-Atlantic, to contribute its fabulous setting to the new ocean and the new continent. Since beliefs and desires persuade, sixteenth-century sailors could seek out and sometimes "see" the holy shores, which appear on maps throughout the sixteenth century, promising paradise to the west.

St. Brandan becomes no less saintly when his voyaging gets turned to the practical purpose of supporting an English claim to the discovery of "Virginia." In this, he joins King Arthur, King Malgo, Prince Madoc of Wales, and an adventurous magician called the Friar of Oxford, all of whom are brought into an argument about national rights, written by Purchas and printed in 1625 under the title of "Virginias Verger." Purchas admits "something fabulous . . . something uncertain" in his evidences, but advances them anyway.

The Friar, Nicholas of Linne, did his exploring in the year 1360, by means of "magical art," which took him beyond the northern islands. The great geographer, Mercator, used his design of the polar regions as it came down through other writers across two centuries. With his astrolabe, the Friar "mapped out and measured" a north polar continent divided by four canals which flowed into a central whirlpool "that if vessels once enter they cannot be driven back by any wind. . . ." His magic must have saved him from catastrophe, since he got back to Oxford and his books. His contribution to American letters may well have been the handing on to Edgar Allan Poe, through later intermediaries, the image of a whirlpool-maelstrom into which pour all the waters of ocean.

Somewhat less spectacularly, Prince Madoc of Wales lends himself to political use, by a process of manipulation which neatly illustrates the rules of unreason. The story runs that Madoc, in the year 1170, left his own distressed country, leading a company of Welshmen to a western land, where they settled. This country could be no other than America, there being no other country to the west. Since Madoc was a first discoverer and occupier, and since he was of royal blood, Queen Elizabeth inherited his "ancient right and interest in those countries."

To strengthen the case, Madoc is shown to have given Welsh names to "certain islands, beasts, and fowls . . . as the Island of Pengwin which yet to this day beareth the same." Moreover, the Emperor "Mutezuma" of Mexico told his subjects that according to their history their founding king and captain had left them, and not returned. Madoc must have been this "strange, noble person" because no European nation but the Welsh owns a tradition such as this.

The political twist illustrates the theme of nationality, rather than the description of place, but it is to be noted that Madoc and his followers found in the west "pleasant and fruitful countries" which they preferred to their own. The phrase has a note of practicality, sturdy in its restraint. The extravagances of fable are much more typical, dominating even the records of experience, cruelly earned.

The golden cities long outlived the men who died looking for them. The modest fairytales of Madoc and Nicholas of Linne and the learned proofs according to Atlantis are little effective either as portrayal or persuasion compared to Cibola or Quivira or their kindred illusory cities, which seem to be born spontaneously in answer to men's desires. Dec-

ades after Narváez and De Soto and Coronado had lost
their hopes and the lives of their men, and—perhaps more
astonishing—fairly close to the time when Luna and Menéndez and the Spanish raiders in the west had found nothing but disappointment in their searches, the marvelous cities and magical mountains decorate America. As the succinct Raleigh put it, "The desire of gold will answer many
objections."

Let "La grand Copal" represent the image which suc-
ceeds to Quivira and Cibola in the late sixteenth century,
since it can be shown to cross the boundaries of national
consciousness, dazzling the minds of Spanish, English, and
French. An Englishman, Henry Hawks, who lived in New
Spain for five years, testifies to the Spanish "Copalla"—
"they have used much labor and diligence in the seeking of
it: they have found the lake on which it should stand, and a
canoa, the head whereof was wrought with copper curiously, and could not find or see any man nor the town
which to their understanding should stand on the same
water, or very near the same."

The close relationship to the Seven Cities is obvious, but
Copal is even more richly endowed, being surrounded by
mountains where "there is great store of crystal, gold, and
rubies, and diamonds." So states a Frenchman brought
home from St. Augustine by Francis Drake, adding "that a
Spaniard brought from thence a diamond which was worth
five thousand crowns, which Pedro Menéndez the marquis,
nephew to old Pedro Menéndez that slew Ribault, & is now
governor of Florida, weareth." Hawks adds further, and
even more significantly that the mountains "shine so bright
in the day in some places, that they cannot behold them,
and therefore they travel unto them by night."

Forever invisible by day, appearing and reappearing
under different names—to the north Saguenay and Norumbega, in the middle continent not only Copal but Cosa—the

magnificent cities not only defied the finding, but defied disbelief, perdurable in the night's landscape.

If Ptolemy had not taken explorers directly to Asia, he had made it inevitable for Asia to come to America.

17 / Nature as Concept and Commodity

Fantasy, born of science and tradition, was beyond doubt the chief creator of the original American setting. Nevertheless, the traveler-writers who subscribed to and described these lands and waters of the imagination, with their cities and stupendous wealths, were for the most part the men who had seen the actualities as well as the visions. They had walked the beaches which were not gold, picked up the pebbles which were not diamonds, looked at mountains which were not crystal, and found mines more likely copper than any more precious metal.

Their factual comments are usually brief. The coast offers good harbors, or poor anchorage; it is low, sandy, and barren, or wild and rocky, or forested and fruitful. There are many rivers or few, their currents swift or slow, their beds deep or shallow. Such and such are the islands, promontories, peninsulas. The soil is fertile or sterile, bearing a heavy growth, or nothing but scrub. In either case, it is desert, that is to say, solitary and uncultivated.

Most of the description of this sort shows practical intent. Pilots had to know their courses, their shores, and seamarks. The records they kept were professional. Much of Cartier's first voyage is pilotage. On the Pacific coast, Cabrillo is a surveyor. His interest—or, more accurately, that of his journalist—in a land the margins of which he saw comes from the fear of shipwreck. Francis Drake, farther north on the Pacific coast, looking for a passage back to Europe, meets with severe cold, so that his men complain and he has to turn back "and seek the land . . . finding it not mountainous, but low plain land." Since he knows now that he must prepare his ship to cross the Pacific, he anchors in a "fair and good bay," and christens the country "Nova Albion . . . in respect of the white banks and cliffs, which lie towards the sea." His nephew's later rendering, perhaps to excuse his not finding the much-wanted strait, condemns the landscape. "Besides, how unhandsome and deformed appeared the face of the earth itself! showing trees without leaves, and the ground without greenness in those months of June and July." Even drought, or a cultural antipathy to wilderness can hardly explain such other descriptive terms as "the general squalidness and barrenness of the country," "those thick mists and most stinking fogs," or the hills covered with snow in midsummer.

The Vizcaíno expedition of 1602—not so far north—had no such extremes to report. "This realm of California," Father Ascensión writes, "is very large and embraces much territory. . . . It has a good climate, is very fertile, and abounds in many and various kinds of trees." In his California, he finds "abundant pastures of good grazing land." His wording is that of an observer, but since he usually refers to Lower California, he is more cordial than accurate.

Far to the east and long before him, Cabeza de Vaca had suffered by sea and land. He has little praise for a Gulf country "very thinly peopled and difficult to travel for the bad passages, the woods and lakes . . . dense forests, immense deserts and solitudes." His words show his fear of the southeastern wilderness, just as, farther to the west in the arid regions, his constant search for food, his bare aim of survival, reveal the landscape in its desolation. Yet, even more remarkable, the sparseness of his comment testifies to his little attention. His world of nature exists only for its benefits to men.

Coronado's troopers at the Grand Canyon try to measure and reach its depths; its size moves them, its magnitude, but not its magnificence. On the plains of Kansas, they observe the huge sweep of the earth, pasture for incalculable numbers of buffalo, but Coronado's descriptive phrase reads, "these barren lands." Over fifty years later, the Oñate travelers find little more to celebrate—Father Escobar's New Mexico is "poor and cold." To the east and north they add something to Coronado's description, praising this or that small river, its banks thick with walnut trees, its land a "good country, bounded on both sides by the coolest of rivers and by pleasant groves." Once again, they wonder at the buffalo, and once again they scant the "description of the country."

Their compeers on the Atlantic coast are rarely more generous. John Smith vigorously enjoys his Virginia, but his early comment is likely to be limited—"The most of this country though desert, yet exceeding fertile; good timber, most hills and dales, in each valley a crystal spring." Later, in *A Map of Virginia*, he presents what is literally a verbal map of the area he has explored, but his first response is succinct enough to suggest unconcern if not indifference.

In sum, then—with exceptions duly to be noted—many of the early writers of northern America deserve the comment which Gilbert Chinard made about the seventeenth-century Jesuits—they traveled through the spectacular landscape like blind men. Their compatriot Champlain is typical enough. He finds the Saguenay a "fine" river, with a great waterfall; its banks "of mountains and rocky promontories" he terms "a very unattractive country . . . mere wastes." The Lachine Rapids fill him with fear, reasonably enough since they have just drowned two men. Of admiration or enjoyment of their wildness, he shows not a trace.

To expect him to do so is anachronistic. The romantic revolution lay nearly two centuries ahead. The neoclassical reading of virtue in the natural scene, however tempered, was nearer by, but still of a future era. Nor would such men as Champlain have responded readily to concepts and images alien to their experience.

Their school of nature might indeed be named the empirical. The desert or wilderness, unsubjected or little subjected by men, they find both dangerous and hostile. They see neither beauty nor virtue in falls of water which are killers; nor in equally mortal snow and ice; nor in deadly swamps and dark forests. Their effort is to survive, not to celebrate. Not only did they not see the grandeur they confronted, they suggest in their few words or the lack of them that they often did not look. Where they are close and specific in observation, they have usually some special purpose to serve. John Smith pauses to describe an ideal site for the building of a city. Spanish priests, whatever the actuality, will praise the soil upon which they wish to establish missions.

The main purpose to be served by both description and praise was colonization. As projects of settlement shape up, their planners turn much closer attention to the land and its growths. To recognize their practicality is not to deny their enthusiasm. Ribaut, with the planting of Charlesfort before him, can still write in a spirit wholly genuine, "We sailed and viewed the coast all along with unspeakable pleasure, of the odorous smell and beauty of the same"; or, "we entered and viewed the country thereabouts, which is the fairest, fruitfulest, and pleasantest of all the world, abounding in honey, venison, wild fowl, forests, woods of all sorts, palm trees, cypress and cedars, bayes the highest and greatest, with also the fairest vines in all the world. . . ."

Barlow's "delicate garden" of some twenty years later comes out of the same sort of sensibility. The response is not typical of the age but does renew the supernal image which Columbus first sketched in. Barlow's paradise not only suggests the earlier tropical Eden of discovery, but is reminiscent as well of the fabulous luxuriance of St. Brandan's Island.

The acceptance, once made, is complete. Whatever the menaces of tropics and subtropics, they did not appear at first sight. David Ingram's realistic Florida is "most excellent fertile and pleasant," its "great plains" varied with "great and huge woods. . . . And after that plains again, and in other places great closes of pasture environed with most delicate trees." Palms, bananas, pepper, grapes, herbs, flowers, and "maize" decorate his landscape for him. And if some items of the list are the fruits of wishes rather than crops of the soil, none are more fanciful than license permits, while the fairytale monsters of the narrative offer no threats in Elysium.

The tensions of a double interpretation are hinted at for the south, rather than written out. Ribaut's hurricane is duly recorded but not presented as the destroyer in Eden. Barlow admits no natural violence. His spoiler, barely suggested, is war among the Indians. Ralph Lane, early rejoicing in the "goodliest soil under the cope of heaven," touches later upon "casualty of contrary winds or storms," but puts no stress upon the chance of trouble, nor does he make any point of the destructiveness of the storm which finally defeats him. His Virginia remains, according to Hakluyt, "this paradise of the world."

Even in the far north, where the juxtapositions of natural bounty and natural malice, in feast or famine, ease or suffering, were sharp, the voyager is likely to let his contrasts speak for him. He offers no concept of a nature both friendly and hostile. Cartier's "land God gave to Cain" is a country literally so stony and so wild that he refuses to call it earth. It is ground fit only for beasts and outcasts, its "treshautes" mountains savage also.

But the Cartier journalist, if he offers no interpretation of nature, does pay attention to his particulars. Low, level ground meets his taste, and therein he celebrates the most beautiful fields it is possible to see, or magnificent trees and meadows. Cedar, pine, elm, oak, and willow make the air sweet, while in the grass grow white and red grapes, and strawberries, and grains ripened in the sun's heat and fed on by a multitude of birds.

A year afterwards, along the St. Lawrence in summer, he resumes his lyric of praise for the goodly trees and land, the "smooth, level, and tillable ground," the great mountains interspersed with rich valleys, and the grand, broad, and extensive rivers with their "falls of water," the tumultuous "saults," impossible to pass. He is a poetic landscapist, endowed with purity of vision and of style.

Where abstraction is concerned, he makes the same simple, never-worded assumption. The natural world exists for the use of men. Neither a philosopher nor—beyond the piety of a devout Roman Catholic—a theologian, he represents an attitude which was common enough to call for no reminder and to need no definition. If Cain inherited the desert wastes, the sons of Abel were rightful heirs to a fruitful wilderness.

The utilitarians were, however, by no means the only group to respond to the American scene. The more bookish, and sometimes more scholarly, writers of Europe both early and late are likely to pick up the theme of paradise and translate it into classical terms. Their landscape is that of the Golden Age, the generous playground of a happy people. Peter Martyr employs and enjoys the concept, though evidence makes him qualify it. In a very different setting, Nicholas of Linne revives by his geography the classical

theme of the hyperboreans, the gay and handsome people of
the Pole and its whirlpool. John Davis, practical seaman of
the late sixteenth century, echoes him, giving the classical
fable a Christian and Platonic twist, the Polar race being of
"a wonderful excellency," and possessed of an "exceeding
prerogative . . . for they are in perpetual light. . . ." In
such references, the new world concept of nature takes on
the luster of poetry, the idealization of learned authority.
The turn is, of course, to fable once again. The utopia of a
long past time becomes the utopia of far distance. The land
is "mighty," or "large," and always "fruitful." Atlantis is
the prototype, but Aristotle's island discovered by Cartha-
ginians, and the "mighty island" of Diodorus Siculus, and
Virgil's land beyond "ultima Thule" add to the connotations.

Among those who actually walked the earth of the new
world, the classicist above all is Lescarbot. A mindfulness of
the Golden Age and its utopian setting pervades his text.
The landscape of his new world is healthful, beautiful, in-
vigorating, rich, and wholly enjoyable if men will live in an
honest association with it. For him, nature becomes, if not
the teacher of virtue, at least its nursery. The scene wherein
men are demonstrably happy is that in which they may become good. Its original children, the Indians, are not wholly
sinless, though virtue prevails in them. "They follow nature;
and if we curb anything of that instinct, it is the commandment of God which makes us do so, whereunto many stop
their eyes."

If he could not grant a nature wholly perfect in a philo-
sophical sense, he could find no fault in the physical scene.
"This port is environed with mountains on the north side:
towards the south be small hills, which (with the said mountains) do pour out a thousand brooks, which make that
place pleasanter than any other place in the world: there
are very fair falls of waters, fit to make mills of all sorts. At

the east is a river between the said mountains and hills, in the [which] ships may sail fifteen leagues and more, and in all this distance is nothing of both sides the river but fair meadows . . . the said port, for the beauty thereof was called Port Royal."

Lescarbot's philosophic qualification of natural excellence is clearly religious. The curb upon nature is the commandment of God. The theological doctrine reads that all nature fell with Adam, and is depraved. In logic, then, Lescarbot's social and his theological doctrines are incompatible. Because he is not a strict thinker, he makes no recognition of this, and if he had, could very likely have written his way out of his dilemma. His effort is less towards argument than persuasion, his appeal to senses and enthusiasms rather than reasonings. Yet, inevitably, into his pages comes the violence of the landscape he so warmly praises. Cartier's horrific winter of ice and snow, the fearful storms of the south, and the suffering from starvation among the Indians, all are parts of his narrative, but he puts little stress upon them.

The English voyagers to the north are those who most closely word what can be called the medieval or theological concept of nature, in which nature is satanic—at the worst extreme—or at best, God's instrument for the punishment and amendment of sinful humanity. Nature is thereby either an antagonist or a scourge. George Best, Frobisher's captain, records the escape from shipwreck on a sunken rock, from crushing islands of ice, from fog, snow, high seas and winds, with the devout comment, "as their dangers were great, so their God was greater." In his landscape of "very high lands, mountains . . . covered with snow" he does not directly place Lucifer, but makes note that the people are "great enchanters, and use many charms of witchcraft. . . . And they made us by signs to understand, lying groveling with their faces upon the ground, and making a

noise downward, that they worship the devil under them."
A contemporary of Best's is less pictorial. His devil may or
may not be subterranean; he is simply "that spiritual Phar-
oah, the devil" who holds captive the people of Newfoundland.

In a strict reading, Best and his fellows are saying that
God is on the side of men, whom He helps and preserves
against nature and Satan. However, they also offer that
other interpretation by which a hostile natural world is
God's instrument to teach sinners and to bring them to repentance. Best expresses the former conviction and hints at
the latter when he describes the escape of storm-driven
ships, thrown against the rocks. "Many times also by means
of fog and currents being driven near upon the coast, God
lent us even at the very pinch one prosperous breath of wind
or other, whereby to double the land and avoid the peril,
and when that we were all without hope of help, every man
recommending himself to death, and crying out, Lord now
help or never, now Lord look down from heaven and save
us sinners, or else our safety commeth too late: even then
the mighty maker of heaven, and our merciful God did deliver us: so that they who have been partakers of these dangers do even in their souls confess, that God even by miracle
hath sought to save them. . . ."

Thomas Ellis is even more explicit. His nature is the tool
and instrument of the divine will. In storm, God administers
punishment "for amendment's sake," and in calm after
storm, gives "consolation." He thereby uses winds and seas
to exercise not only justice, but mercy. "For through the
darkness and obscurity of the foggy mist, we were almost
run on rocks and islands before we saw them: But God
(even miraculously) provided for us, opening the fogs that
we might see clearly, both where and in what danger we
presently were, and also the way to escape: or else without
fail we had ruinously run upon the rocks."

The landscape of the Northwest Passage is by necessity for the most part seascape. To the south lies the "supposed continent" of America, to the north Asia. Both show mountains of bare rock, and lands of desolation, ice- and snow-covered. "There is very little plain ground and no grass, except a little which is much like unto moss that groweth on soft ground, such as we get turfs in. There is no wood at all. To be brief there is nothing fit or profitable for the use of man, which that country with root yieldeth or bringeth forth. . . ."

Once again the geography is Ptolemaic. The phrase "nothing fit or profitable for the use of man" once again brings the doctrine of nature back to a doctrine of use. The repetition is valuable not only in itself, for emphasis, but also for the recognition that the four interpretations of nature, however contradictory in logic, were concurrent. Moreover, a particular writer, such as George Best, may assume that God intends the natural world for the use of humanity, that Satan attacks mankind through natural forces which men can resist only with God's help, and finally that God himself commands the elements to strike his wayward people, for their redemption. Best even shows faint vestiges of the classical concept in his insistence upon "temperate and commodious habitation under the poles," though he nowhere names the hyperboreans and nowhere in the polar regions finds a nature wholly benevolent. Like Columbus, he puts his Earthly Paradise in the tropics. He had, after all, suffered with Frobisher in the Arctic.

If any one concept of nature prevails over the others, it is that of usefulness. Nature is the provider for men, in the cosmic scheme. Whatever embellishments and profundities classical scholarship and religious belief may offer, few writers fail to look to the landscape for food or exploitable wealth. A country which yields "nothing fit or profitable" does not excite admiration. A coast such as Verrazzano finds along the Atlantic—of "most sweet savours" promising "drugs, or spicerie, and other richesse of gold"—is that which is as well aesthetically pleasing. Barren lands are ugly as well as threatening.

When projects of settlement advanced, the "commodities" of the landscape took on a sharper importance. Early and late, the voyagers delightedly found them to be Asian. Silks in the form of "silk grass," spices—cinnamon, nutmeg, pepper, cloves—and drugs such as rhubarb, benjamin (or benzoin), and cassia offered promises of wealth, along with Asian gold, silver, and jewels.

These hopes and wishes persisted long after they were for the time being proved false. Cartier's third voyage to Canada, made in preparation for Roberval's settlement, continues them. The writer barely draws breath between his report of practicalities—the growing of cabbages, turnips, and lettuce and the finding of ground "apt for tillage"—and the gathering of stones "esteemed to be diamonds," and of "certain leaves of fine gold as thick as a man's nail."

For Florida, John Sparke provides close description. "The land itself . . . flourisheth with meadow, pasture ground, with woods of cedar and cypress, and other sorts, as better cannot be in the world. They have for apothecary herbs, trees, roots and gummes great store, as storax liquida [liquidamber], turpentine, gum, myrrh, and frankincense." He is skeptical of local gold and silver, believing that the Indians have got theirs from Spanish wrecks; however, "it is not unlike, but that in the main where are high hills, may be gold and silver as well as in Mexico, because it is all one main." Pearls he knows there are. With equal certainty, he knows the country produces "unicorns horns," because he finds "many pieces" among Laudonnière's Frenchmen. Needless to say, he is naming one of the most valuable of commodities.

Food is a more immediate necessity, however. Along the

forested Atlantic coast, say all the reports, fish abound. The Newfoundland and New England areas provide "incredible quantity, and no less variety of kinds of fish in the sea and fresh waters, as trouts, salmons, and other fish to us unknown: also cod . . ." Whales, herring, bonito, turbot, flying fish, oysters, lobsters, mussels "with others infinite" add to the bounty of the sea, richer off Massachusetts—so, in 1602, John Brereton's *Relation* boasts—than in the more famous banks further north.

As "incredible" are the flocks of birds which especially throng the many bird islands, where a ship could replenish her stores of food with no risk or effort. Madoc's Penguin Island justifies its name by the "great number" of the fowl, and the "infinite number" of their eggs. Elsewhere, cranes, herons, bittern, geese, ducks, teal "and other fowls, in great plenty" crowd the shores.

The list of game animals and animals to be valued for their furs becomes a convention of the narrative. Later writers are likely to be somewhat more skeptical than David Ingram and John Sparke. Pring, sailing the New England coast, names stags, fallow deer, bears, wolves, foxes, lynx, "and (some say) tigers," as well as porcupines, long-nosed dogs, and "many other sorts of wild beasts."

The Indians are renowned as hunters on land or water. For Florida, Le Moyne's drawings show them deer stalking, and killing crocodiles. They make snares and traps for game and build fish weirs and are expert spear fishermen. They make gifts of venison or bear, oysters, mussels or clams, shad, cod, and mackerel. The explorers and settlers of Europe know that these, together with the fields of maize and squash, beans and potatoes, make the foods of the savages, but comparatively seldom do they themselves undertake to hunt or plant. Spurred by hunger they occasionally do so, but are more likely to depend on stores from home, or on trade with the Indians, or levies or raids against them.

Wealths of these practical kinds were nevertheless given importance, so that within the single voyage there is likely to be a group of paragraphs describing the produce of the country. Best's assemblage of voyages devotes a section of the text to the purpose, as does Smith's *Map of Virginia*. In the expansion, an essay begins to shape up to a degree of independence. By the seventeenth century, such an essay readily becomes a small book. John Josselyn's *Voyages to New-England*, or William Wood's *New Englands Prospect*, or Daniel Denton's *Description of New York*, or Thomas Budd's *Good Order Establish'd in Pennsylvania and New Jersey* will develop subject and form together, not through the working of influences, but through the dictates of the experience and its record.

Within the sixteenth century, even, the evolution accomplishes itself, but only in a single instance. Thomas Harriot's *A briefe and true report of the new found land of Virginia* (1588) achieves the full essay form, developing the subject of "commodity" as a defense of Raleigh's plans for Virginia. Having disposed of those who have "slandered" Roanoke, Harriot proceeds, reasonably, to put before reasonable men the harvests they may expect, so that they may judge how their "dealing therein," by trading or planting, may bring them "profit and gain." To this end, he divides his commodities into two groups, those "merchantable" and those "for victual and sustenance of man's life."

Because Harriot was a highly trained observer, and a man of balanced judgment, his lists offer the best possible evidence not only of what men found in Virginia but also of what they expected and wanted to find. "Silk of grass, or grass silk" comes first, followed by "worm silk," flax, hemp, minerals, resins, drugs, dyes, wine, oil from walnuts, furs, civet, and pearls. He is hopeful of growing sugar cane, oranges, lemons, and quinces. He suggests even higher hopes.

"Many other commodities by planting may there also be raised, which I leave to your discreet and gentle considerations: and many also may be there, which yet we have not discovered. Two more commodities of great value, one of certainty, and the other in hope, not to be planted, but there to be raised and in short time to be provided, and prepared, I might have specified." His nod and wink to the knowledgeable leaves him uncommitted to gold and silver, but very likely committed his readers more strongly than any forthright claim.

Such being the merchantable goods, Harriot proceeds to describe the goods "of victual and sustenance," Indian corn, beans, squash, oranges (to which Pliny assigns fourteen remedies), sunflowers, roots of various sorts, nuts, fruits, and finally game animals, fowl, and fish. Among the herbs, he highly recommends tobacco for "many rare and wonderful experiments of the virtues thereof." Like most of the vegetables, it was unfamiliar to the English palate. The meats, fruits, and fishes would have been less strange. Whatever the category, he offers the statement or implication of plenty. Yet he knew, having himself hungered with Lane, that Englishmen at Roanoke had come near to starving, for all the abundance of Virginia.

He employs the same sort of reticence in writing about the Indians, hardly touching upon their eventual hostility to the English but putting his attention and his intelligence to the understanding of this new race of men. However much of his knowledge he held back, he does present his savages with a broad understanding of their differences in behavior and thought. He condescends to them, without doubt, but at the same time considers them deserving of his close scrutiny. They are not to be feared, he assures his readers, but neither are they to be scorned, since "in their proper manner (considering the want of such means as we have), they

seem very ingenious." He then briefly sketches in "their natures and manners" in peace and war, their religious convictions, their fear of the English as supernatural beings,
and—somewhat disingenuously—their willingness to submit themselves to a stronger people.

Harriot's essay is that of a highly trained and orderly
mind. Clearly organized and consistent in its parts, it veers
from its subject only in including the Indians among the
commodities of the new country. It is no doubt unfair to
dwell upon the possible significance of this grouping, although even Harriot—for all his tolerant attention—in-
clines to think of the native peoples as part of a landscape.
The reason for the break in structure is, however, more
likely to be the one which Harriot himself suggests. He
needs not only to encourage planting for its profits, but also
to allay the fears of Indian attack upon the plantations. He
does this by suggesting that the savages are timid, weak,
and somewhat cowardly, and hold the English "in wonderful admiration."

The briefe and true report may originally have been composed as part of a larger and fuller "discourse" which Harriot declares that he wrote but which has never been found.
As the present text stands, the voyage pattern has completely disappeared, leaving only a trace of itself in the title
and subtitles, in its argument, in an occasional reference,
and in the conclusion. Harriot's ending is significant. Like
John Smith, he emphasizes the infinite possibilities of a
country still known only along its coasts. "Why may we not
then look for in good hope from the inner parts of more and
greater plenty, as well of other things, as of those which we
have already discovered?"

In the next breath, he returns to the theme of Asia, that
possibility which after nearly a century still overshone all
others. "What hope there is else to be gathered of the nature
of the climate, being answerable to the island of Japan, the

land of China . . . and of many other notable and famous countries, because I mean not to be tedious, I leave to your own consideration." Even for a scientist and mathematician such as Harriot, Ptolemy's world survives.

18 / *Brute Neighbors and Higher Laws*

Whatever the realisms, the geographically fabulous American continent offered a rich theatre of equally fabulous monsters. These, too, were often traditional, translated to new soil out of familiar authorities, or out of loosely formulated but firm religious beliefs. Beyond these, the Indians contributed certain inventions. Errors of observation, sensory illusions, misinterpretations, and the like no doubt added to the number. So too, the simple or complex hoax and the wish to entertain, at one extreme, and at the other the need to find adequate images to embody stress and terror. Social and moral purposes, as well, could create or re-create abnormalities and aberrations among animals and men.

By the evidence, chronology made little change in the process. If, by the end of the sixteenth and the beginning of the seventeenth century, the writer felt himself obliged to supply the titillation of a monster or two, even the late writer shows little reluctance to comply. Champlain's demonic "Gougou" of *Des Sauvages* is actually more warmly extravagant than Ingram's earlier "Collochio" or Pigafetta's "Setebos." The Gougou takes the shape of a dreadful woman, a gigantic devourer of human flesh. The huge and horrible beast is provident, however, keeping captive Indians in "his" enormous pouch, ready for appetite. According to Champlain's suggestion, the island of the Gougou is the residence of some devil. Thereby Champlain goes over into the more serious aspect of religious reference. Lescarbot, his contemporary and an equally devout man, nevertheless mocked the story and Champlain for telling it, but his unusual skepticism did not put a stop to the retailing of prodigies, any more than Champlain's credulity had begun it.

Dating, then, can be put out of consideration. Mermaids and mermen live outside of time, though they may be endowed with varied interpretations. Henry Hudson's mermaid of 1608, who looked "earnestly" on the men who watched her, wore a melancholy cast of countenance but offered them no harm. Job Hortop's "monster in the sea" who showed himself "from the middle upward" . . . proportioned like a man, of the complexion of a mulatto, or tawny Indian" is not directly hostile, but sixteen days of "wonderful foul weather" followed his appearance. Thevet, by 1557, had gathered for America a collection of "singularities" from many sources, but chiefly from Pliny. He manipulates his anecdotes rather cleverly, often disavowing conviction but nevertheless reaping the dramatic harvest. He can assert that the savages do not grow fur, and from the denial gain references to those who say they do, and gain a second time by recalling a Frenchman of Normandy who was covered with scales, and still a third by going back to the satyrs. Through ingenious sequences and juxtapositions, he collects for the new world such other rarities as the basilisk and an assortment of demons, native and foreign, as well—of course—as the unicorn.

The unicorn was especially sought after, and as to its horn regularly found. In itself, the gentle (to maidens) animal was more likely to be heard of than seen on land; on

the ocean, the narwhal became the sea unicorn. Frobisher
took back its single, magical tusk, countervailent to poisons,
as a "jewel" for Queen Elizabeth's "wardrobe of robes," a
gift particularly appropriate because of the unicorn's
affinity for virgins.

Three quarters of a century earlier than Frobisher, and
much better schooled, Peter Martyr none the less eagerly
looked for marvels in the new Indies, and because returning
adventurers talked freely to him he had no trouble collect-
ing them. In a black sea off the gulf of Panama "swam fish,
as large as dolphins, singing melodiously, as is recounted of
the Sirens." Answering the disbeliever, Martyr finds it necessary to defend the color of the water—nature is capable of
infinite variation—rather than the melodies heard upon it.

He is, of course, going back to an old story, of which St.
Brandan's voyage provides another version, in which the
fish listen to music instead of providing it. Homecoming
sailors no doubt confirmed the anecdote. Very likely they
also told him the story of Matu, the friendly manatee,
which is Pliny's dolphin in American dress. Peter Martyr's
cucurio (the cucuya, or fire beetle), however genuine,
evokes in him no more and no less wonder than the half
truth of Matu or the full falsities of harpies and sea serpents
upon which he expatiates elsewhere. "O admirable fertility!" he exclaims, and lets enthusiasm have free way.

For Florida, John Sparke matches him and provides a
scientific rationale. "Of beasts in this country besides deer,
foxes, hares, polecats, conies, ounces, and leopards, I am not
able certainly to say: but it is thought there are lions and tigers as well as unicorns; lions especially; if it be true that is
said, of the enmity between them and the unicorns; for
there is no beast but hath his enemy, as the cony the pole-
cat, a sheep the wolf, the elephant the rhinoceros; and so of
other beasts the like: insomuch, that whereas the one is, the
other cannot be missing."

The full course of sixteenth-century writing is equally fertile in providing wonders of every category. Beyond a point, accumulating them becomes an antiquarian amusement, the critical value of which lies in the recognition that while there is little change in the fabulous testimonials, the presenting of them seems—as has been suggested—to become a requirement upon the writer about America, a literary convention not to be ignored. It is impossible to puzzle out with what eyes Champlain studied the West Indian bird of paradise, to discover that it had no feet and therefore "must remain continually in the air without ever coming to the earth till it falls dead." His editor suggests that he never saw a live one, but only footless feathers readied for the market. This is not Champlain's presentation, however, and simply spoils the fun. No such reduction to plausibility will allow for his best creation, the "dragons of strange figure"—eagle-headed, bat-winged, lizard-bodied, and scaly tailed. The figure is strange indeed, with the forequarters of a griffin and the hinder parts of a cockatrice. Champlain accurately assures his readers that the creatures "are not dangerous, and do no harm to anybody, though to see them, you would say the contrary."

The likelihood is that such items were offered and accepted not only for belief but for poetic pleasure, like Charlie Brown's Snoopy, and so exempted from scrutiny. Literary flourishes, as harmless as Champlain's monster, they gave satisfactions and thereby should have existed if they did not.

The human prodigies of the new world point to different and ultimately to serious significances. Equally fantastical accounts of them exist, of necessity, since the European was trained to look abroad for monstrous peoples. Even Marco Polo reported "male" and "female" islands in the Eastern oceans, while André Thevet in discussing the inhabitants of

America felt compelled to deal at length with the Amazons of the "Pacific coast." Where on the Pacific coast, he does not say. He had perhaps picked up Cortés as authority, who in turn had the authority of the Indians, that north of Mexico "there was an island inhabited only by women." He certainly knew tales of the Orellana who navigated the river named for them. He may have heard of the Amazons "of Chile." His vague attribution—"the Spaniards aforesaid"— comes into the Brazilian sequence, but is generous enough to take care of Amazons wherever met. So too his description requires only water scenery for "these warlike women" who live apart, on islands walled by tortoise shells, from which they hurl threats and arrows at their invaders. Thevet's illustration shows them, as his editor puts it, clothed only in their modesty and their weapons. Wherever their "terrifying" faces looked out upon the Spaniards, with the disagreeable expressions he ascribes to them, he moves rapidly to more absorbing questions. Did they or did they not burn their breasts in order to be more dextrous in war? Did the Scythian Amazons maintain their lineage by prostituting themselves?

By such ingenious verbalisms, Thevet decorates the unusual Asian women whom he had inherited, whom Columbus got news of on his first voyage with their male counterparts nearby, and whom Peter Martyr placed with assurance on the island of Martinique. Later narrators, in turn, kept them alive and shrewdly peculiar, on the page if not on the Pacific coast.

Among like heritages in something resembling human form, pygmies at war with cranes perform for Roberval along the St. Lawrence River, while giants, cannibals, and demons multiply until they become acceptances of the landscape. Others, now creatures of tradition, now exaggerations or inventions, join the more normal abnormalities.

The outstanding group is arranged by Father Escobar of the Oñate expedition to California:

> "The Indian Otata told us . . . of a nation of people with so large and long ears that they dragged on the ground, and that five or six persons could stand under each one . . .
>
> ". . . there was another . . . whose men had virile members so long that they wound them four times around the waist . . .
>
> ". . . other people . . . dwelt on the shore of a lake, and . . . at night they all slept under the water.
>
> ". . . there was another nation . . . whose people sustained themselves solely on the odor of their food . . . because they lacked the natural means of discharging excrement from the body."

He includes also the less spectacular fur growers, unipeds, and tree sleepers, and hedges his own credulity—"each one may believe what he wishes"—but commits himself to an honest report. "I dare to tell what I heard a multitude of Indians report in my presence, for I must uphold the truth of what I saw with my own eyes, and I shall do so." His logical leap from hearing to seeing has a certain grace.

These reports, like those of fabulous animals, might contribute merely to entertainment, if it were not for the linkage. They put the "naturals" among the brutes, not in the human kingdom. Thevet, with a consistency unusual for him, applies such terms to the Americans as "pauvres brutaux," and "bestes irraisonnables," who live altogether without faith, law, creed, or culture. Yet he is kind, tolerant, hopeful of their amendment, and ultimately not consistent at all. Others, such as Henry Hawks, the Englishman in Mexico who writes of "wild" and "tame" savages, offer the kind of assumption which is stronger than statement.

The delineation is by no means the only one, nor that which necessarily prevails. Columbus, it is to be remembered, found the Indians whom he met as comely as their

groves and hills, fit inhabitants of his Elysian island. Yet he
instantly thought of them as idolaters and slaves, while he
called them wholly innocent, little short of moral perfection.
When, on his second voyage, he returned to Hispaniola to
find his garrison massacred, he faced his own dilemma and
was faced with the single, active definition of his followers,
that the Indians were subhuman, fit only for labor and extermination.

The complexities of attitude towards the aborigines increase rather than diminish. As they were being killed off in
the islands, Europe was restoring to them their idyllic character, and finding in their ways of life a contrast to cor-
rupted civilization. Peter Martyr puts his first emphasis
upon ideality. The savages "go naked, they know neither
weights nor measures, nor that source of all misfortunes,
money; living in a golden age, without laws, without lying
judges, without books, satisfied with their life, and in no
wise solicitous for the future." He admits, however, that not
even the dwellers in an earthly paradise are free of "ambition and the desire to rule," and reflects that even in the age
of gold "there is never a moment without war." He does not
resolve the contradictions which he recognizes, but lets his
"golden age" analogy prevail over realism, to outlast by
many generations the short physical term of those who first
suggested it.

In constant repetition, it becomes a stereotype which is
sometimes identified with the eighteenth-century Rous-
seauistic assertion of natural virtue and nobility. Apart from
the distortion of Rousseau, the identification is doubtful. In
the Golden Age—or age of Saturn or Chronos—the question of virtue is hardly raised; rather, the state of happiness.
Free of care and labor, its people are fed by fruits and herbs,
and devote themselves to games, songs, and dances, living
wholly without malice, sickness, or the fear of death, in an
innocence which is without temptation. Columbus's inno-

cent savage, like Peter Martyr's, is a child, gay rather than noble, simple rather than profound, nourished by rather than attuned to elemental forces.

The classical image, taken over to kinds and scenes wholly alien to Greece and Rome, wears an incompatibility which did not trouble its translators. Nor did another sort of incongruity disturb them, if they were bent on ideality—to the north, a realism of cold, hunger, and disease, or, everywhere, a subjection not only to the hostilities of men, but to those of storm, drought, heat, and flood. After a century in which firsthand knowledge of the Indians had accumulated, Lescarbot, who had himself lived among the Indians, could repeat the Age of Saturn analogy, while he wrote down Cartier's account of them, assembled his own, and presented other incongruous interpretations. Neither Cartier's singing, dancing forest creatures, greedy for toys and instinct with fears, nor his famished, desperate, carrion-eating beggars; neither Lescarbot's shrewd, friendly Membertou, nor his "sauvages tousjours en crainte" and subject to "faulses visions et imaginations" fit the pattern. And yet . . . and yet . . . wherever the reference appears, it holds, because it enforces the contrast to European depravity. Montaigne, more than half a century after Peter Martyr and nearly half a century before Lescarbot, used even the "cannibals" of Brazil to castigate the vices of civilization. The theme of American purity and European corruption was born early, and born in the old world, not the new.

For all of that, the brutish portrayal of the Indian persisted, so that he emerges with a double identity. The ignoble counters the noble Indian in an antithesis far from clear, intellectually speaking, posed and developed by writers hardly aware of the process in which they were taking part.

19 / The Indian Is a New Man

The voyager among unknown men is usually constrained to describe them in the terms of his own culture. Only rarely can he rest satisfied with the physical persons he meets, but edges over into distortions, and into condemnation or praise on social, moral, or religious grounds, the measurements of which he has brought with him. So the writer in America begins at once the attempt to assimilate the Indian, whom he wishes to present as fact and in being, into his own conventions. He may even do so by a complete rejection. In a more complex process, he adapts the strange to the familiar, and thereby alters both.

A minor illustration of the process appears in the discussion of skin color. The majority of observers report the Indian complexion as a matter of sunburn, dyes, or paint. George Best is one of the few who consider it a "natural infection," and Best knows that he must supply evidence to support his opinion, or he will not be believed. Likewise the origin of the Indians, once they cease to be Indians of India, may be given over to the Ten Lost Tribes, the Welsh, the early Greeks, or almost any group the writer's fancy and training elect.

By an inevitability of history, religious beliefs presented the sharpest incompatability between Indian and European. The Christian of whatever creed could have no tolerance for the Indian as pagan; as a convert, however, he gained immediate sufferance. Persistent idolatry made him vulnerable on religious, social, and intellectual grounds. Columbus humbly saw himself as God's agent for the conversion of the savages and the propagation of the faith, without which the Indian was damned. For Columbus, the Indian's heathenism, not his race or the color of his skin, committed him to subjection and slavery. In the event, it often condemned him to death.

His conversion remained an obligation upon believers of every establishment or sect. Both Protestants and Catholics, however divergent otherwise, agreed in this duty, while Englishmen, Frenchmen, and Spaniards, whatever their political and national differences, were unanimous in declaring that the savages must be taught religious truth, although they varied widely in defining the nature of that truth.

When the converted Indian gains his entitlement to salvation, he should in reason also gain his entitlement to full humanity. Indeed the proselytizing effort implicitly admits his humanity, but also gives justification for conquest, while Indian resistance to Christian dominance confirms, for others besides Villagrá, his brutish and even satanic nature. In defeat he becomes a captive in war, and may legally be enslaved on that ground.

Thereupon the confusions of attitude and behavior multiply. From the Spanish beginnings, both secular and religious authorities insisted that he be brought into the church. Quite early he was officially, though not effectively, protected from abuse. Slavery was forbidden but widely used. By a royal decree of 1573, invasions of Indian territory became "pacifications," not conquests. The nomenclature

did not change the event. The rebel Indian emerges as the
devil's child, the submissive Indian as a serf, ward of a government which had words but not means to protect its
many adopted children from the natural offspring of its culture. A Villagrá can respond to the noble epic defiance of
the satanic Indian hero, or the touching pastoral simplicity
of the faithful Indian woman, but meet the Indian on any
ground but his own, he cannot.

For the English, Sir George Peckham in *A true Reporte, Of
the late discoveries* (1583) sketches in the rationalizations
about as clearly as anyone. When he named Christopher
Columbus "the first instrument to manifest the great glory
and mercy of Almighty God in planting the Christian faith,
in those so long unknown regions," he was merely echoing
Columbus himself, and most of Columbus's successors.
Peckham went on to require that Englishmen also meet this
duty, thereby making "traffic and planting . . . unto the
savages themselves very beneficial and gainful," their conversion being the means "whereby they may be brought
from falsehood to truth, from darkness to light, from the
highway of death to the path of life, from superstitious idolatry to sincere Christianity, from the devil to Christ, from
hell to heaven."

Peckham's argument, in the course of which he never
puts aside the religious obligation, proceeds from the lawfulness of peaceful trade and planting to the lawfulness of
Christian defense against savage violence. Recourse to the
"Law of Arms" he can justify by citing the children of Israel
in the Old Testament, and—after Christ—"mighty and
puisant emperors and kings." Religion propagated by conquest becomes a historic duty of princes, which England
cannot refuse.

He is equally intent upon the "profitability" of the new
countries, both to the realm and to the individual. Is not the
workman—messenger of "God's great goodness and

mercy"—worthy of his hire? Moreover, the savage will gain a worldly benefit as well, "being brought from brutish ignorance to civility and knowledge," shown how to till the ground, taught "honest manners," trained in "mechanical occupations, arts, and liberal sciences," defended from cannibal neighbors, and preserved from human sacrifice.

Peckham's Indians are never people of a golden age. He does not call them such, nor does he explicitly condemn them. He merely wants them transformed, politically into submissive and useful subjects, economically into willing producers, and socially into pliant, imitation Englishmen. Wherever and whenever his persuasions fail him, or may not overcome the reluctances of his audience to abuse a helpless people, he returns to his religious theme, and regains certainty—"by Christian duty we stand bound." This he can assert, fearless of contradiction.

The statement is axiomatic, and requires no proof. If he had examined his reasoning, or collected wider evidence to support it, he would still have remained blind to its fabulous origins, by which the war in heaven has transferred itself to earth. The new world is Satan's. Indeed the fallen angels have taken refuge there, and from its fastnesses continue their awful rebellion. Thereby the Indians have taken them for their gods.

In Mexico, "Mutezuma" worships and consults with the devil. Henry Hawks reports of the "wild" as well as the "tame" people of New Spain. "They use divers times to talk with the devil, to whom they do certain sacrifices and oblations." The devil helps them in witchcraft, so that they have been able to hide the seven cities and "Copalla" from the Spaniards, who declare "that the witchcraft of the Indians is such, that when they come by these towns they cast a mist upon them, so that they cannot see them."

Hawks' pronoun confusions do not obscure his meaning. Moreover, he can tell two stories of mines made to disappear by sorcery. Since each instance shows greedy Spaniards trying to rob poor savages, the devil carries out the laws of justice. Hawks does not go so far in his analysis, but concludes his anecdotes with the comment, "and many other things have been done in this country, which men might count for great marvels."

The satanic interpretation led devout and merciful Spanish priests to their work of conversion, and some of them to the condemnation of a very different diabolism. For saintly men like Bartolomé de Las Casas, God created these native peoples "to be the happiest in the world." In ignorance of "matters of the faith," which they are eager to learn, they are nevertheless virtuous, "very simple, without subtlety, or craft, without malice, very obedient, and very faithful." Humble and peaceful, gentle, tender, and meek, they are natural Christians.

Satan's agents in the new world are not the savages, but the European invaders, the Spanish who have entered upon these "lambs" as killers, "incontinent . . . as wolves, as lions, and as tigers most cruel of long time famished: and have not done in those quarters these forty years past, neither yet do at this present, aught else save tear them in pieces, kill them, martyr them, afflict them, torment them, and destroy them by strange sorts of cruelties never neither seen, nor read, nor heard of the like. . . ."

Thereafter, Las Casas presents a history of atrocity so consistent and so appalling that it is still difficult to read without disgust. That he created what is called the "black legend" of Spanish ferocity is easy to believe. By the black record—however exaggerated his numbers—he did well to reverse the concept of satanism, informing his king about the king's own subjects, "that in those regions there are not any Christians, but devils. . . ."

The historical consequences of Las Casas' vehemence came about in official regulations, outlawing Indian slavery and attempting to control forced labor. In literature, the Indian as innocent victim remains, both in actuality and image; and in presenting him through his "kings" Las Casas loosely sketches in the noble savage as well. "The king and lord . . . Guarionex was very obedient and virtuous, naturally desirous of peace, and well affectioned." Guancanagari, who welcomed Columbus, received him "so graciously, bountifully, and courteously . . . that he could not have been better made of in his own country of his own father." The king of Xaragua, Behechio, governed a realm which was "the diamond over all the other realms in language and polished speech, in policy and good manners, the best composed and ordered. For as much as there were many noble lords and gentlemen, the people also being the best made and most beautiful."

Las Casas is among the earliest, then, to reverse the religious condemnation. The figure with which he replaces the brutish worshipper of Satan is ideal. For the same embellishment, Garcilaso de la Vega uses the vocabulary of the courtly romance. Verrazzano's hospitable Indian monarch, who entertains his visitors with sports, anticipates the fabulous Indian nobles of the Coronado cycle who enjoy the music of golden bells, and the feather-robed kings of Florida, carried in litters by their subjects.

Like mermaids and mermen, idealizations defy chronology and contradiction. The noble Indian neither supersedes the ignoble, nor yields to him. Laudonnière can record "the wonted perfidiousness of those wild people" while both he and Jacques Le Moyne present the ideal figure of the Indian king—that Athoré who was "handsome, foresighted, virtuous, robust, and great in stature . . . given to a grave modesty." Beside the august savage, the Europeans are the lesser men, subjects who have to acknowledge in their native host "majestas spectabilis"—kingship visible.

The two extremes of condemnation and admiration are

common. The Hakluyt voyages illustrate the wide range of judgment, and the confusions between the one and the other. On paper, the Indian might quite easily be Europeanized—as Peckham suggests, passing over the actualities too lightly; in the wilderness, acculturation was a different matter. Indeed, the evidence suggests assimilation the other way, when the European was pressed by hunger.

On the whole, however, neither way of living yielded to the other, except as the Indian was destroyed. The devout, self-sacrificial priest, from whom the saving of souls demanded every risk of life, made few converts and these of dubious faith. The practical English aim of trade was hardly as yet more successful. In motive and behavior, the Indian remained incalculable, a curiosity, a reality but with many of the qualities of an imaginary being.

His reality was not altogether ignored. Among the early narrators, Cabeza de Vaca manages to free himself, first of his preconceptions, and second of final judgments. Although his pitying savages "howl like brutes," he goes no further in reducing their humanity, but rather shows their humaneness. He finds in them no ideality beyond a generous kindness in a hunger-driven life. Probably because he shared their necessities for many years, he could come closer than many of his fellows to the unskewed report.

For the English, Thomas Harriot notably keeps to moderation. His savages are "simple," untaught but ingenious. Their ignorance may be mended, he thinks, and their idolatry redeemed. His account is cautious, balanced, reasonable, and devoid of large ideas.

Within the Roanoke group, not Harriot but John White the artist best delineates the actual Indian. Released from the connotations of language, he presents men, women, and children to the life indeed, in pose, movement, and expression. His figures are strange enough in their costuming, but their attitudes and faces are familiar. Humorous or responsible or austere, his "chiefe Herowans" are distinct individuals. His family group he makes not simply an assemblage of oddities, but a grouping of persons shown each according to his nature, gross, somber, dull, absent-minded, attentive, lively, or elegant. One of his women is foolish if not moronic, another amiable, another modest, and still another self-possessed. White must have been a man of wit, as he certainly was a shrewd genre painter, who had only Lescarbot for serious rival in Indian characterization.

Three attitudes, then, make for three interpretations of the savages. A benevolent enthusiasm idealizes them—they are people of a golden age or "natural" Christians; a scornful rejection brutalizes them—they are animals, and since they have human shape they are monstrous among beasts; an objective geniality realizes them as discrete personalities within a new kinship of the human race, whose novelty does not exile them from mankind. The last of the three is rare.

None of the three is likely to appear without confusions and even contradictions. And all of them are likely to contradict, confuse, and blur the fourth attitude, with its interpretation—that of social revolt, which begins negatively, in the rejection of European society, and moves forward to the acceptance of the Indian as archetype of natural virtue, and prefiguration of a new man, whether European or American. Within his landscape, with its fresh and generous fertility, he offers the future an image by which men may measure and perhaps recreate themselves, while his European counterpart within the same landscape of forest and field, following the prototype, can escape the sins and disfigurements of a vile and destructive social order.

As such an image he is—needless to say—a creature of the imagination, who emerges gradually and partially from sixteenth-century writing, never arriving at complete portraiture. The repeated comment reads that the Indians live wholly according to nature. This is not always a reference to the Golden Age, or an assignment to brutishness. Thevet, for an instance, wavers in his first general judgment of animalism to praise the savage restraint of appetite, the freedom from covetousness and envy, the equality of possessions, or—in sum—the "wealth" of contentment within poverty which requires no governance by men. All this, he suggests, is admirable, but does not go so far as to wish such virtuous satisfactions for himself or his readers. Other writers touch upon the Indian's generosity in giving, in hospitality, in friendliness; his immunity from property and its vices; his loyalty and good humor and his avoidance of quarrels and rancors within his tribe. All these qualities spare him human laws, while nature does him its honest justice. His dignity and courage become proverbial. His endurance, his hardihood, his indifference to pain—the list becomes long, and the praises many. A terser tribute grants that he may be murderous but is never mean.

Lescarbot, who carries the utopian Indian as far as the early development takes him, is quite ready to accept the Indian realities while he cultivates the vision. His new social order and its men are to be born of the fertile landscape he so warmly enjoyed. Time and again he celebrates the prosperity, literally the hopefulness of a land which waits only for tillage to come to full fruit.

> Car les iles Fortunées
> Sont certes infortunées
> Au pris de celles ci . . .
> Veu la grand' felicité
> Qui s'y voit de tout côté.

> For the Fortunate isles
> Are unfortunate isles
> Compared to these here . . .
> In view of happiness. Here you may see
> At every hand, felicity.

For Lescarbot, these more than fortunate isles are to become the birthplace of a new and virtuous man, indifferently Indian or European. Let the Indians become Christian; let Frenchmen learn from them to follow nature. Let both kinds cultivate the generous soil—

> *La terre y est plantureuse*
> *Pour rendre la gent heureuse . . .*

> The earth there is kind
> To make content mankind.

Admonishing his fellow countrymen, he writes, "If we did content ourselves with their simplicity, we should avoid many troubles that we put ourselves unto to have superfluities, without which we might live contentedly (because Nature is satisfied with little) and the coveting whereof makes us very often to decline from the right way and to stray from the path of justice."

He pays as close a care to "ces peuples vagabons qu'on appele sauvages," for whom he rejects the term.

> *Ce peuple n'est brutal, barbare, ni Sauvage*
> *Si vous n'appellez tels les hommes du vieil âge,*
> *Il est subtile, habile, & plein de jugement,*
> *Et n'en ay conu un manquer d'entendement,*
> *Seulement il demande un pere qui l'ensiegne*
> *A cultiver la terre, à façonner la vigne,*
> *A vivre par police, à être menager,*
> *Et souz des fermes toicts si-aprés heberger.*
> *Au reste à nôtre égard il est plein d'innocence*
> *Si de son Createur il avoit la science.*

> His race is not beastly, barbarous, nor savage,
> If you do not so call men of the ancient age;
> Subtle, adroit, and in appraisement clever,
> Dullness he never shows, poor understanding never.
> Give him a father, him to teach
> To dress the vine, the sod to breach,
> A rooftree for his house to raise,

Firm shelter for domestic days.
In all else harmless, free of blame,
Were he but schooled his God to name.

Reasonable enthusiast though he is, Lescarbot's simple
requirements were beyond the reach of both sorts. Of each
he demands amendment. No primitivist, he wishes his forest
innocents to stop their wanderings, to raise their crops, to
live under roofs and by decent custom, and to learn to know
their Creator. The Frenchman, for his part, is to practice
moderation instead of excess, to obey the creed he professes,
to recognize his own barbarism and cure it by the example
of those whom he calls savage. By honesty in living, both
will gain happiness.

Thus Lescarbot poses a large role, and within it a large
theme for his native peoples of America—

> *Hôtes de ces forêts & des marins rivages . . .*
> *Qui aiment le travail, qui la terre cultivent,*
> *Et, libres, de ces fruits plus contents que nous vivent . . .*

> Hosts of these forests and these ocean coasts . . .
> Who love to work, who plant the ground, and, free,
> By its fruits live happier than we . . .

He is, then, a Christian, an agrarian, and a humanist,
prophet of a future golden age so easy to achieve that it has
never been reached. Lescarbot might have read its frustration in his own, by which he had to leave the world in
which he rejoiced to return to that which he despised.

20 / *Theme and Myth in America*

Within their many undertakings, the sixteenth-century writers of America notably express certain themes. The term is here used to mean an explicit general statement, drawn from the particulars. The central and pervading theme is best described by a single word—revelation. Every early American writer has heard and obeyed and echoed the commandment given to John: "Write the things which thou hast seen, and the things which are. . . ." Many of them have turned their pens to the third of the orders of vision—"the things which shall be hereafter." For all his pilgrims, and for himself as well, Purchas provides the text, "I also have been an Athenian with these Athenians, one delighting to tell, the others to hear some new thing."

From Verrazzano's boast that he has gone to a "new land" never seen before to John Smith's admission of ignorance, the process of disclosure and its ruling idea move through the sixteenth into the seventeenth century. Smith's inverse wording—his "three thousand miles, more than half . . . yet unknown to any purpose, no not so much as the borders of the sea . . . yet certainly discovered . . ."—

defines the search. His "they err, that think everyone that
hath been in Virginia or New England, understandeth or
knoweth what either of them are . . ." challenges the
imagination.

"What either of them are. . . ." In such a phrase, Smith
admits not only ignorance and the urging to knowledge, but
also the theme of infinite possibility, often imaged in fable,
and nearly as often in history and geography, and in landscape and its creatures. Peter Martyr had every reason to
exclaim, "Oh, admirable fertility!" in celebration of the
new Indies. When Columbus looked for—more exactly,
found—King Solomon's mines on Hispaniola, and saw
there an earthly paradise, his eyes widened to look for *the*
earthly paradise. His Asia-America, a revelation, provided
him with the setting for greater revelations.

The gold and silver of Mexico and Peru having been
counted and weighed, and the mines of Zacatecas and Po-
tosí found to be inexhaustible, the likelihood of still richer
hoards becomes a certainty. The catalogue repeats itself
and lengthens. Cosa, Chaunis Temoatan, Norumbega,
Copal, Lago de Oro, Cibola, Saguenay—no arithmetic
could contain their wealth, nor did scales exist to weigh it.
"For the rest, which myself have seen," Raleigh wrote of
Guiana, "I will promise these things that follow, which I
know to be true. Those that are desirous to discover and to
see many nations, may be satisfied within this river, which
bringeth forth so many arms and branches leading to several countries and provinces, about 2000 miles East and
West, and 800 miles South and North, and of these, the
most either rich in gold, or in other merchandises. The common soldier shall here fight for gold, and pay himself instead of pence, with plates of half a foot broad, whereas he
breaketh his bones in other wars for provant and penury.
Those commanders and chieftains that shoot at honor and
abundance, shall find there more rich and beautiful cities,

more temples adorned with golden images, more sepulchres filled with treasure, than either Cortez found in Mexico, or Pizarro in Peru: and the shining glory of this conquest will eclipse all those so far extended beams of the Spanish nation."

Not in treasure alone did the Americas admit the impossible. Raleigh's Orinoco, huge enough in all reality, merely pays tribute by exaggeration to the sense of hugeness. Herrera, the Spanish historian, in the same spirit proclaims an immeasurably large America. His American continents make "the fourth part of the world," whose "greatness . . . hath set the people in great admiration." To the south, his new world extends beyond fifty-two degrees (as indeed it does), "and goeth so high to the North that it hides itself under the Pole Artike, without knowing any end."

Such wealths and such an expanse of land stir the ambitions of kings and their subjects. In history, these lead to occupations and conquests; in literature to the theme of empire. In neither can the possibility of sovereignty over this fourth part of the world be ignored. The possibility of empire becomes the right to empire, a right which adheres originally to first discovery; later, to first occupation; and always to power. The general statement is expressed in religious as well as political terms. The Christian king has the pre-eminent claim over the "pagan" natives, and the duty to exercise that claim. He will enjoin his subjects to enter only "pure" lands, and forbid them to encroach upon territories held by other Christian majesties, unless, of course, the rival realms are at war. Queen Elizabeth, secure in her western entitlement through the discoveries of King Arthur, St. Brandan, Madoc son of Owen Gwined, and others including the Cabots, grants Sir Humphrey Gilbert "free liberty and license . . . to discover, find, search out, and view such remote, heathen and barbarous lands, countries and territories not actually possessed of any Christian prince or people. . . ." Against the idolater, Gilbert possesses the Christian right of subjugation. Politically, he is Elizabeth's vassal, and must pay her homage and the royal fifth of precious metals.

The promise of empire begins with Columbus, to become thereafter a stereotype, either as persuasion or as boast of accomplishment. Prospects of wealth and glory strengthen the ambitions of kings, but for Robert Thorne, in exhorting Henry VIII, glory is the first mover. "Experience prooveth that naturally all princes be desirous to extend and enlarge their dominions and kingdoms. Wherefore it is not to be marvelled, to see them every day procure the same, not regarding any cost, peril, and labour, that may thereby chance, but rather it is to be marvelled, if there be any prince content to live quiet with his own dominions. For surely the people would think he lacketh the noble courage and spirit of all other." Henry was not unmoved, though unmoving. Hakluyt speaks for the king's "intention . . . to have done some singular thing in this case," had death not prevented him.

Both king and subject celebrated the glory of empire. The Zenos' Prince Zichmni and the Welsh Prince Madoc are, however, the only royal personages known to have looked to the west for utopia, though many subjects of the throne found the ideal country there or about to be created there, well within the possibilities. The Antilia of the seven bishops, Plato's Atlantis, St. Brandan's blessed islands, and the kingdom of Ania to the north of the great strait are as little imaginary as maps and minds can make them. Raleigh's emissary, Laurence Keymis, can forgive England for doubting Columbus—"perhaps it might be imputed for some blame to the gravity of wise men, lightly to be carried with the persuasion and hope of a new found Utopia"—but he cannot forgive his countrymen their doubts of Guiana, that second millennial country of "a new world abounding with great treasure."

Far to the north, Lescarbot defined his utopianism differently, envisioning a humane race whose contentments come from satisfying their needs, who demand no more. Free of the cupidities which make some men bloodsuckers upon the needy, devourers " 'who eat up my people as they eat bread,' " the wise man can cure himself of "the misery which we see in the majority of men." In a new world of simple abundance, he can become free of those "great tyrants" of civilized life, the "excesses of the belly and of bodily ornament, which if we could cast off, it would be a means to recall the golden age. . . ." Free by right of reason, Lescarbot's new man lives in utopia because he is himself a utopian.

The utopia of wealth and power and the utopia of the wise touch the borders of the utopia of the poor, who therein cease to be poor. Raleigh's common soldier, and the psalmist's and Lescarbot's devoured people can claim companions in the Spaniards who, according to Peter Martyr, "go eagerly anywhere they are called by a nod or a whistle, in the hope of bettering their condition."

For the English, Hakluyt speaks in a tone that is benevolent, but in an approach somewhat short of idealism. His "Discourse on Western Planting" recommends the employment in colonies of "decayed merchants" who are jailed for debt. Such as are detained "maliciously, wrongfully, or for trifling causes," along with others "that hide their heads," should be set free and employed, "for so they may be relieved, and the enterprises furthered." In a longer passage, he argues that thieves, vagabonds, and such persons as crowd the jails "where either they pitifully pine away, or else at length are miserably hanged, even twenty at a clap," may be usefully employed in the plantations. The infirm among them may work at home, making trade goods for the savages.

If Hakluyt is practical, Sir George Peckham is brisk. He looks forward to the setting to work of idle men—"burthenous, chargeable, and unprofitable to this realm"—and of children "of twelve or fourteen years of age, or under. . . ." He adds to his list "our idle women (which the realm may well spare)." He joins Hakluyt in an offhand kindliness towards the unfortunates who will find "great relief and good employments" in the "Newfound Lands," but he takes a still greater interest in curing "the common annoy of the whole state."

John Smith is more generous. Appealing to rich and poor, he shows "what honors and rewards, the world yet hath for them [who] will seek them and worthily deserve them." In his New England, "necessity doth in these cases so rule a commonwealth, and each in his several functions, as their labours in their qualities may be as profitable, because there is a necessary mutual use of all." He too would free England of its idle people, but he promises them, in return for industry, that "by their labour" they "may live exceeding well." With land to be had for the working, "it seems strange to me, any such should there grow poor."

Bookkeeping aside—though Smith was always a practical utopian—he presents a landscape of contentment not unlike Lescarbot's. "What pleasure can be more, than (being tired with any occasion ashore, in planting vines, fruits, or herbs, in contriving their own grounds, to the pleasure of their own minds, their fields, gardens, orchards, buildings, ships, and other works, &c.) to recreate themselves before their own doors, in their own boats upon the sea . . . ?"

Now and again, Smith touches upon the reversal of utopia, in which the all-promising country becomes, to those who delude themselves, a "death," a "hell." The equivocal presentation is not uncommon, though the ambiguity is usually inherent rather than expressed. Fray Marcos can set down his little pastoral, knowing that the pueblo Indians have killed his companion Estevanico. Ribaut and Arthur Barlow write their idylls of the American landscape, and Hakluyt prints them. Soon following, he prints the narratives of hunger and distress at Fort Caroline and Roanoke. George Percy can praise the fruitful soil of Virginia in a prelude to his list of those who died there, "for the most part . . . of mere famine."

The contradiction is implied, not stated, so slightly touched upon that it was perhaps not recognized. The opposed portrayals of nature, as bountiful or as deadly, likely enough reflect experience rather than conscious explication. The likelihood is the greater, because nature as a theme rarely appears, and when it does belongs to the classicist. Lescarbot and Thevet and Peter Martyr can and do treat of nature as a generality and make nature and the laws of nature their themes, within the golden-age metaphor, or (in Thevet's case) in ambivalence. Beyond that range, capitalized Nature is not discussed, much less apostrophized. Repeatedly catalogued, the natural fact—Purchas was to call all such the bricks and stones of the divine creation—makes much of the American writer's subject, who is as yet satisfied with the particular.

If the humanistic assertion of the excellence of nature is rarely spelled out, so too the doctrine of the depravity of nature is left latent. A Thomas Ellis or an Edward Hayes will hold the concept, or some modfication of it, in his mind, without enlarging upon it as a theme. Modify it, they do. If, for them, nature is God's instrument for the chastisement and correction of sinful humanity, it becomes part of a holy purpose, and cannot be utterly depraved. If Gilbert's death shows God's judgment upon a presumptuous pride, after the punishment is carried out Gilbert is "refined and made nearer drawing unto the image of God," and the divine will

resumes its purged and perfected creature. The phrasing
reflects a humanistic Platonism. Yet the scholastic theme of
a depraved natural world retains its image in the earlier apparition of the devil on the sea, "yawning and gaping
wide," bidding the ships farewell in "a horrible voice."

The theme of nature and its patterning remain limited
and unclear. As a conceptual heritage from classical learning it is readily defined; as a doctrine of medieval theology,
easily identified. The incompatibility between the two be-
quests is obvious. A second incompatability, perhaps even
deeper, divides off the realism of the American writer. However often a fabulist, he describes and reports this plant, this
creature, this scene of a nature which is immediate and secular, not an idea but an experience, from which he draws
no general theme, but out of which new concepts and
themes are slowly to emerge.

Whereas theme is an abstraction, myth is here taken to
be its opposite, being figurative, in representing an action of
large significance, throughout which places, persons, and
events image a cultural dogma. The great cultural acceptance which translates itself from Europe to sixteenth-century America is that of the divine order.

Again Purchas is helpful, in the title of his first publication, of 1613: "Purchas his Pilgrimage or Relations of the
World and the religions observed in all Ages And places discovered, from the Creation unto this present. In four Partes.
This first containeth a theological and Geographical Historie of Asia, Africa, and America, with the Islands Adjacent . . ."

Geography and its discoveries thus ally themselves with
the science of religion. Purchas remains faithful to the joining. In the opening paragraphs of his *Pilgrimes* of 1625, at
the beginning of the address "To the Reader" he explains
that "Divine things are either natural or supernatural," the

latter being the "proper subject of theology, and not the peculiar argument of this work." The former, "natural
things," but no less divine, are his "more proper object,
namely the ordinary works of God in the creatures, preserv-
ing and disposing by providence that which his goodness
and power had created." Amiably putting aside argumen-
tation, and ignoring the theme of depravity in nature, he
offers "Individual and sensible materials (as it were with
stones, bricks and mortar)" to "universal speculators for
their theoretical structures."

His avowals and disavowals have their significance here,
in that "individual and sensible materials," and indeed
"stones, bricks and mortar" have been shown to occupy a
large part of the American subject. They do not, however,
contribute to sixteenth-century American mythology. The
thesis of divine manifestation in "natural things," in history,
and in geography most definitely does. The Christian discoverers, confronted by "deserts," however fertile, and by
idolaters, however virtuous, at once translate their experience in Christian terms. Since this is not God's kingdom,
or these his subjects, both must be Lucifer's. Here, Peter
Martyr says, while he praises it extravagantly, is Satan's
realm. The idols which the natives worship "are images of
deceiving demons who, because of their pride, were driven
from heaven." The fallen angels have become the rulers of
the new continents.

Their general dominance in heathendom had long been
accepted, recently for Asia, and remotely for Greece and
Rome, where the Olympians were the princes of darkness,
masquerading to deceive mankind. "These wicked spirits
the heathens honored instead of gods." So wrote Richard
Hooker. He could have changed his tense, and turned the
same judgment to the Americas. The Indians thereby become the cohorts of the Adversary, themselves, by imperative ruling, adversaries to be destroyed. In positive terms,

the invaders and occupiers carry the banners of heaven.
The issue is clearly between absolute good and absolute evil.

The myth was to be powerful and long-enduring. When
Hawthorne's Goodman Brown met the fiend in the dark
New England forest, he found the rebel angel where Puri-
tan divines and Spanish priests had always known him to
be. Sixteenth-century piety demanded his defeat in a new
celestial war, now on earth, in which his unregenerate followers deserved no mercy.

By good fortune, the issue was clear in logic only. Such
men as Las Casas made the humane refusal to carry on the
war of God against Satan in such terms, and Las Casas
himself reversed the parts. The humanistic shift away from
the doctrine of depravity in nature and the men of nature,
such as Purchas records, could sometimes also reverse it.
The emphasis upon the divine creation of "natural things"
calls for their acceptance and even for admiration. Perhaps,
in the upshot, the strongest opponent of logical and theological damnation was the normal muzziness of the human
mind. Few, even among the writers about the new world,
spelled out the myth or its consequences. Many of the individuals who obeyed it would not have read it strictly, but
simply have known their divine mission. Yet when Gilbert
found Satan in the western sea and knew him for the
enemy, the most ignorant of sailors could have understood
and agreed.

No single, complete presentation of the myth exists in sixteenth-century American letters. For the seventeenth, Mil-
ton had American counterparts, though not rivals. In the
earlier period, Villagrá comes closest to its explication.
Granted that he falls short of achievement, he nevertheless
clearly shows his understanding of its epic quality.

A paradoxical pair to the myth of the war between
heaven and hell, the myth of the golden kingdom—equally

evidenced and equally significant—puts on different images though it shows itself in many of the same actions. A quest myth, its actor has to achieve his destination by undergoing certain trials in which, for good success, he must show himself the possessor of certain qualities and of skills in ritual behavior. Lacking the necessary qualities and skills, he condemns himself to failure.

The imaginary voyages supply the pattern, of which St. Brandan's affords the pre-eminent example. His humbler but engaging brother, the Friar of Oxford, is probably the more primitive instance, since his "magical art" took him to "all the regions situate under the North pole," his spells demonstrably effective and presumably not unhallowed.

History, only less marvelous, fills in the outline with places, persons, and events. Antilia, wherever it may be; the Northwest Passage and the Strait of Anian, roadways to glory and Asian riches; Mexico and New Mexico, Saguenay and the Island of the Amazons—all offer the same reward, and in the event offer the same tests and tribulations. Whatever the end of the action, whether Cortés' triumph, or the defeat of Coronado and Oñate, whether Columbus's discovery or Prince Zichmni's deterrence, whether the achievement of Cuzco or the never-satisfied search for the court of Queen Calafia, the progression of the myth remains the same.

It includes within it many of the themes of American writing—of possibility, empire, utopianism, ambivalent nature—and sometimes crosses over to merge with its opposite, theological pair. Apart from the war of good and evil, its gold may be metal and ordinarily is, but along with "abundance" Raleigh offers his "commanders and chieftains" the bait of "honor" and of "shining glory," while Columbus is the Christ-bearer.

Many of the "historical" kingdoms were illusory, and

some of them were never searched for. Some underwent transmutations. The Kingdom of the Saguenay was to become the Hudson's Bay Company, hardly mythical though scarcely less rich. Some are peripheral to northern America but nevertheless shape its mythology.

Of these the most evident is El Dorado, the golden man or golden country whose name appears in the northern continent, but whose physical existence—if any such ever was —belongs to South America. There, according to the anthropologist Bandelier, on the plateau of Cundinamarca, in modern Colombia, the golden king had an actual existence, his treasure having been taken by the Spaniard, Gonzalo Ximenes de Quesada, in the year 1537.

Quesada did not, however, capture the *dorado* himself. Instead, the man disappears and the gilded figure transmutes himself into the mythical king of a mythical kingdom of gold which migrates eastward, eventually as far as Guiana, where in 1595 Sir Walter Raleigh desperately sought both "abundance" and "shining glory" to redeem his own ruin, only to confirm it.

For *el dorado* as the king who dusts his body with gold and then washes in the sacred lake, the evidence shows an Indian origin. Manoa, his city, grows around him. The lake called Parima, on which stands "that rich city," is of salt water and stretches for two hundred leagues. The Spaniard, Juan Martinez, becomes the first, in 1531, to "see" Manoa, "the seat and residence of Inga the emperor." After him the mythical place captures the treasure hoards of Peru and the imagination. If the golden king and his court were drunkards who caroused while servants gilded their bodies, their intoxication was infectious, fevering the minds and the pages of generations after them.

In northern America, the several cities of gold are less extravagantly decorated than Manoa, and are still rich enough. Their richness is of the Orient as well as the south, but the pattern of the myth remains the same—the quest after wealth, and along with wealth, glory. The search, always disappointed in the historic record, keeps its perennial vitality through all the failed successes, while the figure of *el dorado,* the gilded man, takes his place beside the golden kings of Asia, to personify whatever greed or triumph the general mind might shape in him.

The two American myths oppose each other. The latter presents an earthly paradise, the former an earthly hell. The complexities of contradiction multiply, as paradise nurtures devils, and as Satan's kingdom offers utopia. If the original patterning of each is neat, the clarities soon blur with confusions and inconsistencies. The first countervailents remain, however, with all their implications of sanctification and damnation, of absolute grace and absolute wickedness, of prosperity and overthrow both unmitigated, of a world of gold, always there, but here, stony ground.

21 | *Towards a New Atlantis*

A discussion of pre-colonial American literature can arrive at no exact and unequivocal stopping point. No conclusion of this earliest period can be fixed, no arbitrary line drawn between sixteenth- and seventeenth-century writing, or even between the pre-colonial and the colonial eras. A change does occur, but it is gradual. Older forms persist, while the new have already begun to emerge, discernible by the evidence of the future.

Individual writers, even, produce work which overlaps any strict division. Champlain, Smith, and Lescarbot are notable contributors to the transition, and could be discussed—as indeed Champlain and Smith usually have been—as colonialists. That argument can be sustained (to little profit for the one side or the other), although their books reveal their deeper involvement with the voyage and with discovery than with the settled, enduring community. Each of them looks forward as well as back, however, in act and idea, in subject and in structure.

The early Jamestown writers, other than Smith, might entirely reasonably be placed with him, and in history must be so placed. Nevertheless, such men as George Percy,

Ralph Hamor, and William Strachey join themselves to settlement and society, rather than to discovery, and do more to illuminate a later Virginia than an earlier. Others, not studied here, continue to write in the voyage pattern. Such New England discoverers as Martin Pring, James Rosier, and James Davies, or Robert Juet for New York, have historical and regional claims to recognition. They contribute little new to literature. Their writing often makes pleasant and interesting reading but does not depart in any valuable way from the conventional voyage form, or—beyond an occasional passage—offer an action new in itself or in interpretation. They confirm already traveled courses, from which they undertake no departures.

They confirm as well the dominant property of American letters—the close association between history and literature, the subjects of both being the same, however the methods and aims may differ. This distinguishing characteristic persists, to be made out as readily in Henry James and Edgar Allan Poe as in Washington Irving or Hamlin Garland, in Ernest Hemingway and Walt Whitman as in Thomas Jefferson or Charles Brockden Brown, in Benjamin Franklin and Nathaniel Hawthorne as in James Fenimore Cooper and Henry Adams. The few exceptions merely strengthen the general law (and with a little critical ingenuity, even they can be brought in under it).

Inevitably, then, the American writer offers both information and entertainment. For the first century and a third, his information could be assumed to entertain, but the assumption does not preclude his efforts to capture and hold his readers. His success may be complete or incomplete, according to his gifts and skills. It is likely to be the latter, since this is a period of beginnings in which only the form of the voyage affords a pattern, and even that is confusingly flexible.

His power is nonetheless great, when he is read by the

measures of his own intentions. If he is held to those of an
aesthetic alien to him, he is likely to come off poorly. He is
part of a process of becoming, not one of being. Indeed the
twentieth-century critical theory that America is process becomes him well. His one voyage links itself to another in the
ease with which one strip of a cartoon joins another, or one
movie or television episode leads into another, or one essay
in *Walden* or *A Week on the Concord and Merrimack Rivers* flows,
by time or the river, into its successor. His voyaging, like
that of the Zeno "Discoverie," or of *The Grapes of Wrath,*
need never end.

He is likely to be untidy, admitting the irrelevant and the
confused, perhaps because, as a journalist, he thinks he
must; perhaps because he is aware that the overneat is shallow, and that the inconsequent can give depth or even consequence. Just as his dedication to the real, to the "truth" of
what he saw, permits him the freedoms of fantasy, so fidelity
to the course of his voyaging vouches for his departures from
it. Fray Marcos can look across at storied, gleaming Cibola,
Smith can be rescued by Pocahontas, and Cartier can arrive at the verge of Asia, by the same virtue through which
the Connecticut Yankee can mount the knights of the
Round Table on bicycles, or Whitman in *Democratic Vistas*
can discuss the quality of being or the "shows and forms" of
Nature. The truth of probability overrides the truth of fact,
and nothing is irrelevant to a subject largely conceived. The
clear and complete statement demands confusion.

No such theorizing moved the seventeenth-century
writer. He provides the bricks and stones of an aesthetic, not
the edifice. For justification he claims simple realism and
writes the honest report. Experience is his teacher, even
such experience as he never had.

Under that guidance, he is inevitably a regionalist. Language and nationality are likely to group him with his compatriots, although they cannot work strictly when an Italian

sails and writes for Spain or France, an Englishman for the Netherlands; or when a French voyage, such as Cartier's or Ribaut's, survives in Italian or English rather than in its native tongue. Translation, moreover, could make common property of a narrative. De Bry translates into Latin, and follows his originals with English, French, and German editions. Regionalism was, then, less a matter of language than of geography. French Canada, with northern New England and New York; the southeast, with Florida, the Gulf states, and the lower Mississippi; the west and southwest, from California to western Texas, begin to shape up into areas distinct from each other. They are dominantly French and Spanish. English Virginia is a late intruder. A very different sort of regionalism begins to separate off the narratives of the sea.

One literature distinguishes itself from another as much by what it is not as by what it is. The notable lack for sixteenth-century America is the lack of personal relationships, familial and social. Families only rarely took part in the ventures, but they did sometimes. The wives and children of Luna's married soldiers and those unfortunates of Fort Caroline whom Menéndez spared earn the barest of mention. Laudonnière's chambermaid survives by virtue of gossip and hardihood, but gains no attention otherwise. A lady who accompanied Oñate gets listed because of her wardrobe and other accouterments—"nine dresses . . . trimmed; . . . two silk shawls with bead tassels . . . one damask and velvet hoop skirt; four ruffs; four gold coiffures . . ." Beyond her possessions, she is no more than a name; no final end is given for her or her clothing.

The few women who do play active parts are Indian. Barlow's pitying hostess, Garcilaso's Indian queens, Pocahontas, Doña Antonia—even the list of these is short. The others are likely to get fobbed off with tags, so-and-so's Indian woman, a young woman, an old woman, and so forth.

Sex, beyond the rare instances of Roberval's niece and
Doña Antonia and the posturings of the courtly romance, is
never a subject or a theme. By the evidence, it was too common and wanton a practice to hold literary interest. Along
with intellectual rejection, religious prudery, at first Roman
Catholic and later Protestant, likewise forbade the description of sin.

Not only is there a lack of relationship between the sexes,
but even between friend and friend, follower and leader.
Where such associations are spoken of or shown, they are
likely to be hostile. The Drake-Doughty conflict, the various
mutinies or protests of the common people against their
leaders, Laudonnière's victimization by his men, and the
quarrels between Smith and his fellow councilors make for
some sort of character portrayal, but only the first suggests
subtleties. These appear notably and uniquely in Pricket's
accounting of Hudson's crew, and make for much of its
power. To a lesser degree, Smith achieves personality and
sometimes character through Powhatan and Pocahontas,
and through the reflections of his followers. Circumstances
and Solís de Merás fill out the portrait of Menéndez.

Humphrey Gilbert gains identity, not by his associations
but by the literary device of the "character." Before Hayes
turns to it, Gilbert is one of the many figures of leadership
—bold, ambitious, and steadfast. The stereotype is firm
enough to withstand all vicissitudes. Whatever the evidence
of event, De Soto or Oñate remains the hero to his chronicler. Frobisher and Davis need no further explication.
Monts, Poutrincourt, and Cartier show themselves suffi-
ciently within the category, even for an observer as acute as
Lescarbot.

The paradox stands that even in this era of high individ-
ualism, interest in individuality hardly appears. The common man is usually without face or name. The one person
who is ordinarily revealed is the writer, sometimes—such is

the case with Cabeza de Vaca and the Gentleman of Elvas
—because of his restraint in revealing himself; sometimes by
such expansiveness as that of Smith or Lescarbot or Castañeda or Villagrá. In either case, under the strictures of reporting, he is helpless to rid himself of his function as observer, or—in terms of the techniques of fiction—the use of
point of view. Thereby he has to portray himself, and
thereby he loses impersonality, while his record becomes a
biased one, through selection and interpretation.

With such exceptions as Raleigh, Harriot, Lescarbot, the
Inca, and perhaps Hayes, he cannot be accounted a man of
letters, much less a scholar. The quality of his work is therefore likely to be uneven, and it is. He can achieve the deli-
cacy and purity of Cartier's tapestry landscapes or the dull-
ness of his sailing directions, the eloquence of Smith's
exhortations or the clutter of his diatribes, Lescarbot's liveliness or his overburdened analogies.

The ranking of this writer above that, or this voyage
above the other is in all likelihood profitless, except as a
matter of individual taste. The critical fact is that no one
voyage achieves, much less outdoes, the value of the whole.
Hakluyt and Purchas were critically correct in grouping
their narratives, the one of which complements and enhan-
ces the effectiveness of another. When they let go or dis-
turbed their sequences, they lost not only continuity but enrichment.

If the quality of the whole body of writing is higher than
that of any of its parts, the quality exists, notwithstanding.
A reader who comes to it after a familiarity with cleverer
artifice and more conscious manipulation may question the
existence, and must be left to answer his own question. For
the negative, the statement is likely to be that these narratives are not works of the imagination. It is too easy to reply
that neither, then, is the Bible. "Imagination" requires
definition, and one way of defining the term is to go back to

its root. That the pre-colonial literature of northern America supplies many, if not most, of the images of the culture is beyond doubt.

The recognition once again brings in the subject of continuity. With the later Jamestown, with Plymouth, and Massachusetts Bay the truly colonial narratives and journals begin, showing as compared to those of the earlier settlements some of the same and some very different emphases. Personal associations and the concerns of fixed place—politics, social life, and the setting-up of institutions, to name only a few—lead to new structures in writing, new subjects, and new interpretations. To a surprising extent, however, the older shapes, matters, and renderings persist. The journal remains the basis from which accounts both of settlement and of exploration are written. The literature of the voyage grows larger and more varied, a progress which actually, by date, begins while Champlain, Smith, and Lescarbot are writing. The great series of the *Jesuit Relations* opens during their era, and before Plymouth.

Three years after that plantation, the Recollect friar, Gabriel Sagard Theodat, undertook his long journey to the country of the Hurons, to publish his classic of the inland voyage in 1632. Meanwhile, the West India Company of the United Netherlands had occupied the Hudson, and its settlers and wanderers began to contribute their sea and land farings to the traditional development, varying it as their needs and interests required.

The linkages and kinships are many, whatever the changes in subject and character, in scene and event and motive. Notably, the original themes persist, however altered. New England's utopianism is not Guiana's, nor Philadelphia's St. Brandan's, but the vision of "that great city," the idea of the earthly paradise, manifests itself in both. Above all, the central theme of revelation renews itself. Purchas, in his "Conclusion" of 1625—as he worded it in his beginning—rewords it for a Virginia of "high and steep mountains . . . rich with mines of gold, silver, and copper" and "another sea lying within six days journey beyond them." Indeed, Asia has come nearer than before. Fixed settlement notwithstanding, the text still reads, "no not so much as the borders of the sea are yet certainly discovered." Estotiland and Icaria are still mapped. The Indian, noble and ignoble, is still a new man. Florida offers a landscape for another fictitious savage nation, the Apalatci, while by the west Canada nurtures the equally fictitious Gnacsitares and Mozeemleks who inhabit the Arcadian "River Long," which leads—where else?—still further west to Tartary.

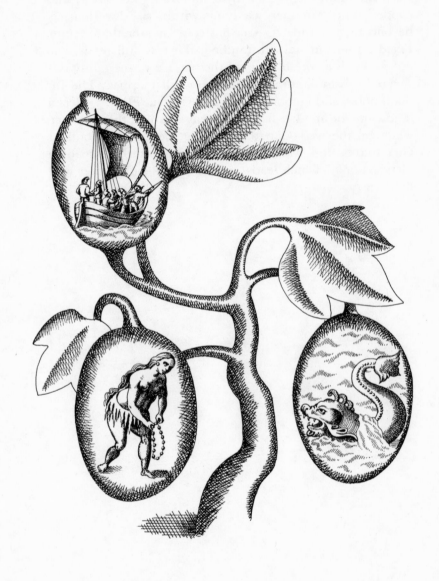

Chapter References

A selective bibliographical listing of the great voyage collections follows the chapter references. The chapter bibliographies refer by short title to the publications of Ramusio, Hakluyt, Purchas, Ternaux-Compans, Pacheco and Cárdenas.

2 Eastward in Eden (pages 6–21)

For the writings of Columbus, see Ramusio III; M. F. de Navarrete, *Colección de los viages y descubrimientos que hicieron por mar los españoles desde fines del siglo XV*, 5 vols. (Madrid, 1825–1837), vol. I, "Viajes de Colon," reprinted in *Biblioteca de Autores Españoles*, vol. 74 (Madrid, 1954); R. H. Major, ed., *Select Letters of Columbus*, Hak. Soc., 1st ser., Nos. 2, 43 (1847, 1870); Clements Markham, ed., *The Journal of Christopher Columbus*, Hak. Soc., 1st ser., No. 86 (1892); E. G. Bourne, ed., *The Northmen, Columbus, and Cabot*, 985–1503, Or. Nar. (New York, 1906). These English texts are based on the Spanish of Navarrete. The more recent edition by Cecil Jane, *Select Documents Illustrating the Four Voyages of Columbus*, 2 vols., Hak. Soc., 2nd ser., Nos. 65, 70 (1929, 1932), is based on the more accurate texts provided by Cesare de Lollis, *Scritti di Colombo*.

The Verrazzano "Relation" was first printed in Ramusio III (1556); trans., Hakluyt 1582. The Magliabecchian mss., in original and trans., appears in *Col. N.-Y. Hist. Soc.*, 2nd ser., I (New York, 1841). Lawrence C. Wroth, *The Voyages of Giovanni da Verrazzano, 1524–1528* (New Haven, 1970) [Cèllere Codex].

The Cartier bibliography is complex beyond usefulness here. The following titles show original publications, early English translations, reasonably available reprints in French, and the outstanding scholarly editions in English: *Brief Récit et Succincte Narration, de la navigation faicte es ysles de Canada* . . . [second voyage] (Paris, 1545); Ramusio III (1556), "Prima Relatione di Jacques Cartier della Terra Nuova detta la Nuova Francia" [first voyage] and "Breve et succinta narratione della navigation fatta . . . all' Isole di Canada . . ."; trans., John Florio, *A Shorte and briefe narration of the two Navigations* . . . (London, 1580); trans. into French from Ramusio, first voyage only, *Discours du Voyage Fait par le Capitaine Jaques Cartier aux Terres-neufves* . . . (Rouen, 1598); trans., Hakluyt 1600 (with third voyage for which Hakluyt is the only source); Ternaux-Compans I, II; James Phinney Baxter, *A Memoir of Jacques Cartier* (New York, 1906); H. S. Burrage, ed., *Early English and French Voyages* . . . Or. Nar. (New York, 1906); H. P. Biggar, *The Voyages of Jacques Cartier* (Ottawa, 1924).

3   Passage, O Soul, to India! (pages 22–36)

For Sir Humphrey Gilbert, the authoritative text is D. B. Quinn, ed., *The Voyages and Colonizing Enterprises of Sir Humphrey Gilbert*, 2 vols., Hak. Soc., 2nd ser., Nos. 83–84 (1940); see also Humphrey Gilbert, *A discourse of a discoverie of a new passage to Cataia* (London, 1576) reprinted in Hakluyt 1589,

1600, Everyman V; Edward Hayes, "A report of the voyage and successe thereof, attempted . . . by Sir Humfrey Gilbert . . ." Hakluyt 1589, from mss.; reprinted in Hakluyt 1600; Everyman VI; H. S. Burrage, *Early Eng. and Fr. Voyages.*

Of the several Frobisher chroniclers, only George Best writes of all three voyages in *A true discourse of the late voyages of discoverie, for the finding of a passage to Cathaya by the Northweast* . . . (London, 1578) reprinted in Hakluyt 1600; Richard Collinson, ed., Hak. Soc., 1st ser., No. 38 (1867), which also includes an anonymous "First Voyage" and Edward Sellman's "Third Voyage"; Everyman V. For Thomas Ellis, *A true report of the third and last voyage into Meta incognita: atchieved by . . . Martine Frobisher* . . . (London, 1578), see the reprints in Hakluyt 1589, 1600, and Everyman V.

The three voyages of John Davis are described in narratives by various writers, printed from mss. in Hakluyt 1589; reprinted in Hakluyt 1600, C. R. Markham, ed., Hak. Soc., 1st ser., No. 59 (1880), Everyman V.

Henry Hudson's first two voyages made attempts at a polar or northeastern passage; his reports of them are without literary value. All four Hudson voyages were published in Purchas, 1625; reprints: G. M. Asher, ed., Hak. Soc., 1st ser., No. 27 (1860). For Robert Juet's "The third Voyage of Master Henrie Hudson . . . to New-found Land . . . and thence to Cape Cod, and so to thirtie three degrees . . ." see the above and *N.-Y. Hist. Soc. Col.*, 2nd ser., No. 1, and J. Franklin Jameson, ed., *Narratives of New Netherland, 1609–1664* (New York, 1909) Or. Nar. [incomplete]. Abacuk Pricket's "A larger Discourse of the same [the fourth] Voyage, and the successe thereof" appears in Purchas and Asher (see above).

4   Westward the Star of Empire (pages 37–48)

The Spanish literature of exploration is extensive. Bibliographies are here given only for the writers discussed in this essay.

Alvar Núñez Cabeza de Vaca, *La relación que dió Aluar Núñez Cabeça de Vaca de lo acaescido en las Indias en la armada donde yua por gouernador Pamfilo de Narvaez* (Zamora, 1542, Valladolid, 1555); reprints in translation, Ramusio III, Purchas (paraphrase), Ternaux-Compans VII; T. Buckingham Smith, *Relation of Alvar Núñez Cabeça de Vaca* (Washington, 1851), ed. in F. W. Hodge and T. H. Lewis, *Spanish Explorers in the Southern United States, 1528–1543*, Or. Nar. (New York, 1907); A. and F. Bandelier, ed. and trans., *The Journey of Alvar Núñez Cabeza de Vaca* . . . (New York, 1905).

[Gentleman of Elvas], *Relaçam verdadiera dos trabalhos* . . . (Evora, 1557); trans., Richard Hakluyt, under title of *Virginia richly valued* . . . *Written by a Portugall gentleman of Elvas* . . . (London, 1609 and 1611 [as *The Worthye and Famous History, of the Conquest of Terra Florida*]); reprint, Peter Force, *Tracts* IV (Washington, 1846); trans., T. Buckingham Smith, *Narratives of the Career of Hernando de Soto* . . . (New York, 1866), edited by E. G. Bourne, *Narratives of the Career of Hernando de Soto* (New York, 1904), and by Hodge and Lewis, *Spanish Explorers* . . .

Fray Marcos de Niza, "Relación del descubrimiento de las siete ciudades," (written 1539); first printing, trans., in 1556 in Ramusio III; Hakluyt 1600; Ternaux-Compans IX; Pacheco and Cárdenas III (in Spanish); trans., Bandelier, *Journey of* . . . *Cabeza de Vaca*; G. P. Hammond and Agapito Rey, *Narratives of the Coronado Expedition, 1540–1542* (Albuquerque, 1940).

Pedro de Castañeda, "Relación de la jornada de Cibola
. . . la cual fue el año de 1540," trans. Ternaux-Compans
IX; trans. from mss., G. P. Winship, "The Coronado expedition, 1540–1542," *Fourteenth Annual Report, U. S. Bureau of
Am. Ethnology*, Pt. I (Washington, 1896); reprints: *The Journey of Coronado* (New York, 1904); F. W. Hodge, ed. (San
Francisco, 1933); Hodge and Lewis, eds., *Spanish Explorers*;
independent trans., Hammond and Rey, *Narratives . . .Co-
ronado.*

For an extended bibliography of the Spanish materials, see
H. E. Bolton, *Coronado* (New York and Albuquerque, 1949).

5   Hazards of New Fortunes (pages 49–60)

Obregón's chronicle history of 1584 remained in manuscript, in the Archivo General de Indias, until 1924. It has
since been published under various titles—*Historia de los descubrimientos antiguos y modernos de la Nueva España*, Mariano
Cuevas, ed. (Mexico, 1924); *Obregón's History of 16th Century
Explorations in Western America*, G. F. Hammond and Agapito
Rey, trans. and ed. (Los Angeles, 1928); the mss. title is
cited as *Cronica, comentario ó relaciones de los descubrimientos antiguos y modernos de N. E. y de Nuevo Mexico.*

Because Alarcón's narrative got its first printing in Italian,
it carries a title in that language, "Relatione della naviga-
tione & scoperta che fece il capitano Fernando Alarcone
per ordine della illustrissimo signor Don Antonio di Men-
dozza vice re della Nuoua Spagna," Ramusio III (1556);
trans., Hakluyt 1600, Ternaux-Compans IX, Hammond
and Rey, *Narratives . . . Coronado.*

The Cabrillo–Ferrelo–Juan Paez "diary" carries the cursive title, "Relación ó diario, de la navegación que hizo Juan Rodríguez Cabrillo con dos navíos al descubrimiento del paso del Mar del Sur al norte . . ."; printed from mss. in T. Buckingham Smith, *Colección de Varios Documentos* . . . (London, 1857); from another mss., Pacheco and Cárdenas, XIV (Madrid, 1870); H. E. Bolton, *Spanish Exploration in the Southwest, 1542–1706*, Or. Nar. (New York, 1916); Henry R. Wagner, *Spanish Voyages to the Northwest Coast of America* (San Francisco, 1929).

The Sebastián Vizcaíno "diary" has no formal heading beyond the opening words of the mss.: "Reynando El rrey . . ."; first printing, Francisco Carrasco y Guisasola, ed., *Documentos referentes al Reconocimiento de las Costas de las Californias*. . . . (Madrid, 1882); trans. and printed as "Diary," in H. E. Bolton, ed., *Spanish Exploration*.

For the same voyage, Fray Antonio de la Ascensión wrote, in 1620, his "Relación breve . . . del descubrimiento que se hizo en la Nueva Espana, en la mar del Sur"; printed from mss. in Pacheco and Cárdenas VIII; trans., Bolton, *Spanish Exploration*. Wagner, *Spanish Voyages*, gives a full bibliography of the various versions (notes, chap. 11).

The later land voyages, to 1584, are summarized in Obregón (q.v.). Among them, the following require listing:

Hernán Gallegos, "Relación y concudío de el viage y subseso que Francisco Sanchez Chamuscado con ocho soldados sus companeros hizo en el descubrimiento del Nuevo Mexico en Junio de 1581"; trans. from mss. in G. P. Hammond and Agapito Rey, eds., *The Gallegos Relation of the Rodríguez*

Expedition to New Mexico, Hist. Soc. of N. M. Pubs. on Hist., IV (Santa Fe, 1927).

Antonio de Espejo, "Relación del viage que yo, Antonio de Espexo . . . hice á las provincias de Nuevo Mexico . . . en fin del ano de mil e quinientos ochenta e dos" (written 1583); printed, Pacheco and Cárdenas, XV; trans., Bolton, *Spanish Exploration.*

———, "El Viaje que hizo Antonio de Espejo . . ." included in Juan González de Mendoza, *Historia . . . del gran Reyno de la China . . .* (Madrid, 1586) [Hak. Soc., 1st ser., Nos. 14–15 (1853–1854)]; reprinted in Hakluyt 1600; trans., *New Mexico. Otherwise the Voiage of Anthony of Espeio* (London, 1587).

Diego Pérez de Luxán, "Journal," trans. in G. P. Hammond and Agapito Rey, eds., *Expedition into New Mexico Made by Antonio de Espejo, 1582–1583*, Quivira Society Pubs., I (Los Angeles, 1929).

Geronimo de Zárate-Salmerón, "Relaciones de Todas las cosas que en el Nuevo Mexico se han visto y Savido, asi por mar como por tierra, desde el año 1538 hasta el de 1626," written 1626; printed from mss. in *Documentos para la Historia de México*, 3d ser., Mexico, 1856; trans. and ed., Charles F. Lummis, *Land of Sunshine*, XI, XII (1899, 1900); retrans., incomplete, Bolton, *Spanish Exploration.*

Juan de Oñate's "Act of Possession" got its first printing in Villagrá's *Historia*, Canto 14 (q.v. chap. 6); the official version appears in Pacheco and Cárdenas XVI, and in D. Vicente Riva Palacio, *México á Través de Los Siglos*, 4 vols., (Mexico, n.d.), II, 455–456.

The Oñate documents and relations are collected in G. P. Hammond and Agapito Rey, eds., *Oñate, Colonizer of New Mexico*, Coronado Cuarto Cent. Pubs., V, VI, 2 vols. (Albuquerque, 1953).

6   Epics of America (pages 61–76)

The three narratives discussed here can be found, each in its differing versions, as follows:

Gaspar Pérez de Villagrá, *Historia de la Nueva México* (Alcalá, 1610); reprint, [Luis Gonzales Obregón, ed.] for the Museo Nacional de México, with appendix, 2 vols. (Mexico, 1900); trans., Gilberto Espinosa, Quivira Society (Los Angeles, 1933). The translations of quotations provided here are not Mr. Espinosa's.

Garcilaso de la Vega ["el Inca"], *Historia del Adelantado Hernando de Soto, Governador y capitan general del Reyno de la Florida, y de otros heroicos cavalleros Españoles e Indios* [La Florida del Ynca] (Lisbon, 1605); E. G. Bourne describes various nineteenth-century paraphrases in his introduction to *Narratives . . . de Soto* (q.v. chap. 4, under "Gentleman of Elvas"); the first translation of the complete text is that of Jeannette Johnson Varner and John Grier Varner, eds., *The Florida of the Inca* (Austin, 1951).

David Ingram, *A true discourse of the adventures & travailes of David Ingram . . .* (1583) [no surviving copy]; reprints: Hakluyt 1589; *Mag. of American History* IX, 1883 (from Bodleian mss.).

7   Episodes of America (pages 77–84)

The "Petition of the married soldiers" is printed in H. I. Priestley, ed., *The Luna Papers, 1559–1561*, 2 vols., Florida State Hist. Soc., No. 8 (De Land, Fla., 1928), in which the documents are transcribed, translated, and printed in the order in which they came from the transcriber. For the "Petition," see I, 132–135.

Fray Luis Cancer and Fray Gregorio Beteta have earned as little praise in literature as in history. Their jointly constructed martyrdom has not been translated into English. Written in 1549, under the manuscript heading, "Relación de la Florida para el Il^{mo} Señor Visorrei de la N^a España la qual trajo Fr. Greg° de Beteta," it is printed in trans. (French, text altered), in Ternaux-Compans, *Recueil de Pièces sur la Floride* (1841); in Spanish, from mss., in T. Buckingham Smith, *Colección de Varios Documentos para la Historia de la Florida y Tierras Adyacentes* (London, 1857).

The obscurity of Hernando de Escalante Fontaneda (or Fontanedo) is better deserved. For his "Memoria de las cosas y costa y indios de la Florida" see Pacheco and Cárdenas, V; Ternaux-Compans, *Recueil*; Smith, *Colección*; trans. in T. Buckingham Smith, *Letter of H. de Soto and Memoir of H. de Escalante Fontaneda* (Washington, 1854).

8   The Peopling of Paradise (pages 85–99)

Since no French original survives, perhaps because none was ever written, the French cycle of Florida begins with the English version of Jean Ribaut, *The whole and true discov-*

erye of Terra Florida, (englished the Florishing lande.) . . . (London, 1563); reprint, Hakluyt 1582; fac. ed., Jeannette Thurber Connor, with transcript by H. P. Biggar from Sloane mss., Florida State Hist. Soc., No. 7 (De Land, 1927).

The cycle continues with:

René de Laudonnière, *L'Histoire notable de la Floride situees es Indes Occidentales* . . . Martine Basanier, ed. [with Gourgues, "Reprinse," see below] (Paris, 1586); reprint, Ternaux-Compans, *Recueil*; trans., Richard Hakluyt, *A Notable Historie Containing foure voyages . . . unto Florida* (London, 1587); reprints: Hakluyt 1600; B. F. French, ed., *Historical Collections of Louisiana and Florida*, new series (New York, 1869); *Voyages en Virginie et en Floride* (Paris, 1927).

Nicolas le Challeux, *Discours de l'histoire de la Floride* (Dieppe, 1566), reprinted as *Histoire Memorable du dernier voyage aux Indes . . . fait par le capitaine Jean Ribaut* (Lyons, 1566); Ternaux-Compans, *Recueil*; trans. of Dieppe ed., *A true and perfect description, of the last voyage or Navigation, attempted by Capitaine John Rybaut* (London, 1566); "modernized" text in Stefan Lorant, *The New World* (New York, 1946).

Jacques le Moyne de Morgues, *Brevis Narratio* . . . (Frankfort, 1591) [Le Moyne's narrative and captions trans. into Latin from French (no surviving French mss.), and published with engravings of Le Moyne's sketches by Theodor De Bry as Part II of his *America*]; trans., F. B. Perkins, *Narrative of Le Moyne* (Boston, 1875); trans., L. Mingler, *Voyages en Virginie et en Floride* (see above); trans. from Latin, Lorant, *New World*. The New York Public Library holds the one available Le Moyne/De Bry original, which raises too many questions of time and state of composition to be commented on with any confidence.

[Dominique de Gourgues], "La Reprinse de la Floride" included in Laudonnière [Basanier, ed.], *L'Histoire notable de la Floride* . . . (Paris, 1586), and in Hakluyt, *A Notable Historie* . . . (London, 1587); Hakluyt 1600; Ternaux-Compans, *Recueil*.

The Spanish story is to be found in:

Francisco Lopéz de Mendoza Grajalas, "Relación de la jornada de Pedro Menéndez de Avilés en la Florida" (n.d.), printed in Pacheco and Cárdenas III; reprinted in Eugenio Ruidíaz y Caravia, *La Florida: su conquista y colonización* . . . 2 vols. (Madrid, 1893); trans., Ternaux-Compans, *Recueil*; French, *Collections*, 2nd ser. (New York, 1875); Old South Leaflets, Gen. ser., vol. IV, No. 89 (Boston, 1897).

Gonzalo Solís de Merás, "Memorial . . . de todas las jornadas y sucesos del adelantado Pedro Menéndez de Avilés . . ." (written c. 1567), first printing (incomplete) in Andrés Gonzáles de Barcia Carballido y Zúñiga, *Ensayo Cronologico para la Historia General de la Florida* (Madrid, 1723) [see chap. 9]; in full in Ruidíaz y Caravia, *La Florida*, I; trans., Jeannette Thurber Connor, *Pedro Menéndez de Avilés* (Gainesville, 1923), reissued with intro. by L. N. McAlister (1964).

Bartolomé Barrientos, "Vida y hechos de Pedro Menéndez de Avilés" (written 1568), first pub. from mss. in Genaro García, *Dos antiguas relaciones de la Florida* (Mexico, 1902); trans. with intro and fac., Anthony Kerrigan, *Pedro Menéndez de Avilés, Founder of Florida, written by Bartolomé Barrientos* (Gainesville, 1965).

9   The Meeting Point Between Savagery and Civilization (pages 100–113)

The Florida/Virginia narratives are referred to, summarized, or quoted (from the Spanish point of view) in Andrés Gonzáles de Barcia Carballido y Zúñiga, *Ensayo Cronológico para la historia general de la Florida* (Madrid, 1723); trans., Anthony Kerrigan, *Barcia's Chronological History of the Continent of Florida* . . . (Gainesville, 1951).

All the Roanoke texts are published in David Beers Quinn, ed., *The Roanoke Voyages, 1584–1590*, 2 vols., Hak. Soc., 2nd ser., No. 104 (London, 1955).

For individual printings, see:

Arthur Barlow, "The first voyage made to the coastes of America . . ." Hakluyt 1589, 1600, Everyman VI; Burrage, *Early English and French Voyages*; paraphrased in Lorant, *New World*.

Ralph Lane, "An account of the particularities of the imployments of the English men left in Virginia . . ." Hakluyt 1589, 1600, Everyman VI; Burrage, *Early English and French Voyages*; paraphrased in Lorant, *New World*.

Thomas Harriot, *A briefe and true report of the new found land of Virginia* (London, 1588); reprinted in Hakluyt 1589, 1600, Everyman VI; Burrage, *Early English and French Voyages*; paraphrased in Lorant, *New World*. For publication, 1590, and captions for John White's drawings, see De Bry, *Virginia* (below); reprint of De Bry, intro. by Paul Hulton (New York, 1972).

John White, "The fourth voyage made to Virginia, with three shippes, in the yeere, 1587," pub. from mss. in Hakluyt 1589; reprints: Hakluyt 1600; Everyman VI; Burrage, *Early English and French Voyages*; paraphrase in Lorant, *New World.*

————, "The fift voyage of M. John White into the West Indies and parts of America called Virginia, in the yeere 1590," printed from mss. in Hakluyt 1600; Everyman VI; Burrage, *Early English and French Voyages*; paraphrase in Lorant, *New World.*

————, Drawings. At Hakluyt's instigation these were turned over to Theodor de Bry, who engraved twenty-three of them, and published them with captions by Thomas Harriot and Harriot's *Briefe and true report* as the first volume (*Virginia,* 1590) in the *America* series of the De Bry volumes (Frankfort, 1590–1634). The engravings, together with the De Bry engravings of Le Moyne (see chap. 8), became the standard depictions of the American Indian. The White drawings themselves were lost to general knowledge until the mid-twentieth century, kept in mind only by occasional reference and—for a few of them—unsatisfactory reproductions, the earliest in 1882. The first attempt at complete publication was made in 1946, in Lorant, *New World.* The definitive publication is that of Paul Hulton and David Beers Quinn, *The American Drawings of John White 1577–1590,* 2 vols. (London and Chapel Hill, 1964).

10   The Pathfinder, or, The Inland Sea (pages 114–123)

Two complete editions of Champlain have been issued, the first of which is definitive:

C.-H. Laverdière, ed., *Ouevres de Champlain*, 6 vols. (Quebec, 1870). Henry P. Biggar, ed., *The Works of Samuel de Champlain*, 6 vols., Champlain Society (Toronto, 1922–1936). Particular titles have appeared as follows:

Brief Discours des Choses plus remarquables que Sammuel Champlain de Brouage a reconneues aux Indes Occidentalles (written 1601); trans. from mss. by Alice Wilmere, Norton Shaw, ed., *Narrative of a Voyage to the West Indies and Mexico*, Hak. Soc., 1st ser., No. 23 (London, 1859); first printing in French, Laverdière, ed., *Oeuvres*, I.

Des Sauvages, ou Voyage de Samuel Champlain de Brouage, faict en la France Nouvelle, l'an mil six cens trois (Paris, n.d. [1604]); trans., Purchas; C. P. Otis, E. F. Slafter, eds., *The Voyages of Samuel de Champlain*, Prince Soc., 3 vols. (Boston, 1880–1882); reprint of Purchas, E. G. Bourne, ed., Trailmakers Series (New York, 1906).

Les Voyages du Sieur de Champlain . . . ou Journal tres-fidele des observations faites és descouvertures de la nouvelle France . . . (Paris, 1613); trans., Prince Soc. (see above); W. L. Grant, ed., *Voyages of Samuel de Champlain, 1604–1618*, Or. Nar. (New York, 1907); A. A. Bourne, E. G. Bourne, eds., *The Voyages and Explorations of Samuel de Champlain, 1604–1618, Narrated by Himself*, 2 vols. (New York, 1922).

Voyages et Descouvertures faites en la Nouvelle France, depuis l'année 1615 jusques à la fin de l'année 1618 par le Sieur de Champlain . . . (Paris, 1619); trans., Prince Soc.; W. L. Grant, ed., *Voyages*; Bourne and Bourne, *The Voyages . . .* (for all three translations, see above).

Les Voyages de la Nouvelle France Occidentale, dicte Canada, faits par la Sr de Champlain . . . et toutes les Decouvertes qu'il a faites en ce Pais depuis l'an 1603 jusques en l'an 1629 . . . (Paris, 1632).

11 The Evangelist of Fish (pages 124–138)

The collected writings of Smith appear in Edward Arber, ed., *Travels and Works of Captain John Smith* (Birmingham, 1884), 2 vols., 1895; reprint, with emendations by A. G. Bradley, 2 vols. (Edinburgh, 1907, 1910).

The bibliography of individual titles is complex. The following citations are chosen for usefulness and accessibility:

A True Relation of such occurrences and accidents of noate as hath hapned in Virginia since the first planting of that Collony (London, 1608); reprints: Charles Deane, ed. (Boston, 1866); L. G. Tyler, ed., *Narratives of Early Virginia*, Or. Nar. (New York, 1907); F. C. Rosenberger, ed., *Virginia Reader* (New York, 1948); Philip L. Barbour, ed., *The Jamestown Voyages Under the First Charter, 1606–1609*, 2 vols., Hak. Soc., 2nd ser., Nos. 136, 137 (Cambridge, 1969).

A Map of Virginia. With a Description of the Countrey, the Commodities, People, Government and Religion (Oxford, 1612); reprints: Smith's *General Historie* (q.v.); Purchas [abridged]; Tyler, *Virginia*; B. C. McCary, ed., *John Smith's Map of Virginia . . .* (Williamsburg, 1957).

A Description of New England: or the Observations, and discoveries, of Captain John Smith in the North of America 1614 (London, 1616); reprints: Peter Force, *Tracts*, II (Washington, 1838); Charles Deane, ed. (Boston, 1865); G. P. Winship, ed. (New York, 1905).

New Englands Trials (London, 1620, 1622); reprints: 1st ed., Charles Deane, ed. (Cambridge, Mass., 1873); 2nd ed., Force, *Tracts*, II; Charles Deane, ed. (Cambridge, Mass., 1867); Purchas [abridged].

*The Generall Historie of Virginia, New-England, and the Summer
Isles* (London, 1624, *et al.*); reprints: 2 vols. [with *True Travels*] (Glasgow, 1907); excerpt ("the fourth booke"), Tyler,
Virginia.

*The True Travels, Adventures and Observations of Captaine John
Smith, in Europe, Asia, Affrica, and America, from Anno Domini
1593 to 1629. Together with a continuation of his generall History*
(London, 1630); reprints: [with *Generall Historie*] Glasgow,
1907; J. G. Fletcher and L. C. Wroth, eds. (New York,
1930). For "Francisco Ferneza" narrative, in first published
form, see Purchas.

*Advertisements For the unexperienced Planters of New-England,. or
any where* (London, 1631); reprints: Col. Mass. Hist. Soc., 3d
ser., III (1833); Charles Deane, ed. (Boston, 1865).

12   The American Is a New Man (pages 139–151)

Marc Lescarbot, *Histoire de la Nouvelle France Contenant les
navigations, decouvertes, & Habitations faites par les François ès
Indes Occidentales & Nouvelle-France* (Paris, 1609). And [separate publication] *Les Muses de la Nouvelle France* (Paris, 1609).
Reprints: 1st ed., excerpt, trans. [see *Nova Francia*, below]
(London, 1609); 2nd ed. (Paris, 1611, 1612), "reveuë, corrigée, & augmentée"; 3rd ed. (Paris, 1617), "enrichie de plusieurs choses singulieres"; 1612 ed. [Book V only] trans.,
Purchas; 1612 ed. in full, Librairie Tross (Paris, 1866);
1617 ed., trans. [except for *Muses*] and ed. by W. L. Grant,
intro. by H. P. Biggar, 3 vols., The Champlain Society (Toronto, 1907, 1911, 1914).

————, *Nova Francia: or the Description of that part of New
France, which is one continent with Virginia* . . . Trans. from

French into English by P. E. [Pierre Erondelle] (London, 1609) [Books IV, V, VI of *Histoire*, 1609]; reprint, H. P. Biggar, ed. (New York, 1928).

Peter Martyr D'Anghera, *De Orbe Novo*, trans. and ed. by F. A. MacNutt, 2 vols. with bibliog. (New York, 1912). The bibliography is complex beyond usefulness here, except for the following: Richard Eden, *The History of Travayle in the West and East Indies* . . . (London, 1577) [prints in trans. three of the eight decades]; reprinted in Edward Arber, *The First Three English Books on America* (Birmingham, 1885) [also includes passages from Oviedo, Gómara, and others]; all eight decades reprinted in Latin, Hakluyt (Paris, 1587); trans., Michael Lok (London, 1612, 1625).

The Spanish historians present an extensive literature; Purchas, cutting and condensing, still includes long passages from such writers as Acosta, Gómara, Oviedo, Las Casas, and the Portuguese Antonio Galvano.

André Thevet, *Singularitez de la France Antarctique autrement nommée Amérique* . . . (Paris, 1557); trans., *The New found worlde, or Antarctike* (London, 1568); reprint, Paul Gaffarel, ed. (Paris, 1878).

13   Narrative and Action (pages 152–160)

George Best, *A true discourse* . . . see chap. 3, bibliog.

Richard Clarke, "A relation . . . Written in excuse of that fault of casting away the ship and men, imputed to his oversight." Bibliography repeats that of Edward Hayes (see chap. 3) except that Clarke's "Relation" is not in Burrage.

William Strachey, "Letter to a Noble Lady" (written 1610) appears under the title of "A true reportory of the wrack, and redemption of Sir Thomas Gates, Knight; upon, and from the Ilands of the Bermudas . . ."; first printing, Purchas; reprint, Louis B. Wright, ed., *A Voyage to Virginia in 1609* (Charlottesville, 1964).

Sir John Hawkins, *A true declaration of the troublesome voyadge of M. John Hawkins to the parties of Guynea and the West Indies* [1567–1568] (London, 1569); reprinted in Hakluyt 1589, 1600; C. R. Markham, ed., Hak. Soc., 1st ser., No. 57 (1878); Burrage, *Early English and French Voyages*; Everyman VII.

————, "An Account of Hawkins' Third Slaving Voyage, 1569" (a "fuller" version); printed in J. A. Williamson, *Sir John Hawkins* (London, 1927).

John Sparke the younger [on Hawkins' voyage of 1564–1565], "The voyage made by the worshipful M. John Hawkins, Esquire, now knight . . . begunne in An. Dom. 1564"; pub. by Hakluyt from mss., 1589; further bibliography follows that for Hawkins, *A true declaration . . .* (see above).

For Sir Francis Drake in California, the bibliography is confused and confusing. Certain copies of Hakluyt 1589 contain the so-called "Drake leaves" (see Quinn, ed., *Principall Navigations*, I, intro.) and some do not; reprints: Hakluyt 1600; Vaux, ed., *The World Encompassed* (see chap. 14); Burrage, *Early Eng. and French Voyages*; Everyman VI, VIII.

14   Narrative and Fiction (pages 161–168)

For Gentleman of Elvas, see bibliog., chap. 4; for Garcilaso, bibliog., chap. 6.

The Drake-Hakluyt bibliography is complex beyond usefulness here. It is discussed in Quinn and Skelton, eds., *Principall Navigations*, q.v.; Drake narratives appear in Hakluyt 1600 and in Everyman, VI and VIII (see bibliog., chap. 13). For later editions, the following titles are relevant: [Sir Francis Drake, the nephew] *The World Encompassed By Sir Francis Drake . . . out of the Notes of Master Francis Fletcher* (London, 1628); W. S. W. Vaux, ed., with the journal of Francis Fletcher and the narrative of John Cooke "entituled 'For Francis Drake,' " both from mss., Hak. Soc., 1st ser., No. 16 (1854); Sir R. C. Temple, ed. (London, 1926).

15   The Imaginary Voyage (pages 169–178)

[Nicolo Zeno], *De i Commentarii . . . Et dello scoprimento dell'-Isola Frislanda, Eslanda, Engrouelanda, Estotilanda, & Icaria, fatto sotto il Polo Artico, da due fratelli zeni . . .* (Venice, 1558); reprint, Ramusio III (Venice, 1574); trans., Hakluyt 1582 under the title, "The Discoverie of the Iles of Frisland, Iseland, Engroueland, Estotiland, Drogeo, and Icaria, made by M. Nicolas Zeno, Knight, and M. Antonio his brother"; reprints: Hak. Soc., 1st ser., No. 7, J. W. Jones, ed. (London, 1850); *The Voyages of the Venetian Brothers Zeno*, Hak. Soc., 1st ser., No. 50, R. H. Major, ed. (London, 1873).

[Juan de Fuca—Apostolos Valerianos], "A Note made by me Michael Lok the elder, touching the Strait of Sea, commonly called Fretum Anian . . ." first printed by Purchas

1625; reprint, Henry R. Wagner, "Apocryphal Voyages to the Northwest Coast of America," American Antiquarian Society, new ser., No. 41 (April, 1931).

Lorenzo Ferrer Maldonado, *Relacion del descubrimiento del Estrecho de Anian, que hice yo el capitan Lorenzo Ferrer Maldonado el año 1588* . . . trans., Wagner, "Apocryphal Voyages . . ." (see above). Wagner gives the bibliography of the Spanish printings of the text, all of them difficult to come by.

Sir Walter Raleigh, *The Discoverie of the Large, Rich, and Bewtifull Empyre of Guiana, with a relation of the great and Golden Citie of Manoa (which the Spaniards call El Dorado)* . . . (London, 1596); reprints: many, among them Hakluyt 1600; Hak. Soc., 1st ser., No. 3, R. H. Schomburgh, ed. (London, 1848); W. H. D. Rouse, ed. (1904, 1905, 1913); Everyman VII.

[R. M.], *Newes of Sr. Walter Rauleigh. With The true Description of Guiana* . . . *Sent from a Gentleman of his Fleet* . . . *1617* (London, 1618); reprint, Force, *Tracts*, III, No. 4 (Washington, 1844).

16   Ptolemy's America (pages 179–191)

[John Rastell?], "A new interlude and a mery of the nature of the iiii. elements &c" (c. 1519). The verses which refer to the New World are quoted in Edward Arber's preface to *The First Three English Books on America* (Westminster, 1895). For edited texts, see *British Museum Catalogue*, under "INTERLUDE."

Of the large bibliography of historical geography, only a few titles can be mentioned here: Henry Harrisse, *The Dis-*

covery of North America (London, 1896; reprint, Amsterdam, 1961); W. H. Babcock, *Legendary Islands of the Atlantic*, Am. Geographical Soc. Research Ser., No. 8 (New York, 1922); for the Pacific coast, see Wagner, *Spanish Voyages*; for sixteenth-century Atlantic exploration, Samuel Eliot Morison, *The European Discovery of America: The Northern Voyages* (New York, 1971). Most of the maps mentioned in the text are printed in Emerson D. Fite and Archibald Freeman, comp. and ed., *A Book of Old Maps delineating American History* (Cambridge, Mass., 1926); reprint (New York, 1969). These texts offer a wide range of reference.

For Zárate-Salmerón, see bibliog., chap. 5.

Henry Briggs, "A Treatise of the North-West Passage to the South Sea, through the Continent of Virginia, and by the Fretum Hudson," makes up pp. 45–50 in *A Treatise of the Declaration of the State of the Colony and Affairs in Virginia* (London, 1622); Purchas 1625 reprints the Briggs argument.

Rio de Losa, see bibliog., chap. 5, for Oñate; ref. to *Oñate, Colonizer*.

Gilbert, *Discourse*, see bibliog., chap. 3.

For Castañeda, consult bibliog., chap. 4; for Ingram, bibliog., chap. 6.

[St. Brandan] Thomas Wright, ed., *St. Brandan, a Mediaeval Legend of the Sea, in English verse and prose*, The Percy Society (London, 1844); Jessie L. Weston, ed., *The Chief Middle English Poets* (Cambridge, Mass., 1914); Morison, *European Discovery*.

[Nicholas of Linne or Lynn] Gerardus Mercator, *Nova et*

Aucta Orbis Terrae Descriptio (Duisburg, 1569); Hakluyt 1589, 1600, Everyman I.

[Madoc] Sir George Peckham, *A true Reporte, Of the late discoveries, and possession, taken in the right of the Crowne of England, of the New-found Landes: by Sir Humfrey Gilbert* (London, 1583); reprints: Hakluyt 1589, 1600, Everyman VI.

Henry Hawks, "A relation of the commodities of Noua Hispania, and the maners of the inhabitants, written . . . 1572," printed from mss., Hakluyt 1589, 1600, Everyman VI.

17   Nature as Concept and Commodity (pages 192–207)

All but three of the citations here are covered by bibliographies for earlier chapters. See, for Drake, chap. 14; Vizcaíno-Father Ascensión, chap. 5; Vaca and Coronado, chap. 4; Ribaut and Le Moyne, chap. 8; Barlow, Lane, and Harriot, chap. 9; Smith, chap. 11; Lescarbot, chap. 12; Best, Ellis, and Settle, chap. 3; Sparke, chap. 13.

The narrative of Cartier's third voyage survives only as a fragment in Hakluyt 1600, q.v.

John Brereton [Brierton], *A Briefe and true Relation of the Discoverie of the North part of Virginia: Made this present yeare 1602, by Captaine Bartholowmew Gilbert* . . . (London, 1602); second and enlarged issue, 1602; reprints: (first issue) Burrage, ed., *Early English and French Voyages*; (second issue) G. P. Winship, ed., *Sailors' Narratives of Voyages, along the New England Coast* (Boston, 1905).

Martin Pring, "A Voyage set out from the Citie of Bristol . . . for the discoverie of the North part of Virginia, in the yeere 1603 . . ." printed from mss., Purchas 1625; reprints: Winship, ed., *Sailors' Narratives* . . . (1905); Burrage, *Early English and French Voyages.*

18   Brute Neighbors and Higher Laws (pages 208–215)

Henry Hudson, "A second Voyage or Employment of Master Henry Hudson . . . written by himselfe," Purchas 1625 (first printing); reprints: Asher, *Henry Hudson . . .* , and appropriate items of bibliog., chap. 3.

Job Hortop, *The Rare Travailes of Job Hortop, an Englishman* . . . (London, 1591); reprints: Hakluyt 1600 under the title of "The travailes of Job Hortop, which Sir John Hawkins set on land within the Bay of Mexico . . . 1568"; Everyman VI; Purchas (paraphrase); G. R. G. Conway, facsimile (Mexico City, 1928).

For Father Escobar, see Hammond and Rey, *Oñate, Colonizer* (bibliog., chap. 5).

For the other writers quoted, consult the following bibliographical sections: Thevet and Peter Martyr, chap. 12; John Sparke, chap. 13; Champlain, chap. 10.

19   The Indian Is a New Man (pages 216–226)

All but one of the writers referred to here have appeared in earlier bibliographies. See, for Peckham and Hawks, chap. 16; Vaca, chap. 4; Harriot and White, chap. 9; Lescarbot, chap. 12.

Newly cited: Bartolomé de Las Casas, *Brevissima relación de la destruccion de las Indias* (Seville, 1552); trans., M. M. S., *The Spanish Colonie, or Briefe Chronicle of the Acts and gestes of the Spaniardes in the West Indies* (London, 1583); abridged in Purchas.

20   Theme and Myth in America (pages 227–239)

Again, bibliographical references are largely given in previous chapters: Smith, chap. 11; Raleigh, chap. 15; Lescarbot, chap. 12; Peckham, chap. 16; Ellis, Gilbert, and Hayes, chap. 3.

First reference is made to the following:

Robert Thorne, "A declaration of the Indies and lands discovered . . ." Hakluyt 1582; reprints: Hakluyt 1589, 1600; Everyman I.

Lawrence Keymis, *A Relation of the second Voyage to Guiana* . . . (London, 1596); reprints: Hakluyt 1600; Everyman VII.

Richard Hakluyt, "A Particuler Discourse . . . written 1584"; first printing, L. Woods and C. Deane, eds., "A Discourse on Western Planting," *Documentary History of the State of Maine*, vol. II, Maine Historical Society (Cambridge, Mass., 1877).

[George Percy], "Observations Gathered out of a Discourse of the Plantation of the Southerne Colonie in Virginia by the English, 1606," first printing, Purchas 1625; reprints: E. Arber and A. G. Bradley, eds., *John Smith*; Tyler, ed., *Nar. . . . Early Virginia* (Or. Nar.); D. B. Quinn, ed., *Observations Gathered out of 'A Discourse . . . .'* Assoc. for the Preservation of Virginia Antiquities (Charlottesville, Va., 1967).

Selective Bibliographical Listing
of Voyage Collections

(in order of publication)

Giovanni Battista Ramusio, *Navigationi et viaggi* . . . 3 vols. (Venice, 1550–1559). Volume III, of which there are several issues, contains the American voyages. Referred to as Ramusio. See *Library of Congress Catalog of Printed Cards* (1943) for full bibliography.

Richard Hakluyt, *Divers voyages touching the discoverie of America and the ilands adjacent to the same* (London, 1582); reprint, Hakluyt Society, 1st ser., No. 7 (1850); photo-offset, Burt Franklin (New York, n.d.). Referred to as Hakluyt 1582.

————, *The Principall Navigations, Voiages and Discoveries of the English Nation* . . . (London, 1589); facsimile, intro. by D. B. Quinn and R. A. Skelton, modern index by A. Quinn, 2 vols., Hakluyt Society, Extra series, No. XXXIX (Cambridge, 1965). Referred to as Hakluyt 1589.

————, *The Principal Navigations, Voiages, Traffiques and Discoveries of the English Nation* . . . 3 vols. (London, 1598–1600); reprint, Hakluyt Society, Extra series, Nos. I–XII, 12 vols. (Glasgow, 1903–1905); photo-offset, Burt Franklin (New York, n.d.); reprint of Glasgow edition (New York, 1971). Referred to as Hakluyt 1600. The Everyman edition of *The Principal Navigations*, 8 vols. (London, New York, 1907, 1910), prints only the English voyages. Referred to as Everyman.

Samuel Purchas, *Hakluytus Posthumus or Purchas His Pilgrimes Contayning a History of the World in Sea Voyages and Lande Travells by Englishmen and others* . . . 4 vols. (London, 1625); reprint, 20 vols., Hakluyt Society, Extra series, Nos. 14–33 (Glasgow, 1905–1907), photo-offset, Burt Franklin (New York, n.d.). Referred to as Purchas or, where indicative, Purchas 1625.

Henri Ternaux-Compans, *Voyages, relations et mémoires originaux pour servir à l'histoire de la découverte de l'Amérique publiés pour la première fois, en français*, 20 vols. (Paris, 1837–1841). Referred to as Ternaux-Compans.

Joaquin F. Pacheco, Francisco de Cárdenas, *et al.*, *Colección de documentos inéditos relativos al descubrimiento, conquista y organización de las antiguas posesiones españoles de América y Oceania*, 42 vols. (Madrid, 1864–1884). Volume XXXIII contains an index to earlier volumes. Referred to as Pacheco and Cárdenas.

In the twentieth century a number of series of sixteenth- and seventeenth-century voyage narratives have been published, such as the Americana, Broadway, Trailmakers, American Explorers, and Original Narratives of American History. The last, under the general editorship of J. Franklin Jameson, is particularly useful for bibliography and close annotation; certain texts have been cut, and are therefore invalid for literary analysis, but the omissions are always clearly indicated. The individual volumes of the series have been referred to where appropriate, with the designation Or. Nar. in the first citation.

Index

Index